Energy in the Global Arena

Global Issues Series

Series Editors: James E. Harf and B. Thomas Trout
Volume Editors: B. Thomas Trout, James E. Harf,
and Barry B. Hughes

Energy in the Global Arena

Actors, Values, Policies, and Futures

Barry B. Hughes, Robert W. Rycroft,
Donald A. Sylvan, B. Thomas Trout,
and James E. Harf

Duke University Press   Durham, 1985

© 1985 Duke University Press, all rights reserved
Printed in the United States of America
Library of Congress Cataloging in Publication Data
Main entry under title:
Energy in the global arena.
(Duke Press global issues series)
Bibliography: p.
Includes index.
1. Energy industries. 2. Energy policy. 3. Power
resources. I. Hughes, Barry, 1945 –   II. Series.
[HD9502.A2E54397 1985]   333.79   84-21250
ISBN 0-8223-0622-0

Contents

Figures and Tables

Series Preface

This text is one in a series of volumes on contemporary issues in the global environment. The Global Issues Series, of which it is a part, is the result of a multiyear project funded by the Exxon Education Foundation to develop educational resources for a number of problems arising from the shifting nature and growing interdependence of that environment. The issue areas addressed in this ongoing project include food, energy, population, and environment.

Each of these issues has been addressed within a systematic and integrated framework common to all. After establishing the substantive dimensions needed to provide the requisite foundation for inquiry—such as the historical evolution of an issue, its structure within the global system, its basic contemporary characteristics—this framework is applied in separate chapters pursuing four distinct analytical perspectives: (1) Who are the global *actors* involved in the issue and what are the linkages among them? (2) What prevailing *values* are operating and how have the relevant actors responded to these values? (3) What *policies* are applied by these actors at the global level and how are these policies determined? And (4) what *futures* are represented in the values and policies of these global actors? These four perspectives, and the relationships among them, are used to link the analysis of the basic issues: food, energy, population, and environment. Each perspective represents a distinct analytical approach, as shown in figure 1.

In addition, differentiating this project and its product from other texts, each of the single-issue volumes offers exercises that afford the student the opportunity to engage in a variety of active learning sequences—should the instructor so desire—in order to better understand the complexities of the issue.

In realizing its goals the project enlisted the participation of thirty-one prominent scholars who worked together with the proj-

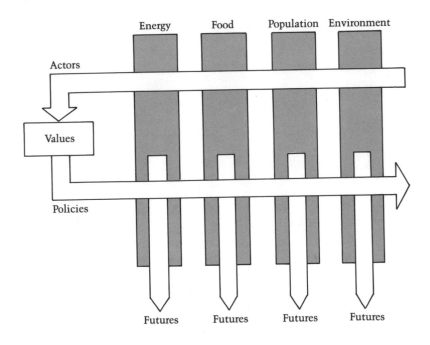

Figure I.   Actors, values, policies, and futures

ect directors. These individuals contributed their substantial expertise both to specific issue areas and to the analytical development
of the project as a whole.

Each volume of the series represents the specific contributions of
several principal authors. One, the issues specialist, was responsible for the substantive introduction and, in some cases, the summary conclusion and for supervising and coordinating the efforts of
the other authors. Those authors applied the components of the
perspective framework—actors, values, policies, futures—to the
issue in separate chapters. The series editors assisted in the writing
of these chapters, then edited each individual volume together with
the relevant issue specialist. The editors incorporated the feedback
from pedagogical and substantive specialists as well as from field
testers.

The project evolved through a series of stages centered on two
development workshops—the first for the "issue" and "perspective" specialists and the second for all participants—and the elaborate field-test network of the Consortium for International Studies

Education. The materials developed in the workshops were produced in field-test editions which were then used across the country in a variety of instructional settings. All the volumes have therefore been revised and refined based on actual classroom experience.

We wish to acknowledge formally the financial support of the Exxon Education Foundation which provided the means to develop this project, and we wish to express our gratitude to several individuals: Roy E. Licklider, Rutgers University, who while serving with the Exxon Education Foundation encouraged us initially to pursue this venture; Richard Johnson who as our contact at the Exxon Education Foundation shepherded this project to completion; and Suzanna Easton of the Department of Education for her enthusiastic support and encouragement not only of this project but of the entire educational enterprise which it represents.

Two books from the Global Issues Project have been published by Holt, Rinehart and Winston: *Population in the Global Arena* and *Food in the Global Arena*. Duke University Press will publish three texts in the series: *Energy in the Global Arena, Environment and the Global Arena*, and *The New Global Agenda*. We are grateful to a number of individuals who encouraged us at various stages of the publishing process. First, we worked with Patrick Powers who as a senior editor at Holt believed in this project. Marie A. Schappert of Holt brought a sound, businesslike style to her task of overseeing the first two manuscripts. We are especially indebted to Richard C. Rowson, director of Duke University Press, who has continuously demonstrated a strong commitment to this project. Reynolds Smith, as editor responsible for the three Duke University Press manuscripts, translated them from final draft into print with a very high level of expertise and sound professional judgment. Both Mary Mendell and Bob Mirandon at Duke Press also contributed materially to the quality of the manuscript. These same qualities were found in our administrative assistant and typist, Edith Bivona, who delivered work of the highest quality under less than ideal circumstances. She brings a pleasant manner and much enthusiasm to her work, making our professional lives much easier. Finally, we would like to acknowledge the support of The Ohio State University's Mershon Center and its director, Charles F. Hermann, who was forthcoming with assistance when needed.

James E. Harf
B. Thomas Trout

Preface

There seems little question that energy is an issue of global proportions. This fact was raised in the public consciousness by the onset of the "energy crisis" in October 1973. At that time the members of the Organization of Petroleum Exporting Countries (OPEC), largely located in the Middle East, seized upon the oil dependency of the industrialized nations of Europe and North America and began a series of moves that would eventually raise the international price of oil by 1,000 percent and lead to the emergence of a worldwide recession. For Americans, this created a sudden and harsh reality. Gasoline, which had been relatively cheap and plentiful, was transformed almost overnight into a scarce and expensive commodity. People were forced to wait hours in lines at service stations and even then only to receive limited amounts of fuel. As the gasoline lines eased, other aspects of the problem became apparent. Nationwide speed limits were imposed, home heating costs skyrocketed, a new bureaucracy—the Department of Energy—appeared and there were countless other examples of the pressure of energy as an issue in everyday life.

With the action of OPEC, energy thus became another of a growing number of issues that have arisen as we approach the twenty-first century, making us aware that we are entering a new global era. We are reminded almost daily of this phenomenon. It is visualized for us most dramatically, perhaps, in the way we now see our earth photographed from space, appearing no longer as a limitless expanse of frontier, rich in resources, but as a blue ball wrapped in its fragile atmospheric envelope, a finite and increasingly constrained representation of the limits of human existence. And so it is now characterized. The earth is seen as a vessel—"spaceship earth"—carrying mankind as common voyagers through space toward an increasingly uncertain future.

It is vitally important that we understand why it is that we consider energy to be a *global issue*. Indeed, what makes an issue global? We must first think in terms of the globe itself. Global issues by definition *transcend the traditional boundaries of the nation-state* or the regional association of nation-state units. We are therefore addressing issues, like energy, whose impact will be felt beyond any clear limits in terms of political or even geographic space. Such issues necessarily affect the judgment and actions of large segments of the world's inhabitants either directly or indirectly. Recognition of that fact, however, simply begs the question again: What are the characteristics of energy which define its impact beyond such previously recognized and accepted limits?

First, such issues are characterized by an *incapacity for autonomous decision*. No single actor, or corporate group of actors, is capable of resolving the issues associated with energy—dependence on oil, limitations in the quantity and distribution of petroleum reserves, constraints on alternative energy sources, current inacessibility of nonrenewable options for large-scale use, and so forth. Energy is an area that exemplifies the worldwide trend toward proliferating numbers and types of actors. The energy crisis and its aftermath demonstrated the impact that new actors can have. OPEC itself was formed only in 1960 for the purpose of redressing what was felt to be an artificially low pricing structure for oil. In little more than ten years, by 1973, OPEC was able to accomplish its objective. But, in increasing the price of oil, OPEC also gave rise to the formation of other institutions, like the International Energy Agency (IEA). IEA was instituted by the industrialized nations of Western Europe and North America together with Japan as a means to counter OPEC's control over the international petroleum market. Within another ten years, by 1983, events in the marketplace— largely through the interaction of supply and demand—seemed again to restore some relative balance to the respective levels of influence between these organizations of producing and consuming nations. But in the meantime other actors had entered the arena as well, with new producers like Mexico challenging OPEC's control of the market by discovering and exploiting new oil fields. There also have been actors, from individuals to international organizations, who have entered the energy arena in order to advocate a wide variety of resources and approaches intended to replace the worldwide dependence on oil that contributed to the current energy crisis. All of these actors have differing agendas, differing points of view, and differing stakes in the outcome. What is more, the energy arena in which they struggle is a highly interdependent one, with complex linkages to other issues (like economic development or food production, both of which are energy-related). The decisions and actions of any one of these actors or of several of them in combination have a clear impact on the action and positions of all of the others. Thus, the issue of energy cannot be resolved by any single actor, but will instead be resolved in the larger global arena through the combined interaction of many different actors (some of which may be outside of the energy field altogether). This characteristic is addressed in this volume by the *actors perspective.*

A second characteristic of global issues is that each possesses a *present imperative* which not only impels various actors to press for resolution, but which encompasses the varied and often competing views as to how that resolution ought to proceed. Nothing can illustrate this point better in the field of energy than the reality that oil, the prevailing worldwide energy resource, is a finite commodity. That is, the total amount of oil available in the world is, with reasonable accuracy, known. The only question is how fast it is used, and as it becomes scarcer, what energy resource will replace it. This situation creates differing roles for energy actors. It is evident that an oil producer such as Saudi Arabia, which possesses 27 percent of the known oil reserves in the noncommunist world, operates with a set of objectives that differ from those held by most other actors. For example, there are other producer states that have far fewer oil reserves and a far greater need for the profits to be made from the international marketplace than Saudi Arabia. Such a nation—and there are several Third World states both inside and outside of OPEC that share those characteristics—would want to maximize the short-term advantage of the current state of oil dependency, therefore preferring to keep prices high and responding to a drop in price by increasing production to maintain a constant share of the market. Saudi Arabia on the other hand would benefit instead by preserving the long-term value of its resource rather than responding to short-term fluctuations. Oil is likely to increase in value as it becomes scarcer. As this scenario has unfolded in the 1980s, Saudi Arabia has in fact sought to keep production low in the face of declining prices, waiting for demand to increase once again. Other OPEC nations, with greater need for short-term earnings, have resisted. Consumer nations of course may seek different outcomes altogether. For consumer nations, what may be most important is the lowest possible cost for oil in order to maintain commitments to continued or restored levels of economic growth. Those countries therefore strive to conserve. There also are energy actors who challenge the dominance of petroleum by supporting alternative sources of energy ranging from other fossil fuels, like coal and nuclear energy, to renewable energy resources, such as wind or solar power. Still other actors may enter the energy arena with nonenergy goals. It is quite likely that these actors will challenge many of the values that govern the action of others. Environmental groups seek to ensure that the choices made in energy will safeguard the environment. Those advocating coal, for example, may be challenged by environmental groups who want laws to ensure that the landscape is not permanently scarred by strip-mining techniques or that the burning of coal will not pollute the atmosphere. There is much at stake in the energy arena today and the issue is still very much unresolved. The outcome will depend on which values, or combination of values, will prevail. Hence, a *values perspective* provides a second analytical focus in this volume.

A third characteristic of global issues, not peculiar to such issues but nonetheless unique in the sequence already defined by actors and values, is that their *resolution requires policy action.* Energy policies adopt several different approaches to the problem. In the short term, the energy problem has been dominated by economic and political considerations. This domination has been evident not only in the emergence of the energy crisis, which was motivated by the effort of OPEC to alter the prevailing pricing structure to their advantage, but also in the efforts to resolve that crisis. The formation of the IEA was intended in part to establish a more integrated approach to the OPEC nations by the industrialized consuming nations of the West. IEA sought to establish petroleum reserves, for example, so that the effects of a sharp cutoff of oil would not have the same devastating impact as the OPEC oil embargo of 1973. IEA also has sought to coordinate the domestic policies of its members with regard to conservation measures adopted for the long term. Indeed, these policy approaches seem to have been successful as oil consumption dropped markedly in the industrialized countries after the peak of the energy crisis of 1979. But, in fact, it appears that the sheer weight of the high cost of oil had as much impact as various policy approaches designed to provide conservation incentives.

As is the case in so many areas involving multiple actors with differing and competing values, energy policy thus tends to be the cumulative outcome of a number of different factors. The success or failure of those policies seems on balance to be less the product of design than the consequence of complex interactions among the wide variety of actors seeking short-term economic or political gain. For policy over the long term, energy is more problematical. In the transition that is taking place from a global system dependent on oil to a system that will rely on other sources, probably in combination, setting clear policy is difficult. The competition for short-term gain tends to retard long-term resolution. The ultimate policy choice will probably be affected by most technological developments that have yet to be fully explored. But initiating those developments is a difficult and demanding task. For each of the several alternatives—nuclear power, coal, solar power, etc.—there will be serious trade-offs for the contending actors in the energy arena and for the society as a whole. Addressing production, distribution, and consumption on a global scale is in itself an awesome task. To try to integrate the competing interests of the many actors on the scene and to try to accommodate the many issues which are affected by energy decisions—like continued levels of economic growth or means to increase food production to meet the rising demand of increased population—make the effort to develop a comprehensive global energy policy even more challenging. The *policies perspective* is therefore critical for understanding the interrelatedness of issues and actors affecting the development of energy in the global environment.

A final element that characterizes global issues is their *persistence*. Energy has proven to be an essential component of human development and human existence. It is an essential component of global survival. There is no clear agreement among experts about the global energy future. Optimists argue that the past decade has proven the capacity to extend the timeline for the transition from oil. Instead of using up the oil reserves available to us early in the twenty-first century, forecasts now focus on a period closer to the middle of that century. In the short term this view is reinforced by the recent reductions in the level of consumption, the exploitation of new fields, and the accompanying decline in the price of oil. Some analysts contend that the impact of demand and supply has shown that there will be energy produced as long as the demand remains. Other analysts take a more pessimistic view. Regardless of the short-term adjustments that have taken place recently in the petroleum marketplace, they argue, the long-term energy problem remains and little has been done to resolve it. They perceive changes over the past decade as retarding the effort to take a clear stand on the energy future. The drop in the price of oil that occurred at the beginning of the 1980s is seen as having an ultimately negative effect. Because of the high price of oil during the energy crisis, a number of initiatives were undertaken in the energy field to find alternative forms of energy. Exploration of new techniques was started to extract energy from nontraditional sources. The established energy institutions saw in the end of the dominance of oil the need to find other bases in order to play a continuing role in the energy picture. The large oil corporations began to diversify their operations into other areas—nuclear power, synthetic fuels, renewable energy sources, etc.—and began to invest in research efforts to seek even newer and more innovative solutions to the energy problem. But as oil declined in price and its prevalence as an energy resource seemed to extend further into the future, such investment became more costly again relative to the development and marketing of petroleum. Corporations began to reduce their efforts. There is no clear sense of the energy future. Many possible alternatives to oil will have to pass the crucial test of commercial feasibility, and for those energy resources that are not ultimately exhaustible—the "renewable" resources—that feasibility seems a long time away. How the energy picture will look after the year 2000 is still uncertain. It is evident that oil cannot continue to play the role that it has played; experts agree generally on that point. But there is no agreement about what will succeed oil as the dominant world energy resource. The trends and consequences of forecasts and alternatives for the global energy system are addressed in the final perspective of this volume, the *future perspective*.

Several individuals played critical roles in this book. Three scholars did the bulk of the writing. Barry B. Hughes, together with the series editors, supervised it from conception to completion—selecting the other principal authors, adapting the general framework to the energy issue, evaluating the reviews, and editing the field-test edition and final manuscript. Hughes also contributed the first chapter, which describes the background and global characteristics of the energy problem. Robert W. Rycroft wrote the chapters that focus on the *actors* and the *policies* perspective. Donald A. Sylvan wrote the chapter on the *futures* perspective and drafted the chapter on *values*. The series editors joined Sylvan in the completed chapter on *values*; the editors also wrote the conclusion. In addition, a number of persons critiqued this volume in draft form and contributed valuable suggestions, and some used it in their classrooms. The material also was used in a series of workshops for faculty across the country, and many insights and amendments were offered. Finally, we wish to acknowledge Robert S. Jordan, Chadwick F. Alger, Richard W. Mansbach, and Dennis Pirages who examined, respectively, the actors, values, policies, and futures chapters.

Exercises designed for student use in or outside of the classroom are available from the publisher.

B. Thomas Trout
James E. Harf
July 1984

1 Energy as a Global Issue

An Energy Crisis

The phrase "energy crisis," which filled the headlines in the 1970s, disappeared in the early 1980s to be replaced by talk of an "oil glut." Lines in front of gas pumps and natural gas and heating oil shortages largely vanished, and widespread shortages became things of the past. And these changes were reflected in public attitudes. When asked in a national poll a few short months after the shortages of spring 1979, "Do you think the energy shortage we hear about is real, or are we just being told there are shortages?" only 37 percent of the respondents felt it was real. The majority, 45 percent, replied that we are just being told this (although 55 percent of the college-educated said it was real). This poll was not truly informative, however, for the question, like many on the issue, was phrased badly. In fact, the public appears to be capable of distinguishing between short-term physical *shortages* and a basic, underlying long-term *problem*, and it is the latter around which the real debate revolves. The public does now believe that there is a long-term energy problem, but the debate still rages among professional observers of the energy scene concerning the reality of that perception.

Let us begin, then, to address the issue: Is there in any sense an energy crisis, and if so in what sense? In a medical sense of the term "crisis," the world has had a bad case of oil dependency, and this malady has reached the crisis stage. And, in that sense one of two outcomes is imminent: either the patient will die, or the fever will break and the patient will recover full health. But one of the characteristics of the illness is that the various attending physicians provide radically different prognoses. In fact, the medical analogy describes the situation too dramatically, although many do depict our alternatives in such stark terms. There is broader agreement, however, for the notion that the world is in the midst of an energy system *transition*, during which the current domination by conventional oil and natural gas will give way to domination by one or more other primary energy sources. From that perspective, the problem sounds móre manageable.

In order to make our own judgments about whether or not there is an energy crisis, and if there is, how severe and long-term it may be, we need a considerable amount of information about energy and the global energy system. The energy crisis extends far deeper than those surface manifestations so familiar to energy consumers around the world, such as lines at gas stations, threats of possible rationing, and appeals to turn down thermostats. To understand how much more profound the energy problem is, we should consider what we mean by energy, know something about historic usage patterns, and outline what exactly is meant by a "global energy system." Further, we need to have an image of the current dimensions of that system and some understanding of how it evolved. At that point we can more intelligently consider the energy "crisis" and its consequences throughout the globe. And we will then be in a position to examine in more detail in subsequent chapters the actors involved in the intense political process surrounding energy, their values, their political interactions, and the energy future they are helping to shape.

The Nature of Energy and the Energy System

Energy is the capacity to do work. Mankind derives the energy it requires from a large variety of sources. The most fundamental and ancient source of energy is food. Fire from wood was the first nonfood energy source used by man, providing heat for cooking and warmth for living space. It also allowed the development of primitive metallurgy.

However, the amount of work that an individual human fueled by food can do is quite limited. Hence, the domestication of animals associated with the beginnings of agriculture about 8000 B.C., allowed about a tenfold increase in the amount of work accomplished under the direction of man. It was not until the first century B.C., that waterwheels were developed and not until the twentieth century A.D., that windmills came into use. These devices allowed a further 100-fold increase in work.

These five energy sources—food, animal labor, wood, water, and wind—provided essentially all of man's energy until about 1700. All were renewable. That is, none relies on a resource base that can be exhausted and that cannot be replaced. All these renewable energy forms derive their energy from sunlight and thus can be characterized as solar.

A New Source

After 1700 the fossil fuels (coal, oil, natural gas, and eventually nuclear energy) began to make contributions to energy needs. These sources facilitated an additional 100,000-fold increase in work (as measured by power output of machines)! Although coal, oil, and natural gas are, strictly speaking, carriers of energy from the sun and are therefore also solar sources, they are not generally classed as such because they are not renewable within periods of time meaningful to humanity. The gradual recognition that nonrenewable energy forms are limited in supply and that our patterns of usage for them will cause us to reach those limits within a meaningfully brief time (such as a handful of generations) have been two considerations redirecting our attention to renewable energy sources. At the same time the search for other so-called eternal sources, such as much more efficient nuclear fission through breeder reactors, or even nuclear fusion, also has intensified.

In addition to the renewable/nonrenewable distinction, the differentiation between commercial and noncommercial energy types is important as well. Especially in the Third World a large fraction of energy never enters the cash economy. Privately owned or gathered animal power, firewood, and cow dung still provide over half of total energy needs in a number of countries. Because almost all of our data collection efforts in energy are tied to commercial energy, it is very difficult to make precise statements about levels of noncommercial energy use or changes in those levels. We do know, however, that significant shortages of firewood now plague much of the Third World and that the firewood energy crisis is a very real one. This volume will be able to tell us little about noncommercial energy, and we will often slip into the developed world view of treating the energy system as if only commercial energy mattered. But the reader should not forget the "other energy system."

The Energy System

Although there have already been references here to "the energy system," the phrase has not been defined. A system is defined abstractly as a set of elements and the pattern of interactions among them. Looking at the energy system in largely physical terms, we would identify basic elements such as oil wells, coal mines, electric generating plants, gasoline burning automobiles, and electric toasters. Interactions could be shown as highways, pipelines, and electric grids.

It is productive to view the energy system in such a manner, but it may be even more useful to impose a set of organizing concepts on it. One such concept has already been discussed, namely the *source* of the energy. We routinely organize our view of the system by differentiating solar from fossil fuels, coal from oil, oil from nuclear power, etc. Another important set of concepts divides the energy system in terms of *function*. Thus, the elements of the system are the production and consumption sides, and the interaction between these two sides is distribution.

This volume relies very heavily on concepts relating to energy source and to energy system function (production, consumption, or distribution). Energy actors are labeled producers (like OPEC, the Organization of Petroleum Exporting Countries), consumers (such as auto owners), or distributors (like the public utilities). The values of each set of actors clearly derive in significant part from their functional roles. Whereas producers normally are concerned greatly with profit and therefore desire high prices, consumers want security of supply and the lowest possible prices. Such values motivate much of the actors' behavior in the policy process and many issues can themselves be characterized as those of production or supply on one hand, or of consumption or demand on the other. When we try to forecast critical aspects of the energy system we normally focus on supply and demand, and to a lesser degree (in part because of methodological difficulties) on distribution. These functional concepts help to organize this volume and will reappear throughout.

Evolution of the Energy System

As suggested in the above discussion of energy, the nature of the energy system in which any individual human being may play a part has undergone several dramatic transformations. When man was a hunter-gatherer and food was the principal energy source, individuals "produced" what was needed for consumption, minimizing the geographic scope and requirements of the distribution system. Distribution was, of course, a very important issue within family and tribal units.

The gift to man of fire by Prometheus in Greek mythology portrayed a dramatic energy system change. More mundanely, so did the neolithic revolution with its spread of agriculture, the establishment of more settled living, and the domestication of animals. The scope of the energy system in which a person was involved expanded, and functional roles became more differentiated. In traditional agricultural societies today we see that some individuals make a living as energy producers by gathering and selling firewood or by owning a windmill or water mill. Each community has its own production sources. A key element of these systems remains, however, in the visible dispersal of the requisite energy source. Many Americans who expect on their first trip to Europe to see agricultural fields covering all available rural space in order to meet the needs of dense populations are surprised to see a great deal of forest area mixed with fields. What they fail to realize is that all those French and German villages required local forest area to provide wood for energy. Elimination of accessible forest would have destroyed the community just as surely as inadequate land devoted to crops would have. This is a critical issue today in Third World countries still heavily dependent upon wood for energy.

The rapid introduction in the last three centuries of fossil fuels to the energy system eliminated the close relationship of local communities to local energy sources. Historically, major cities have almost always grown up on a navigable river or ocean and near to extensive wood supplies. Fossil fuels did not eliminate these linkages completely, as we can see from the proximity of major steel cities to the coalfields, iron mines, and rivers in the eastern United States. But the size of modern western cities like Salt Lake City, Denver, or Phoenix indicates the greatly weakened linkages.

With the dependence on less evenly dispersed energy sources came a system with large geographic scope, much more clearly defined functional roles in the energy system, and an increase in the potential power of producers and distributors relative to consumers. U.S. political history of the nineteenth and twentieth centuries is full of conflicts over railway ownership and pricing policies (not all were energy-related, but many were), battles over electricity and natural gas systems, and struggles to define and shape labor and antitrust policies, frequently with the energy industry as principal motivation.

Heavy reliance upon coal pushed energy system boundaries outward with the scope of the new system soon reaching the edge of national boundaries. In fact, the system began to spill across those boundaries in at least two ways. First, some international trade in coal began. Poland, for example, became tied to a larger international system for the most part because of extensive coal exports (and remains so today). Second, some of the inevitable conflict within the energy system (over control of production, distribution, prices, etc.) began to extend beyond national boundaries. The long-term struggles between France and Germany over control of coal-rich areas in Alsace-Lorraine and the Saar are examples.

But it was oil and natural gas, even less evenly distributed around the globe than coal (and generally scarcer), that made the world a single energy system. With the dependence on petroleum products, entire nations became classified as producer countries and others as consuming countries. Oil companies, which began domestically, evolved into multinational enterprises with key production and distribution functions in overseas areas. Naturally, the explosion of international trade in energy during the twentieth century, which marked the expansion of the scope of the energy system, has been accompanied by the entry of energy into the international political system as a key issue.

The Current Global Energy System

The Overall Structure of the Current System

The current energy system is truly a global system. An auto owner filling his or her tank almost anywhere in the world could be buying energy originating in the Middle East, Africa, Latin America, or Asia. The system is very heavily based on nonrenewable and commercial energy sources. Earlier it was suggested that two important sets of concepts are heavily used to describe an energy system:

Table 1.1.   World energy supply (percentage contributions)

	1965	1980	1990	2000
Oil	48	54	45	37
Gas	17	18	18	16
Synthetics	0	0	2	4
Coal	28	18	20	24
Nuclear	0	3	7	10
Hydro and others	7	7	8	9
Total	100	100	100	100

Source: Exxon Corporation, *World Energy Outlook* (December 1979), p. 11.

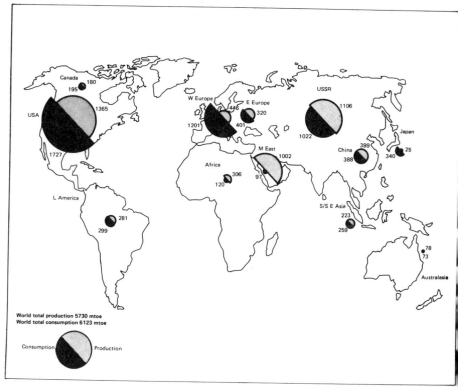

Figure 1.1. World energy production and consumption (million tons oil equivalent). *Source:* David Crabbe and Richard McBride, eds., *The World Energy Book* (Cambridge, Mass.: MIT Press, 1979), p. 200.

energy sources and *functional roles* within the system. We can use both of these in drawing the general outlines of the current global system. Table 1.1 shows how commercial energy supply on a global basis was divided in 1980 into the major energy *source* categories. That table also shows the division in 1965 and two future projections. In 1980, according to the table, oil and natural gas together constituted over 70 percent of global production and consumption as the relative role of coal had fallen sharply since 1965.

Just as table 1.1 provides a view of the global energy system according to the energy source, figure 1.1, which displays the level of production and consumption of all commercial energy by region of the world, helps us understand it by *functional role*. Two important aspects of the current system are illustrated. First, consumption is not at all evenly distributed globally. The bulk of consumption occurs in the United States, Western Europe, and the Soviet Union in spite of the fact that those three regions together contain less than 20 percent of the world's population. This unevenness in consumption must be noted along with the unequal distribution of production in the fossil fuel-based energy system discussed earlier. Inequality of consumption is an issue of great importance to those in the southern half of the globe. Second, it should be noted that the imbalance between production and consumption levels is rather dramatic. Especially noticeable are the very high levels of consumption relative to production in Western Europe (and to a lesser degree in the United States) and the very high level of production relative to consumption in the Mideast.

Figures 1.2 and 1.3 highlight the imbalance between production

Figure 1.2.   World petroleum production and consumption (million tons of oil). *Source:* David Crabbe and Richard McBride, eds., *The World Energy Book* (Cambridge, Mass.: MIT Press, 1979), p. 210.

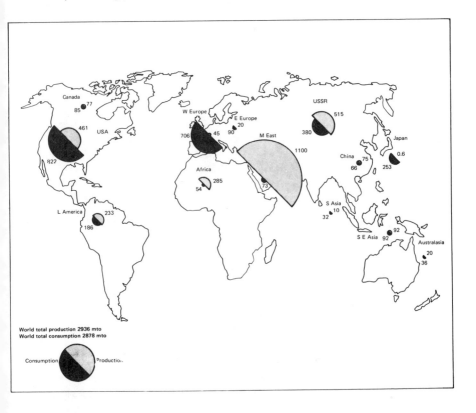

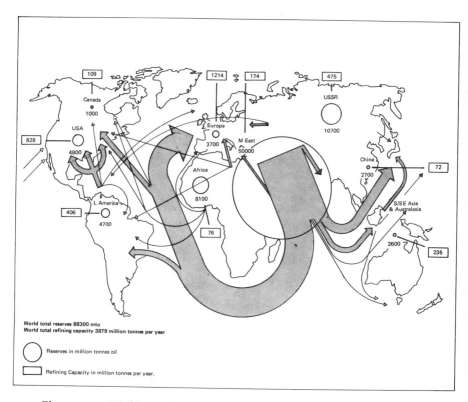

Figure 1.3. World petroleum reserves, refining capacity, and trade movements. *Source:* David Crabbe and Richard McBride, eds., *The World Energy Book* (Cambridge, Mass.: MIT Press, 1979), p. 209.

and consumption of petroleum, the energy source category for which that imbalance is greatest. Figure 1.2 compares actual production and consumption for *petroleum*, while figure 1.3 shows the direction of trade in petroleum and, by using different-sized arrows, indicates different volumes. This latter figure also helps us understand the basis for the imbalance by using different sized circles to represent the oil *reserves* in each region. The dominance of the Middle East appears even more pronounced than shown in figure 1.2 since it is greater with respect to *oil reserves* than it is with respect to *production*. This fact obviously means that the global imbalance between production and consumption will persist or even increase so long as oil remains the key energy source category.

Moreover, these statements about oil can be largely extended to natural gas as well, because oil and natural gas are more often than

not found in the same fields and produced simultaneously. Therefore, as shown in table 1.1, the production-consumption imbalance
accounts for nearly 70 percent of present global energy.

The Dynamic Nature of the Global Energy System

Although the discussion above focused on the current energy system, the changes forecast for the year 2000 in table 1.1 and the
earlier references to historical energy system transformations should
suggest the importance of looking at the system over time. Major
transitions have occurred historically, and the evidence suggests
overwhelmingly that we are now living through another such transformation, namely a shift away from oil and natural gas to other
energy sources. An understanding of the dynamics of energy system
transition is therefore central to any discussion of global energy as
an issue.

Three global transitions   In little more than one hundred years
two important energy transitions have played themselves out, with
very far-reaching consequences for economic, political, and social
organization. In 1850 the United States derived nearly 90 percent of
its energy from wood.[1] Throughout the Civil War and well into the
Robber Baron era of the late nineteenth century, wood remained the
dominant fuel. By that time, however, a new energy source—coal
—was already being adopted. In 1890 coal finally provided 50 percent of our energy (with wood still providing almost all the rest). In
1910 about sixty years after it began its rapid climb, the dominance
of coal peaked at 70 percent of all energy produced and consumed
in the United States. Increasing scarcity of wood played some role
in the wood-to-coal transition (especially in England), but almost
certainly more important were the dramatic benefits reaped from
coal by the emerging industrial system, especially in steel making
and transportation (railroads).

A whole new era in economics and politics thus arose with coal.
The countryside began its movement to the city. The era spawned
entrepreneurial giants, not so much in coal itself as in industries it
supported, most notably again steel and railroads. These industries
in turn gave rise to development of labor organizations. A young
and weak United Mine Workers (UMW) called its first strike in
1900.[2] The energy system based on coal had clearly set in motion
powerful social forces.

But in 1910, when coal reached its peak, oil and gas already
provided about 20 percent of United States energy needs. Sixty

years later, in 1970, these sources had reached the 70 percent level that coal had attained in 1910. A second sixty-year transition had been made. And it, too, left a trail of major economic, social, and political change. Whereas coal companies always remained relatively small, oil's history began with a single major company, Standard Oil, and to date the handful of giants are still known as "majors." We will return later to the social and political transformations that accompanied and in part resulted from the transition to oil.

However, first, it must be recognized that another and third transition is beginning. This does not mean that oil production will henceforth fall, just as United States coal consumption has not fallen (it is now greater than in 1910). But the relative positions of each source have declined. Hence, although global oil production and consumption will continue to rise for some years (as will that of natural gas), its relative position is beginning to decline.

The situation can best be understood by looking at figure 1.4, known as Hubbert's curve. The total *area under the curve* constitutes an estimate of the total global oil volume that has ever been or will be discoverable and retrievable (1.35 trillion barrels). Given the estimate in figures 1.2 and 1.3, global oil production (and consumption) should peak about the year 1990 at a level about 50

Figure 1.4. Cycle of world oil production. *Note:* Cycle of world oil production is plotted on the basis of two estimates of the amount of oil that will ultimately be produced. The higher curve reflects Ryman's estimate of $2,100 \times 10^9$ barrels and the lower curve represents an estimate of $1,350 \times 10^9$ barrels. *Source:* M. King Hubbert, "Energy Resources of the Earth," *Scientific American* (1971):69.

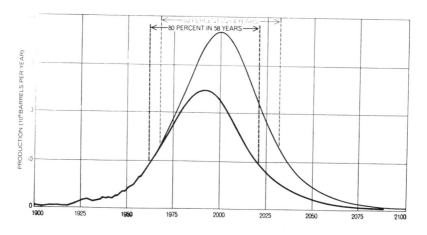

percent higher than current production. One interesting characteristic about Hubbert's curve is that a significant increase in the
assumption about ultimately recoverable resources does not dramatically change the estimate of when production will peak. The
higher curve in figure 1.4 is based on an estimate of 2.1 trillion
barrels, and the peak comes in the year 2000 at twice global production. Both curves suggest that by 2030, or roughly sixty years
after oil attained its dominance within the energy system, petroleum will make only a small contribution to the world's energy
consumption. The situation for natural gas is roughly the same.

Thus, another sixty-year transition appears to have begun.[3] History seldom is so kind to forecasters as to repeat itself so clearly,
however, and there are some significant differences in the coming
transition. For instance, the onset of the recent transition is somewhat premature. It was not geologically necessary that the world
face energy shortages beginning in 1973 because, as we can see
from figure 1.4, less than 25 percent of the oil that most geologists
feel we can ultimately recover had been produced by that time. A
key factor proved to be its concentration; about one-half of currently discovered oil exists in the Persian Gulf–Arabian Peninsula
region. It would have been physically possible to raise production in
that region considerably above the levels attained in the last decade.
In fact, the world's largest producer, Saudi Arabia, had plans in the
early 1970s to more than double its production, rather than to
stabilize it as subsequently happened. Clearly, economic factors,
such as the high "rents" that OPEC members can obtain with restricted production, have interacted with the geological factors to restrict
the growth of global oil production. Instead of continuing up the
Hubbert's curve in the 1970s, as was anticipated, oil production
growth has slowed and almost stopped. And the demand for oil has
not risen as fast as earlier predicted either, as consuming nations
use fuel more efficiently.

A second and related difference between the last two energy
system transitions and the current one is that the world was largely
"pulled" into the earlier two by the more desirable qualities of the
new energy form. Coal was a more concentrated source of energy
than wood. Oil and gas were easier to transport and cleaner than
coal. Now, however, the world is being "pushed" into a transition
and it is not clear what the replacement fuel or fuels can or should
be. Possibilities include: (1) a return to coal, burned directly, transformed into electricity, or as a source of synthetic oil and gas; (2)
nuclear energy, either through current fission technology (i.e., split-

ting a "heavy" nucleus and using the energy released) including breeder reactors, or through the potentially feasible fusion power (i.e., fusing a "light" nucleus into a heavier form and, again, using the energy released), and (3) a variety of renewable energy sources. Many of the renewable sources, which are all in some manner or another a form of solar energy (wood, hydroelectric power, direct solar collection), have strong proponents both because they are environmentally safe and because they constitute a "permanent" solution to energy problems. We shall return to this issue later in the chapter.

The transition to oil   To understand the nature and especially the far-reaching importance of the transition now under way, it is useful to look more carefully at the one that has just been completed.

From the beginning of the oil age there has been a close association between the petroleum industry and the United States. For many years seven major oil companies dominated oil production and distribution, and only two of those—British Petroleum and Shell—are based outside the United States. The other five are Texaco, Gulf (now absorbed by Chevron), Mobil, Standard Oil of California, and the giant Exxon (formerly Standard Oil of New Jersey). The rise of OPEC control over production has somewhat reduced the role of several of these and given rise to a new production giant, the National Iranian Oil Company (NIOC). Nevertheless, there has been a close association between oil and the United States, as well as between the United States and the big companies.

The world's first oil well was drilled in 1859 in Titusville, Pennsylvania.[4] Three years later John D. Rockefeller began Standard Oil, which by 1900 controlled 87 percent of U.S. supplies and 82 percent of refining. Coal is labor intensive, and this fact embroiled that industry in many labor disputes. Oil is capital and technology intensive, so labor issues have never been so important. Those same capital- and technology-intensive characteristics, however, almost always give rise to concentration in an industry, and such concentration in oil has long been a major political issue. Thus, in 1911 Standard Oil was broken into thirty-four companies by the U.S. government after antitrust proceedings.

Another consistent issue throughout oil's history has been overproduction or gluts. Some of this derives from application of the "rule of capture," which means that anyone can pump oil from his own well regardless of whose land is being drained by the well.

Neighbors drawing from the same pool clearly have an incentive to pump as much as possible as soon as possible.

World War I was a period of great United States government–oil industry cooperation in support of the war effort. The expansion of production during that period was one factor that underlay the first oil crisis of the petroleum era—one to which doubters of the physical limits on future oil production still point. In 1919 the head of the U.S. Geological Survey (USGS) predicted exhaustion of U.S. fields in ten years. Ten years later, in 1929, the United States had major oil surpluses. In between, the oil industry was able to obtain from government the famous depletion allowance providing major tax relief. The Hubbert whose name is associated with the curves in figure 1.4 was a latter-day employee of the USGS who produced oil analyses in the 1960s. Many questioned his predictions that U.S. oil production would peak in 1970 and never again attain that level. As of 1984, however, these predictions have been fully supported.

Surpluses prevailed over shortages for decades. The Texas Railroad Commission imposed an allocation system on Texas producers after great violence in the oil fields which required martial law to quell. Because of the size of Texas production, that authority was central to restraining production nationally, and even globally, and to avoiding major price-cutting up to the early 1970s.

Texas also was the center of the petroleum industry's national political strength. For instance, the Petroleum Club in Houston has attracted most post–World War II presidential candidates (even staunch liberals) during their search for campaign funds.[5] Words important to the audience of those speeches included "depletion allowance" and "import quotas." Large campaign contributions often followed until 1976 when changes in electoral laws altered the financial conduct of presidential campaigns.

Although the United States dominated the global petroleum industry, it was not without competition. Major oil strikes were made in Baku on the Caspian Sea in Russia in the 1870s. This area was the first to challenge Standard Oil's dominance of European paraffin sales.[6] The Russian Revolution and World War I greatly reduced the area's competitiveness, however.

In the 1920s Mexico became the second largest producer after the United States, providing 25 percent of world oil. The United States and Great Britain dominated the Mexican industry. Local unrest resulted in the patrol of U.S. naval vessels off the Gulf coast. According to the U.S. secretary of state, this was to keep the Mexicans "between a dangerous and exaggerated apprehension and a proper degree of wholesome fear."[7] The industry was nationalized in 1938, resulting in a boycott by the international companies which helped to keep the Mexican oil industry out of international markets until the recent new discoveries.

In the 1940s Venezuela became a major producer, second to the United States by 1946.[8] A new government in 1958 began to exercise more power over the foreign companies, which again controlled their local industry. Venezuela's international role then dropped and the companies were nationalized in the 1970s.

Iran was the first major producer in the Mideast. The Anglo-Persian Oil Company was formed in 1913. After World War II the U.S. oil industry established its position in Iran. The U.S. industry also dominated during the explosion of Persian Gulf and Arabian Peninsula oil discoveries throughout the 1950s and 1960s. The international (predominantly U.S.) industry purchased "concessions" giving them full exploration, production, and pricing control. At the beginning of the 1970s the new center of global oil production was contributing about $2 billion annually to the U.S. balance of payments through American oil company profits there.[9]

The post–World War II emergence of the Persian Gulf created major global surpluses again, after much tightening of the market during the war, and costs were so low that U.S. domestic producers began to lose control of the domestic market. In 1947 the United States became a net oil importer for the first time; and by 1953, 10 percent of oil was imported. The U.S. oil industry was not happy and pointed to the security threat of foreign oil dependence. In 1954 voluntary quotas were set for oil imports at 12 percent of east-of-the-Rockies oil consumption. In 1959 these quotas ceased to be voluntary. This protection of the domestic market created major windfalls for the domestic oil (and even coal) industries by keeping less expensive foreign oil out of the U.S. market. Although it maintained the United States as the world's largest producer, it cost domestic consumers as much as $4 to $7 billion annually.[10] Domestic crude in New York City was twice the price of imported ($3.00 versus $1.50).

Western Europe and Japan took much fuller advantage of the inexpensive oil, kept even less expensive by self-imposed U.S. exclusion from the market. Thus, cheap oil, partly subsidized by the United States, helped fuel the postwar economic miracles in these countries. It has been argued that this indirect support of Europe by the United States was as important as the Marshall Plan.

The import quota policy, which has since been criticized as one of "drain American first," ran up against growing domestic demand and inability of domestic producers to meet it by 1970. Quotas were loosened in 1970 and 1972, then abolished in 1973 shortly *before* the "oil crisis" began.[11]

The Crisis of the 1970s

The transition from oil The beginning of the transition away from oil was heralded by the emergence of a publicly-recognized crisis in the early 1970s. It is important to understand the bases of that crisis, for several factors contributed. Both American abstinence from foreign oil and the vast magnitude of the discoveries led to the decline of real oil prices by 50 percent from 1950 to 1970.[12] The falling oil prices together with eventual American entry into the world market, the declining slope of Hubbert's curve in the 1970s, and political relationships in the Mideast then influenced the dramatic events of 1973 to 1974.

The 1970s' crisis thus began well before its appearance. In August 1960 the international oil majors unilaterally reduced the posted oil prices, the prices upon which payments to Mideast producers were based.[13] In September 1960 at the urging of Venezuela, OPEC was formed primarily to halt further declines. It was not able to halt the price declines of the 1960s, but it did gradually begin to assert the authority of producer countries. That process greatly accelerated in 1970. In September Libya was able to impose terms on Occidental Petroleum and achieve an increase in posted oil prices. In February 1971 the OPEC countries reached the Teheran Agreement to raise prices cooperatively. The international majors began to lose pricing control. OPEC raised prices again in Tripoli in August. In October 1972 OPEC went beyond pricing control and announced a participation agreement whereby producer countries could purchase 25 percent of their domestic oil industry, rising gradually to 51 percent. Iran went well beyond this in May 1973 and nationalized oil, and this was followed in August by Libya nationalizing 51 percent.

Many people view the Middle East war in October 1973 and the subsequent oil boycott of the United States by several Arab producers as the beginning of the oil crisis. Clearly, however, the dam had already burst. Nevertheless, the earlier oil price increases had been quite minor compared to those in December 1973, when the price of oil per barrel was more than doubled. With that increase, the price of oil had quadrupled since 1970.

In reviewing the longer-term and more fundamental causes of the energy crises, we can probably list four:

1   The fact that the global oil production level reached in the early 1970s what is called the "inflection point" on the Hubbert production curve shown in figure 1.4. That is the point at which the *rate* of annual production increases begins to decline, even though production itself continues to increase.
2   The United States reached the top of its Hubbert curve about 1970 and entered the world market as a consumer with a vengeance in the 1970s, competing with all other importers.
3   Global economic growth in the 1960s was at an all-time high and therefore added considerably to overall energy demand.
4   OPEC, or at least certain of its members, reached a point of economic strength where it could afford to restrict production to support higher prices.

These fundamental factors, plus the political upheaval in Iran that dramatically cut its oil exports in 1979, can also explain the "second oil shock" of 1979 and another doubling of oil prices.

Response to Crisis

The "energy crisis" was no surprise to many energy experts who had been comparing demand and supply trends. In 1973 Congressional Quarterly published a perceptive review of the situation titled *Energy Crisis in America*. But these events did come as a surprise to the public and its leaders. In November 1973 President Nixon responded to the Arab boycott by announcing *Project Independence*, declaring American intent to eliminate oil imports by 1980.[14] The Federal Energy Office was created to alleviate temporary shortages and was succeeded by the Federal Energy Agency.

By 1975 the more fundamental nature of the situation was clearer; and in October President Ford created the Energy Research and Development Administration (ERDA) to attack the technological and economic root issues. Early in President Carter's Administration the perception of the problem changed still more, and the rhetoric escalated. In April 1977 he went before the public to say: "Tonight I want to have an unpleasant talk with you about a problem unprecedented in our history. With the exception of war, this is the greatest challenge our country will face in our lifetimes. . . . This effort will be the 'moral equivalent of war.'"[15]

Carter subsequently announced the most ambitious proposals

yet. The results were the creation of a Department of Energy and the 1978 Energy Bill, which launched a broad attack on the problem, especially from the conservation side. It included phased deregulation of natural gas prices and was followed in 1979 by a presidential decision to phase out oil price controls first installed in 1973. Those controls had protected American consumers to a degree from the major increases in global oil prices but had also slowed the normal economic responses to it (conservation, substitution, and higher production).

U.S. oil imports in volume terms have roughly stabilized since 1977, after the dramatic increases of the 1970s which rose to about 50 percent of total U.S. consumption. But in 1979, partly as a result of political disturbances in Iran that interrupted the oil flow, prices (which had in real terms slightly dropped since 1974) doubled again. The Iran-Iraq war and the interruption of supplies it caused contributed further to an upward price movement. OPEC trade surpluses, which had fallen from $65 billion in 1974 to $5.5 billion in 1978, approximated $40 billion again in 1980.[16]

The United States has, of course, not been the only political actor responding to the price increases. In 1974 the International Energy Agency (IEA) was formed with essentially the same membership as the Organization for Economic Cooperation and Development (OECD). Much of its early effort centered on establishing agreement on floors to be placed under oil prices because it was felt that efforts to encourage private production responses might be undercut by a future sudden drop in OPEC prices. The IEA has, however, reached agreement on automatic sharing of available oil supplies in the case of future shortages. OPEC members generally gained these capabilities during the 1960s. Moreover, the early success of OPEC so strengthened the economic position of many members in the 1970s that even significant drops in sales posed no threat. In fact, the opposite problem had arisen; revenues became so great for a while that many members sought further reductions in output, in part to provide some relief from the economic burdens and possible social turmoil accompanying the tremendous additional income.

The success of the cartel   A cartel's success or failure depends upon important market characteristics. In general, *demand elasticity* should be low. That is, consumers should reduce consumption by only a fraction of a percent for each percentage increase in price. In the case of an oil cartel, this means that overall energy demand should be relatively unresponsive to prices and that oil demand as a portion of energy demand should also be quite unresponsive—

consumers should not be easily able to do without energy or to substitute other energy forms for oil. Also *supply elasticity* should be low. That is, noncartel producers, both of oil and potentially competing energy supplies, should not be able significantly to raise production and thereby undercut the cartel. In the case of OPEC these conditions were met throughout the 1970s. All the elasticities were low. In the early 1980s, however, demand had become more elastic as consumers became more efficient users or simply cut back on consumption. There is great debate and uncertainty among economists and energy experts about the magnitude of these elasticities in the longer run, however. Although short-run supply elasticities, or responses to price, may be low, in the longer run whole new energy systems (synthetic fuels, oil shale, tar sands, solar, even fusion power) may mean elasticities will be much higher. The same is true on the demand side as the long process of transforming transportation systems and even urban designs works itself out.

Still other factors underlying cartel success or failure lie in the character of cartel members and their pattern of interrelationships. OPEC contains members who urgently need additional revenues for economic growth (especially Indonesia, Gabon, and Ecuador, but also Nigeria, Algeria, Iran, and Venezuela) as well as members who have no immediate need for much of the revenue they obtain (like Saudi Arabia, Kuwait, and the United Arab Emirates, and to a lesser degree Libya). The revenue absorbers in the first category cannot afford to cut back production in case external demand falls, whereas the savers in the second category can. The mere existence of the second category is of great value to a cartel (CIPEC, the international copper cartel, has no such members). Relatively greater power is wielded by this category of members, and much depends upon their political relationship with other members. All else being equal, no member has any interest in damaging the cartel; but a number of issues, from the status of Israel to superpower conflict, can also enter into member decisions. So, too, of course, can long-standing conflicts such as that which erupted into war between Iran and Iraq.

During the 1970s the strength and coherence of OPEC seemed to be great. However, in the early 1980s the conditions that sustained the strength of the cartel had shifted, at least temporarily, and the oil marketplace acquired a somewhat different configuration. The world began to experience an "oil glut," meaning that the prices dictated by the high demand and restricted production of the 1970s did not fit the reality of the 1980s market. Oil inventories, purchased as a hedge against continuing price increases, were high, and worldwide consumption had been reduced between 3 and 4 percent between 1980 and 1981, with the sharpest drops occurring in the heavy consumers of the OECD. Both supply elasticity and demand elasticity had been altered. In the face of these changing conditions, those OPEC nations with the need for sustained revenues sought to lower prices; those without such a need sought to resist price declines and to restrict production instead. As a consequence, the coherence of the cartel began to weaken and oil prices began to fluctuate downward. The air of "crisis" that had characterized the oil-dependent energy landscape began to ease and commentators began to speak as if the world were approaching the "twilight of the oil era."

However, there has been some concern among the experts that these trends also will weaken the incentives provided to the consuming nations to respond to the situation. The short-term economic and political measures designed to achieve conservation and the longer-term efforts to find alternative energy sources to shift away from the prevailing dependency on oil were both considered to be prematurely affected by the shift in market conditions. Many argue that the "oil glut" is only a short-term phenomenon created by the response to the crisis of the 1970s and that the energy picture has not substantially changed. Therefore, the importance of the current energy transition should not be disregarded. That transition—unlike those which went before—has a fundamental scarcity component. No superior alternative to oil and gas is animating the transition, and in fact we remain at a loss to identify the next best alternative or set of alternatives. It may be advantageous to stretch out the period of the transition—as was the case when production was being manipulated by the OPEC nations—but that will not occur if it is felt that oil and natural gas are "cheap" once again.

The Broader Importance of Energy

Throughout this discussion thus far a number of references have been made to the relationships between the energy system and our larger economic, political, and social systems. Less abstractly, the events of the last several years have impressed upon us the fundamental importance of energy in relation to a much broader set of issues. In particular, we have become aware of the ties of energy to economic growth and to environmental protection.[17] Only more recently and tentatively have we begun to consider the ties of the energy system to the nature of our society and political system more generally. We want to explore each of these important linkages briefly.

Energy and the Economy

The nearly one-to-one relationship between economic growth and the growth of energy consumption has long been recognized. Specifically, on a global average, every 1 percent increase in gross world product has been accompanied for many years by a little more than a 1 percent increase in global energy consumption. Countries in the process of rapid industrialization (e.g., China, Taiwan, South Korea, Brazil) require significantly more than a 1 percent increase in energy availability. In fact they need as much as 2 percent more energy to achieve 1 percent economic growth. Rapid industrialization emphasizes transportation systems and energy-intensive heavy industry. Economies that are already industrialized (e.g., the United States, Great Britain, France) generally require slightly less energy growth. Specifically, for the 1960s the United States needed about .85 percent additional energy for each 1 percent economic growth. For OECD countries as a whole the figure for the 1960s was 1.13 percent.[18]

The reduced growth rate in global energy supplies since 1973 has had two consequences. First, it has reduced economic growth. Whereas the OECD countries grew at an average annual rate of 4.8 percent between 1951 and 1973, they grew at only 3.8 percent from 1975 to 1979.[19] Most forecasters foresee even slower economic growth in the 1980s, in large part because of lower growth in energy supplies (higher oil prices essentially are equivalent to lower supply growth because users can buy less). However, second, reduced energy growth also has begun to break the global one-to-one, energy-to-economic-growth linkage. In the 1970s and 1980s the United States was using about .7 percent of additional energy for every 1 percent economic growth. For OECD countries the ratio has dropped to .81 percent. The experts really do not know the degree to which the two growth rates can be decoupled. Opinions vary from somewhat more than we have already to a complete stabilization of energy consumption in the United States with no significant effect on economic growth through the end of the century.

The discussion of the growth penalty of energy prices has been quite abstract. It can be made concrete by considering the agricultural sector. The so-called Green Revolution of high-yield agriculture is founded on the use of natural gas or other energy-based fertilizers together with new varieties of grain (also other agricultural inputs). During the 1970s agricultural production per capita actually fell in Africa and did not advance in South Asia. Only imported food maintained dietary levels. The price of fertilizer to a poor farmer is not abstract. For that reason, the transition to a U.S.–style agricultural system, in which more than six times the *food energy output* goes into food production, may never occur in most less developed countries (LDCs). The per capita energy bill for the food chain alone in the United States is four times the total per capita energy use in South Asia.[20]

Growth is by no means the only economic issue. The rise in energy prices also accompanied and partially explained the global inflation of the 1970s. However, that inflation was under way before 1973, so energy is not the only culprit. The Johnson Administration refused to pay for the Vietnam War by cutting other (e.g., Great Society) expenditures. The greater amount of money *pursuing goods and services* in the United States pushed up prices. Much of this money moved abroad as the United States ran inflated balance of payments deficits (and even by 1972, trade deficits) so that we exported inflation. The rapid global economic growth of the 1960s put pressure on raw materials supplies of various kinds, fueling inflation. The agricultural failures of the USSR, South Asia, and North Africa in 1972–1974 also had an impact on prices. Thus, although global inflation cannot be blamed exclusively on energy, it is a major factor. Because energy, like food, is a necessity, this inflation particularly hurts the poor of the world who have not been able to keep up with the rise in prices of either commodity.

Unemployment has resulted both from relative energy scarcity and higher prices and from governmental efforts to control inflation by accepting (on behalf of a portion of their populations) higher unemployment levels. Unfortunately, the trade-off between the two evils did not work in the 1970s the way it had earlier, and the result became "stagflation," that is unemployment *and* inflation. There is growing speculation, however, that in the longer run higher energy prices *might* reduce unemployment as industries substitute human labor for energy. At this point, however, it is an open question as to whether energy and labor are substitutes or complements.

Much of the concern about economic consequences associated with higher energy prices and the energy transition centers on international issues. Many countries have had to borrow to pay for the increased price of oil. After the 1973–1974 price increases Great Britain and Italy were placed in especially precarious positions. The 1979–1980 price increases apparently pushed even Germany and Japan into trade deficits. Throughout the entire period the debt of the LDCs has mushroomed. By 1979 they owed $190 billion to private banks and another $125 billion to governments and intergovernmental organizations like the World Bank.[21] In fact, however, the LDCs have paid a lower growth penalty for high energy prices than have the OECD countries, simply because they have borrowed heavily to avoid the payment. For instance, Brazil had a foreign debt of over $52 billion by the beginning of 1980. Debt for more than half of the LDCs grew in the late 1970s at over 2.5 times the rate of exports. There is considerable fear that private banks cannot justifiably loan more in the 1980s, while at the same time continued LDC problems will require more loans in efforts to protect the earlier ones.[22]

These efforts have used money which the OPEC countries deposited abroad in loans to oil importers, who return the money to OPEC. In each instance (termed "recycling") the total debt continues to grow. Additional money has been created by several oil importers like the United States to assist in payment. The result of that action has been an explosion in international money. Money in the private European currency markets was less than $200 billion in 1972 but was over $1,000 billion by 1979. Currency reserves held by government (money issued by other countries) was also less than $200 billion in 1972 and reached $350 billion by 1979.[23] What is more, the rapid surge in gold prices more than tripled the monetary values of gold held as a stable asset by government (and others) in the last half of 1979. Altogether, these changes mean that, as a result of energy activity, a tremendous amount of international money and debt exists today that did not exist in 1972. The international monetary system is now very different, is still in flux, and is almost unpredictable.

The implications of all this are many. Because of energy requirements, uncertainty and major change make long-term economic planning difficult and rational behavior less likely. Major international monetary panic is a possibility. At the least, this burgeoning of international money will mean more inflation. Inflation helps debtors and hurts creditors. In its difficulties with paying the OPEC bill, the world as debtor helps create inflation. OPEC, in turn, attempts to stay ahead of inflation with price increases.

Energy and the Environment

The severity and immediacy of the economic problems have directed the attention of many away from the environmental issues associated with energy and the transition from oil and natural gas. But these issues—economy, energy, and environment—are so interrelated that they really ought to be studied together. We have already discussed the linkages between the availability and cost of energy, and the economy. The major economic-environmental linkages are obvious; both economic production and consumption have significant and often harmful environmental impacts. Ameliorating the environmental damage often requires either less production-consumption overall or a diversion of some production-consumption to unsatisfying (in terms of our ultimate economic welfare) preventive or corrective activities. For instance, positive reactions to automobile pollution could be less driving, pollution control devices, or (for an individual) moving farther from the city to escape its effect. The only other category of positive reaction is technological advance, which would reduce the problem with no economic cost.

We are primarily interested, however, in energy-environment linkages. Many of these linkages directly involve economics. Because energy problems have reduced economic growth and intensified inflation in the 1970s, there has been less willingness to bear economic costs in correction of environmental problems. Adding stack gas scrubbers to coal-burning electric plants, for instance, is now much less avidly supported, given the already rapidly rising costs of electricity. Eliminating highly inefficient and polluting steel plants is seen as a problem rather than progress when the United States has a trade deficit swollen by energy costs. LDCs have always seen the environmental issue as a "rich man's problem," a perception that has only been reinforced by the economic difficulties raised by energy.

This weakening of commitment to the solution of environmental problems as a result of energy-based economic difficulties is one of the two major bases for the general perception that energy problems are competitive with environmental ones. The other basis is that many proposed substitutes for oil and gas are seen as less "friendly" to the environment. This is the case especially with coal and nuclear power, the two major contenders for the last ten years. There are also environmental problems with oil shale, geothermal power, and even solar energy.

Nuclear power has nearly been eliminated as the primary future energy source in the United States because of environmental issues, including safety. These issues include the danger of the reactor itself under normal and abnormal conditions, an issue which the accident at Three Mile Island made concrete. They also include concern over the security of plutonium in the nuclear cycle, and the threat of its diversion to nuclear weapon construction by terrorists after theft or by governments which obtain it as a by-product of their own nuclear power plants. Pakistan has recently appeared to be following India's lead in this area. The safety and environmental issues further include the disposal of waste heat from nuclear power plants into water or air. Cooling towers were added to nuclear power plants on the upper Rhine to avoid thermal pollution of the river, but may now be affecting weather in the region by release of much water vapor into the atmosphere. Still another disposal issue is, of course, associated with the radioactive wastes that remain dangerous for millenia. In early 1980 the Carter Administration again postponed any "final" decision on permanent waste disposal while initiating an accelerated program to find acceptable means and locations. These issues in total have made the estimates by the Atomic Energy Commission in the 1960s that the United States would have 2,000 gigawatts of nuclear power by the year 2000 now appear absurd. (A gigawatt equals one billion watts, the output of the standard nuclear power plant; hence, 2,000 gigawatts would require about 2.000 average-sized nuclear plants.) Estimates now seldom exceed 300 gigawatts.

Coal also has been battered by environmental issues. Again, it is important to remember that the traditional deep mining of coal is labor intensive. Safety and health issues are of major significance (for instance, the high incidence of black lung disease). The industry has been largely transformed, however, into one based on strip mining, and land reclamation issues have now come to dominate the production-related environmental concerns. New U.S. legislation was passed in 1977 with quite stringent controls. The coal issues relating to consumption center on air pollution. Coal burning is dirty relative to oil and natural gas, and the technology for control of particulate emissions (e.g., stack gas scrubbers) is expensive. Sulfur dioxide has proven to be a major problem; in the atmosphere it combines with water to form sulfuric acid. Sulfuric rains in Sweden have eliminated fish from an estimated two thousand lakes, and such rains in upstate New York have destroyed the fish population in one hundred to two hundred lakes.[24]

Some potentially critical environmental issues may actually be partly resolved by an accelerated transition from oil and natural gas. Smaller and more fuel-efficient automobiles are much less polluting than gas guzzlers. But a potentially even more severe environmental threat is now posed by the increase in atmospheric carbon dioxide. Its concentration in the atmosphere was 290 parts per million (PPM) in the 1880s and 330 PPM in 1977. Estimates are that the concentration could double before 2050 if we continue our patterns of fossil fuel use. Scientists disagree, but many fear a doubling would cause one to two degree centigrade temperature increases through a phenomenon known as the greenhouse effect and produce a long-term ecological catastrophe. Rapid movement from oil and gas, unless coal makes up the difference, could at least slow down the CO_2 concentration growth rate.

Energy and Social Structure

Most of the debate surrounding the energy issue is couched in terms of the economic and environmental impact of various policies and energy systems. Nuclear energy, for instance, is attacked primarily on environmental grounds. Its costs have soared, partly because of environmental pressures, also making it vulnerable on purely financial considerations.

Underlying the energy debate, however, is another set of issues that are not well understood, even by the participants, and that are badly articulated. These issues affect choices between solar and nuclear power, between nationalizing or leaving the oil industry private, between public transit and private autos. The roots of the issues lie in values concerning how society is best organized. We must remind ourselves again of the fundamental impact that the energy system structure has on the social (including political) system throughout history.[25]

The oil and natural gas age can take at least partial credit for a number of phenomena: the existence of some of the world's largest corporations (in oil and automobiles), the undertaking of perhaps history's largest construction project (the U.S. interstate highway system), the surburbanization not only of the United States but now increasingly of major cities everywhere, and even the great expansion of the U.S. global role (including recent strengthening of commitments to real estate in desert areas around the Persian Gulf). We could also name the Green Revolution and the major social and political consequences it has had, and the development of aviation with its impact on global relationships.

We are now in the early and probably critical stages of an energy transition which will have very major consequences for all social systems, including economic and political ones. No collective social choice was exercised in earlier transitions. There were no public institutions that both recognized the occurrence of the transition and possessed the tools to shape it. This time both of these prerequisites of collective social choice are in place, and the debate is under way. Claims and counterclaims of technological feasibility, cost, and environmental impact fly through the media and confuse us daily. These factors are important, but they also often conceal the fact that many positions in the debate are built on less concrete and less knowable social concerns.

Consider some of the social implications of a nuclear power–based society. One of the most obvious is a significant governmental role in the system. Government would need to deal directly with safety issues, including the provision and transportation of fuel and the disposal of wastes. And custody over nuclear materials capable of use in weapons, or century-long control of waste disposal will certainly not be left to private industry. Nuclear energy is a highly centralized power source, and nuclear "parks" with massive generating capabilities (subject to government regulation) have been proposed. Nuclear power requires distribution by power lines, a highly capital-intensive system which is a natural monopoly. Private utilities in that position are subject to constant governmental scrutiny, including price control. It is significant that those countries that have made the largest commitments to nuclear power have strong centralized political systems and share a faith in governmental planning for the economy. These include the USSR, which has the world's most ambitious nuclear program; France, with its active government planning history; and Iran under the Shah, a strong advocate of government planning. Nor does it appear surprising that the U.S. government energy research and development program for 1978 included $3.2 billion for nuclear programs and $1.8 billion for non-nuclear.[26] Decisions being made now in politically centralized societies will naturally tend to reinforce the governmental role.

Consider, in contrast, an energy system based upon small-scale solar collections systems. Whereas the nuclear system would favor centralization of populations (to increase efficiency in distribution systems and even the use of waste heat from the plants), the solar system favors decentralization for collection purposes. Thus, its implications for land use are very different. It favors continued development of the sunbelt over the snowbelt in the United States and perhaps even of the tropical south over the temperate north internationally. Like nuclear power, installation and maintenance of solar energy systems would be capital intensive, but it does not favor only capital concentration. Installation and maintenance would require a large labor force, and the degree to which solar systems need to be specialized would support a craftsman rather than assembly-line labor. The lower grade energy obtained from solar systems (less concentrated than that from nuclear ones) favors smaller-scale and, in today's terms, more primitive industrial processing. Hence, not only is the government role in the energy system much reduced, but large-scale industrial entities are less likely to be attracted. Understandably, such an energy system tends to receive support from those opposed to concentrated governmental or corporate power, and from those who favor more decentralized and, in many respects, more traditional life-styles.

Finally, consider a coal-based energy system. Almost certainly such a system would combine reliance on coal-generated electricity with a synthetic fuels industry producing gaseous and liquid fuels. A society based on such a system appears more similar to our current one than do those based on nuclear power or decentralized solar power. Specifically, the industry would be capital and technology intensive and would provide benefits to highly concentrated capital. Government would probably help provide capital in some cases and at least would need to act so as to reduce the private risk associated with major investments in relatively new energy processes (e.g. coal liquefaction). The system would require the fewest changes in our current energy consumption patterns, including the use of private automobiles and gas-heated private houses. It should not surprise us that many major U.S. corporations see this system as our best answer. It also has begun to look as if this system has characteristics of a good political compromise.

Obviously, we are likely to have an energy system early in the next century which combines several primary fuel resources, and the social impact will therefore be mixed. One interesting feature will be the considerable differences in energy systems among various countries after having experienced a lengthy period in a shared global energy system. At the turn of the century, for instance, Brazil will be heavily reliant upon alcohol (a solar system), France upon nuclear, and the United States (probably) upon coal. Operation of these systems will provide a laboratory for comparing and contrasting the systems. These developments will probably also weaken some international ties. For instance, oil transport now constitutes two-thirds of all ton-miles in international trade.[27]

Conclusion

In summary, we must realize that the energy debate is not simply a consideration of the energy system and how it is changing. It touches our lives in ways too numerous and in many cases too poorly understood to detail. Because of the fundamental importance of the energy transition the debate can be expected to rage for a very long time. Using the emergence of energy as a global issue in the early 1970s as a base point, however, it is possible to roughly identify three periods of public and private response.

In the short term, through the 1970s and into the early 1980s, little was possible besides a political response. The United States did nothing to eliminate its oil imports in the late 1970s. Indeed, those imports had continued to grow for several years after 1973. Other actors found themselves faced with similar trends and rigidities in the energy system and they reacted predictably. Japan and many Western European countries found it desirable to reassess their positions in the Israeli-Arab conflict and to tilt towards the oil-producing Arabs. The Carter Administration, determined to reduce the U.S. role as the world's arms merchant, found it impossible to refuse demands for weapons from those same Arab countries. Mexican oil discoveries helped convince the United States to pay a great deal more attention and to be more respectful to its southern neighbor. Either through appeal or decree, governments everywhere urged consumers to drive less and turn down thermostats.

In the mid-term, however, after delays of five to fifteen years, economic mechanisms can begin to have a noticeable effect on the energy system itself. Thus, a variety of actions taken by governments, companies, and individuals in the late 1970s will bear fruit throughout the 1980s and beyond. Government acceleration of nuclear plant construction in France and legislated automobile mileage targets in the United States are beginning to have noticeable effects on petroleum consumption. Throughout the market economies (and increasingly in the centrally planned ones as well) a major factor behind increased efficiency of energy use and increased non-OPEC energy supply is the existence of higher energy prices and the innumerable small responses made by producers and consumers to those prices.

In the longer term, perhaps twenty to fifty years after the first oil shock of 1973 to 1974, technological change will begin to have its impact in the energy transition. Totally new technologies will appear and further weaken the grip of oil and natural gas on the energy system. The cost of these and the amount of energy they can provide are, of course, uncertain and will determine ultimately whether the transition from oil and natural gas proceeds smoothly. But private and public research and development programs in energy have intensified dramatically around the world and cannot fail to produce some positive results. The breakthroughs of low cost and efficient solar energy and of environmentally friendly nuclear fusion are the ones most ardently desired.

Global energy issues have only been introduced in this chapter with a highly aggregated or "macro" perspective. That is, the focus has been on general trends and issues, major concerns, and possibilities. With this background, it is now possible to begin to look at energy issues with a more detailed and disaggregated "micro" approach. The next chapter begins to do so by refining the categorization of major energy actors and by describing the most important actors. These participants are, of course, driven by values, and it is not possible to understand their behavior without looking at those values. Hence, chapter 3 outlines key values held by the full range of energy actors. With that background, chapter 4 can meaningfully examine the interaction of actors in the policy process. Chapter 5 explores the global energy future that will emerge from this policy process and the associated environment of physical and technological constraints, although such a future is by no means predictable. Finally, in chapter 6 we examine a number of lessons learned that emerge from our analysis of the energy issue.

2 Energy Actors

The preceding chapter showed that it is not accurate to characterize world energy problems solely in terms of the events of the 1970s. Energy as a global issue may be traced to a number of system transitions, from wood to coal and then from coal to a rapid escalation in the demand for petroleum as the preferred fuel. But it was the 1973 oil embargo that focused the attention of the industrialized societies and the less developed countries alike on the need for more comprehensive and coordinated solutions to the latest and potentially the most severe energy crisis—the search for ways to ease the transition away from oil.

The shift toward alternative sources of energy—made even more urgent by the "second shock" upheavals in Iran, continued OPEC oil price hikes, and growing insecurity brought by an oil import dependency[1]—has been accompanied by dramatic changes in those international actors who formulate and implement energy policies. Until the embargo, energy decisions were made more or less independently at various levels of national governments for each of the separate energy resources (oil, coal, natural gas, etc.). With the exception of OPEC, international organizations were weak and much less significant than private multinational enterprises. Since 1973 the varied activities that made up energy decisions have increasingly been centralized at both the national and international levels. In the United States, for example, it has already been noted that the first developments after the 1973 embargo focused on the creation of new federal energy institutions, like the Federal Energy Administration, and the restructuring of established organizations, such as the division of the regulatory and research responsibilities of the Atomic Energy Commission into the Nuclear Regulatory Commission and the Energy Research and Development Administration.

This tendency to rely on economic, administrative, and political centralization as a solution to energy problems has been a typical response of most developed nations; the greater complexities of the international energy situation appear to demand larger, more complex sociopolitical control mechanisms.

The transformation of international institutions has taken a similar course. The 1973 embargo created several serious difficulties for global organizations, including the potential for heightened conflict as a result of problems with the security of supplies, the need to develop institutions that could respond to the financial burdens of higher oil prices, and persistent risks associated with the proliferation of weapons through nuclear energy policies.[2] As in the case of national actors, the response generally has been to create new structures, such as the International Energy Agency (IEA), or to strengthen or expand mature organizations like the World Bank or International Monetary Fund.

Given this organizational response to energy issues, it is necessary to focus on who these actors are, how they have changed over time, and what roles they play in efforts to resolve energy problems if one is to understand fully the complex area of energy policy making. In the sections that follow, the major structural and functional categorizations of energy actors are outlined; the historical evolution of the most significant actors is discussed according to the structural categories; and some illustrations and examples of the interaction of these global actors are delineated according to the functional categories.

Types of Actors

Most approaches to the classification of actors in modern international relations emphasize the importance of structural factors. That is, it is important to know how a society organizes itself to make authoritative decisions and which patterns of behavior have become standard features of any given social system. The most significant structural factors appear to be the formal position of the actor (governmental or nongovernmental); and the level at which the actor participates (subnational, national, or transnational). By combining these two factors—positions and level of participation —six categories of actors are identified (as shown with examples in table 2.1):

1 Nation-states
2 International governmental organizations

3   International nongovernmental organizations
4   National interest groups
5   Governmental subunits
6   Subnational individuals or interest groups

This chapter will examine these six categories, which are listed in relative order of significance. Sovereign nation-states clearly are the most important actors in the international energy policy system. But while the primary decision makers in most energy issues are national officials, many other participants also have major inputs into the policy process. Second in terms of importance are international governmental organizations (or IGOS), such as OPEC, OECD, IEA, and the United Nations and its associated bodies. Third, international nongovernmental organizations (NGOS) increasingly exercise influence in the global energy system. Examples of NGOS would include not only powerful multinational business enterprises, such as the major international oil companies, but also private foundations and professional associations. Fourth, national interest groups have significant energy policy roles, particularly those performed by environmental or consumer interest groups. And finally, there are subnational groupings of governments and people that do not necessarily fall into any one of the preceding classifications. Subnational government units, scientific and technical elites, ethnic groups, and exceptional individuals often serve to challenge successfully conventional wisdoms throughout the world.

The actors introduced above also perform a range of energy policy

Table 2.1.   Structural definitions of global energy actors

Formal position	Level of participation		
	Subnational	National	Transnational
Governmental	Government subunits (U.S., state, and local governments)	Nation-states (United States, Saudi Arabia)	Intergovernmental organizations (OPEC, IEA, OECD)
Nongovernmental	Individuals, subnational interest groups (Council of Energy Resource Tribes, Amory Lovins)	National interest groups (Sierra Club, Common Cause)	Nongovernmental organizations (Exxon, Friends of the Earth)

functions that may be categorized into the three single areas comprising the global energy system: production, distribution, and consumption. By production, we mean the series of stages of energy resource development required to convert a physical resource base into a usable energy source. These stages generally involve: (1) exploratory activities, in which the resource base is discovered, defined, and sampled; (2) extraction, in which the resource is actually removed; and (3) upgrading, or processing the resource so it can be used. The distribution function refers to the movement or transportation of energy sources among these various production stages and then to the user. The consumption function then refers to final end-use. Hence, for example, production in the development of coal includes drilling exploratory core holes, extracting coal through either surface or underground mining, and processing it through various cleaning techniques. Distribution typically is by railroad, although coal slurry pipelines may be used and other transportation modes (such as trucks) may be called upon for shorter distances. Consumption then may involve a range of end-use activities, depending upon whether the coal is to be used as a solid (burned in a boiler by utilities, for example), liquid, or gas (through various "synfuels" technologies). By using these functional categories, it is possible again to categorize all global activities. Continuing with coal, for example, we see that while companies themselves may be active in virtually every aspect of the process, other actors may not be. Environmentalists may only be concerned with the extraction (mining) or consumption (burning) stages of the process; railroads may participate only in the distribution phase; and government agencies may function only in particular stages of the energy resource development sequence where regulations are applied.[3] Thus, it is possible to construct for each energy alternative (subsystem) a classification scheme which combines structural categories (nation-states, IGOs, etc.) with functional stages of the resource process (producer, distributor, consumer). Such a classification is developed in table 2.2 using the petroleum subsystem as an illustration.

Together, the structural and functional classifications provide a framework within which energy actors can be described and their roles outlined. In the discussion that follows, each of the structural categories is examined in some detail, with the emphasis placed on the ways in which major actors perform as energy-resource producers, distributors, and consumers. The goal is to describe the wide

Table 2.2. Global energy framework: system actors by structure and
functions (examples in parentheses drawn from petroleum)

Structural category	System function Producer	Distributor	Consumer
Nation-states	Net energy-exporting nations (Saudi Arabia, Mexico, Nigeria)		Net energy-consuming nations (United States, Sweden, Bangladesh, the Sudan)
International governmental organizations	Energy-producing cartels (OPEC), regional development organizations (OAPEC)	Global financial bodies (World Bank, U.N. Fund for Natural Resources), producer-consumer multilateral organizations (Conference on International Economic Cooperation)	Organizations of energy-consuming countries (OECD, IEA)
International nongovernmental organizations	Multinational corporations (Exxon, Royal Dutch Shell), global science and technology organizations (International Council of Scientific Unions)	Multinational corporations (Gulf, British Petroleum)	Private foundations (Ford, Rockefeller foundations)
National interest groups	National energy companies (Petroleo Brasileiro, Petro-Canada), professional energy associations (American Petroleum Institute)	National energy companies (El Paso Natural Gas)	Consumer, environmental, and scientific and technical interest groups (Friends of the Earth, Union of Concerned Scientists)
Governmental subunits	Energy-producing regions, states, localities (Texas, Alberta)		Energy-consuming regions, states, localities (Ontario, Massachusetts)
Individuals, subnational interest groups	Scientific and technical elites (Ralph Lapp, Alvin Weinberg), think tanks and research laboratories (Stanford Research Institute), ethnic and racial groups (Council of Energy Resource Tribes)		Ad hoc coalitions (Get Oil Out!), individual scholars (Rachael Carson, Amory Lovins), research groups (Club of Rome)

variety of actors in the international system and the range of roles they play in formulating and implementing energy policies.

Nation-States

The international energy system emphasizes policy making by nation-states. This emphasis occurs despite the considerable impact of science and technology worldwide, an impact that might have been expected to lead to the demise of the nation-state as a global actor. For example, energy science and technology have altered the substance of decisions by providing a greater capability to mine for resources in "frontier" areas, such as offshore on the outer continental shelf or in regions like the Arctic. And the cumulative effect of sophisticated energy technologies has introduced immense change in the global environment, making it more difficult to formulate rules, regulations, and other policies designed to control their consequences. Moreover, science and technology have actually created new issues for the international community of states to address (such as responding to the CO_2 problem or to the increased potential of ocean pollution).

Despite these pressures, however, the nation-state continues to be the principal actor in the energy system. For although economic interdependence characterizes the modern global energy system, that same interdependence has also created tensions among nations and a tendency to seek self-sufficiency as a way to respond to petroleum shortages and higher prices. Concern with supply security has dominated the global energy arena to such an extent that conflict among industrialized societies, as they compete for access to markets, clearly poses a threat to international stability.[4]

For the most part, national actors are important as producers and consumers of energy. As illustrated in the framework in figure 2.2, they are categorized according to the degree to which they are *net* producers or consumers of energy (or, in other words, net importers or exporters). This is not to say that national governments do not have major roles in each function but that certain functional roles by nation-states demand more attention. Thus, some national actors must be discussed in more detail.

Saudi Arabia is the dominant force in energy production in the Middle East, and the United States, as a consumer of almost one-third of the world's energy, exercises considerable influence on global energy consumption patterns. Moreover, because it is at least a partial exception to the typical energy policy-making approach

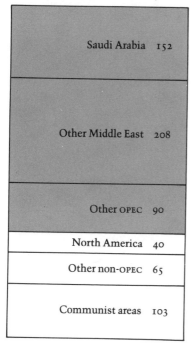

Figure 2.1. World's remaining oil reserves. *Note:* World's remaining oil reserves as of the end of 1975 were estimated *(left)* by *Oil and Gas Journal.* Of the total of 658 billion barrels, 555 billion were in the world outside the communist areas. Note that whereas most of the remaining recoverable reserves were in the Middle East, most of the production of oil up to 1975 *(right)* had been in North America. *Source:* Scientific American, *Energy and Environment* (San Francisco: W. H. Freeman, 1980), p. 21.

of most Western industrial societies, particularly in its attention to the consumption function, Sweden merits attention. And Mexico's potential role in future world energy production patterns deserves mention, not only because of its substantial resources, but also because it is not currently an OPEC member.

Saudi Arabia   In fact, Saudi Arabia is more important for the international energy system than is OPEC itself. This is the case for at least three reasons. First, as shown in figure 2.1, the Saudi oil fields contain about 27 percent of the proven petroleum reserves to be found outside the communist world and about 23 percent of the world's total proven reserves. Second, Saudi excess-production capacity is the greatest in the entire world, with perhaps half the current spare capacity for production in the entire Middle East. And third, the Saudi government has been a moderating influence in OPEC pricing decisions, in part due to its "special relationship" with the United States and in part because Saudi leaders have expressed extreme concern with their inability to maximize demand security (gaining access to markets through long-term contracts, obtaining financial security for investments, etc.) in the face of decreasing domestic requirements for expanding their current revenues.

The historical political foundation for the Saudi position in international energy affairs has been a combination of factors: authoritarian rule within a traditional kinship society, a sensitivity to general trends in regional Arab public opinion, an awareness of the implications of militant revolutionary regimes in the Middle East, and an ethnic and political concern for the Palestinian cause.[5] These factors led to the adoption of a policy of using oil production not only for economic ends but also as a political weapon in the range of conflicts between Arab states and Israel, a posture that eventually supported the 1973 embargo.

In light of the 1979 Iranian revolution, concern has increased in the West regarding the potential threat to world petroleum production posed by possible instability in the Saudi regime. Again, because of the great significance of Saudi Arabia as a producer of that most valued energy source, crude oil, the linkage between energy and national security, always central to Western-Saudi relations, appears likely to gain even more leverage in the policy process in the future. And for the first time in recent years, religion may play a large role in the conduct of Saudi Arabia, as well as the rest of the Moslem world. One study went so far as to observe a few years ago:

> Too little is known about international relations in Saudi Arabia to make any more solid predictions. But experienced "Saudi watchers," men with years of exposure to different strata of Saudi society, including the highest level of the royal family, are increasingly worried about the corrosive influence of instant wealth. Here are some of their comments: "Five years ago (1973), no one heard words against the government; now one hears, 'This government is intolerable and has to go;'" "I judge the government's chance of survival for a half-dozen years to be quite good, and for a dozen years, fairly good. *But there could be a successful revolution this evening.*"[6]

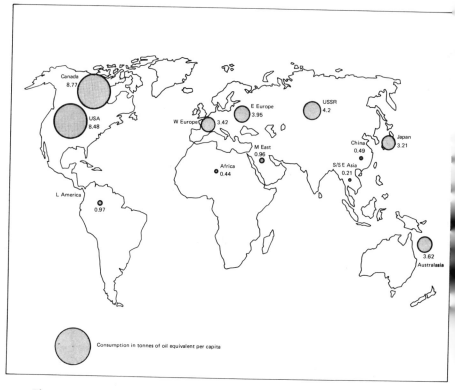

Figure 2.2. World energy consumption per capita (tons of oil equivalent per capita). *Source:* David Crabbe and Richard McBride, eds., *The World Energy Book* (Cambridge, Mass.: MIT Press, 1979), p. 201.

United States   Another important producer of energy is the United States, but it is the enormous, once seemingly unlimited consumption appetite that makes U.S. energy policy of critical importance for the global community. Figure 1.1 in chapter 1 reveals that the United States consumes about 30 percent of the world's total production of energy, and figure 2.2 illustrates the very high energy consumption per capita in America as compared to other nation-states and regions. Two elements of the current American energy situation have created these fundamental problems. First, and most significantly, the nation has suffered from what has been termed the "energy syndrome," a group of symptoms that occur together and that describe a pathology or system malfunction.[7] These symptoms have been: production and consumption practices that require steady increases in energy supply; policies determined to a large extent by the perspectives of producers; and a set of political, institutional, and structural obstacles that limit the search for alternative policies. These symptoms may explain why U.S. energy policies implemented in the last half-decade have not reduced the rapid increase in American consumption and oil import dependence.

The second problem element refers to the national dependence on the least abundant U.S. resources to provide most energy supplies. While domestic oil and natural gas account for almost two-thirds of supply and over half of demand, these two sources together total only about 9 percent of U.S. energy reserves. The increasing reliance on oil imports thus leaves the nation exposed to future supply interruptions from abroad. Over the decade of the 1970s there was a dramatic shift away from relatively reliable western hemisphere sources of oil (Venezuela, for example) to less "secure" eastern hemisphere (Middle East) sources.

One author makes the argument that this situation is a result of an evolving American perception of the energy problem, a changing view of the energy crisis that has gone through at least four stages.[8] First, Americans perceived the foreign energy issue in terms of a "diplomatic threat." That is, the oil embargo was seen as an obstacle to U.S. Middle East policy and a threat to U.S.–Western European relationships. The response to this perception was the Washington Energy Conference in 1974 in which oil-sharing plans were worked out with U.S. allies and the IEA was conceived. The second stage, however, saw American leaders increasingly seeing energy problems in terms of an "economic threat," which emphasized the potential for severe economic dislocations in oil-consuming countries as a result of higher petroleum prices. As a result, American initiatives focused on the IEA's ability to implement cooperative conservation guidelines and on an expanded domestic research and development program. Third, energy came to be seen in terms of a "global institutional crisis," a part of the larger institutional and economic development crisis in relations between developed and less developed nations. The reaction to this point of view featured a broader dialogue with the nations of the Third World, the strengthening of international financial structures, such as the International Monetary Fund, and the creation of new global institutions, like the Conference on International Economic Cooperation. Finally, and only recently, the United States has come to see the energy crisis as a "global resource shortage" in which the demand for energy is perceived as outstripping global supply in the short term (five to eight years). This perspective has given the energy problem a material, technical thrust that contrasts sharply with the more institutional perceptions of the past. And it has led to actions like former President Carter's National Energy Plan in which, for the first time, the reality of the difficult transition from an oil–natural gas system to one based on a combination of conventional (coal and nuclear power) and alternative (solar and conservation) options was recognized.

Sweden An innovative approach to reducing import dependency by turning to an extensive energy conservation program makes Sweden at least a partial exception to the energy syndrome just described. To a much greater degree than other Western industrialized societies, Swedish responses to the rising energy prices and occasional supply shortfalls characteristic of the 1970s focused on expanding citizen involvement in the policy-making process, particularly with regard to the debate and controversy surrounding nuclear power. Thus, an extensive national program of "study circles" brought various interest groups together in town meeting formats to exchange information about nuclear energy issues and to discuss obstacles as part of a comprehensive debate on Sweden's energy future. And Sweden has explored the range of alternative

Figure 2.3. Gross energy use, excluding exports of fuels. *Source:* Lee Schipper and Allan J. Lichtenberg, "Efficient Energy Use and Well-Being: The Swedish Example," *Science* 194 (3 December 1976): 1011.

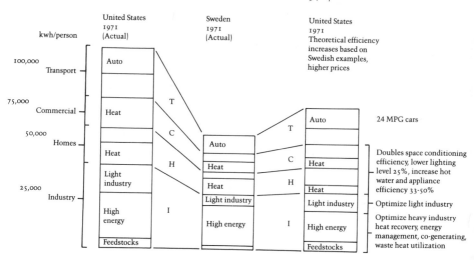

approaches to changing life styles in the interest of improving the efficiency of individual and group energy-consumption patterns. Although the full implications of these policies are still unclear, such initiatives could help avoid such potential consequences of the energy syndrome as constantly increasing energy costs, greater economic and political centralization, and higher risks of global conflict.

Already there are studies that indicate Sweden uses only about 60 to 72 percent as much energy as the United States to generate each dollar of gross national product, while the GNP per capita remains essentially the same. The information displayed in figure 2.3 compares the gross energy use, excluding the exports of fuels, of Sweden and the United States for the year 1971 and illustrates the very significant differences between Sweden as an energy-consuming global actor and the American consumption situation. For each of the major demand sectors—transport, commercial, homes, and industry—Sweden's use of energy appears to be much more efficient. Government policy appears to have played a large role in this end-use efficiency, through the implementation of more stringent building codes, a policy of giving priority to energy conservation in home loans, and taxes on gasoline. The largest difference between U.S. and Swedish energy end-use patterns is in the transportation sector, with the most striking variation appearing in the use of the automobile. Also Swedish use of residential space heating is lower, even when differences in climate are taken into account, because of better use of insulation and less use of electricity for these functions.[9] Figure 2.3 also indicates the level of U.S. energy consumption in 1971 if the country had used energy with the efficiency of Sweden and explains what specific changes would provide that efficiency.

Mexico   The new oil production potential of Mexico has engendered widely differing projections, with optimists contending that proven reserves of 40 billion barrels (about one-fourth that of Saudi Arabia) will dramatically affect the world oil picture. But major obstacles appear likely to constrain even the hopeful forecasts. Not only has Mexico embarked on a cautious and deliberate oil resource development scheme designed to husband this valuable national asset, but because of its large population the Mexican government has emphasized domestic economic development rather than attempting to maximize exports.[10] Moreover, a number of nonenergy issues have clouded Mexican-American discussions regarding possible linkages between Mexico's production potential and the U.S.

oil market. Problems such as American immigration policy and water resource decisions appear likely to hamper efforts to negotiate comprehensive U.S.–Mexican energy arrangements. And recent economic fiascos in Mexico do not help the situation.

LDC *nonproducers*   At this time the situation of the less developed countries without substantial oil resources should be described, for many LDCs share Mexico's development problems without the luxury of an indigenous energy resource base. Developing nations contain about 70 percent of the world's noncommunist population, but they account for only about 15 percent of the total noncommunist energy consumption. Clearly the economic and political implications of the energy crisis have been worse for these Third World actors than for the developed countries. LDCs have been more vulnerable to price increases, which have had large and immediate consequences for foreign exchange reserves, national incomes, and the potential for economic growth in the future.

One of the central issues of energy policy in LDCs is that of financing development. Capital is in short supply, and demands, particularly for electricity, have been fueled by rapid urbanization and industrialization. Some studies have projected as much as $50 billion per year may be required between now and 1985 to overcome this constraint on LDC energy development.

While oil, largely imported, continues to provide the bulk of energy supplies in less developed nations, "noncommercial fuels" such as wood, animal waste, and crop residues are important contributors to the energy sector (sometimes adding as much as 60 to 70 percent of total energy in some countries). And energy use is much different in rural areas of LDCs than in the conventional urban energy systems. Renewable energy sources such as solar power are much more applicable to isolated rural areas with their limited access to power grids and fossil fuels.[11]

International Governmental Organizations

The 1973 embargo created a number of serious problems for international governmental organizations. First, the nationalistic emphasis on securing supplies and the accompanying threat of global conflict demanded some "insurance mechanisms" that could avoid dramatic interruptions to industrialized societies. Second, the financial burden of higher oil prices pressured the international monetary system to develop a capacity to cope with future balance-of-payments deficits and to find some way to recycle petrodollars (the hard currency paid out of the industrialized countries to the oil-producing states). And third, the vulnerability of the Third World demanded a broader global energy dialogue between the developed and the underdeveloped societies. In each of these areas IGOs performed a major role; but with the exception of OPEC these responses plainly have been secondary to nation-state actions aimed at protecting energy availability and supply from possible future disruptions.

The Organization of Petroleum Exporting Countries   This IGO, commonly known as OPEC, is important for energy policy because of its ability to control oil production and pricing decisions. OPEC is presently composed of thirteen LDCs (Algeria, Ecuador, Gabon, Indonesia, Iran, Iraq, Kuwait, Libya, Nigeria, Qatar, Saudi Arabia, United Arab Emirates, and Venezuela), which together produce about 80 percent of the crude oil in world trade. Approximately 60 percent of the petroleum in global trade is produced in OPEC Middle East member states, a fact that was illustrated dramatically in figure 1.3. OPEC also is moving into the "downstream" petroleum resource development activities, but the remainder of the logistical system —tankers, pipelines, and processing facilities—are still in the hands of the industrial countries or their private multinational enterprises for the most part.

Founded in 1960 in response to reductions in the posted price of crude oil by the petroleum MNCs, OPEC was initially characterized as an IGO that only reacted to changes and that never had any role in bringing about modifications in the global energy system. By the mid-1960s, however, the cartel had confounded early predictions of its quick demise by maintaining a very flexible and resilient structure that avoided serious tests of its fragile political consensus while managing to focus its internal efforts on the issues surrounding petroleum pricing. As was noted in chapter 1, the cartel's success has been due to its physical and economic capabilities to constrain production and to the generally low supply and demand elasticities of the petroleum market. But the overall political stability of the cartel also has been a significant factor. Emergency changes in demand elasticity will likely adversely effect the future successes of the cartel.

Recently the oil cartel has been criticized by some energy-poor LDCs because the latter's support of OPEC has not been adequately rewarded with funds for development aid. India, for example, has been especially critical of OPEC resistance to the creation of a two-tier pricing for oil exports that would favor LDCs by providing petroleum at a reduced rate.[12] But the cartel has attempted to respond to issues concerning the financing of Third World development through the traditional international aid mechanism (providing funds to the World Bank, etc.) and by undertaking individual state funding activities (through agencies like the Kuwait Fund for Arab Economic and Social Development), and other innovative forms of assistance (Venezuela's underwriting of Central American coffee sales through a special fund and the use of oil pricing to provide general development financing in that region).

The Organization of Arab Petroleum Exporting Countries   This organization, also known as OAPEC, was established in 1968 to coordinate Arab oil interests and broader regional concerns. Specifically, OAPEC was designed to coordinate the oil policies of its members, and for that reason it is a major energy production actor. OAPEC also provides assistance to members in the exchange of data, expertise, and training to promote cooperative petroleum problem

Table 2.3.   Net oil imports as a percentage of total energy consumption (OECD—West European countries)

Country	1960	1973	1976
Austria	5	41	42
Belgium	28	60	51
Denmark	56	91	82
Finland	26	61	59
France	30	71	68
Greece	76	77	71
Iceland	67	58	45
Ireland	29	77	70
Italy	40	73	68
Japan	31	75	72
Luxembourg	7	35	31
Netherlands	42	44	39
Norway	39	34	−28*
Portugal	59	82	88
Spain	25	64	69
Sweden	48	59	57
Switzerland	36	64	62
Turkey	10	36	44
United Kingdom	26	49	38
United States	5	16	19
West Germany	19	54	51

*Norway is a net exporter of oil.
Source: Ford Foundation, *Energy: The Next Twenty Years* (Cambridge, Mass.: Ballinger, 1979), p. 253.

solving, and to develop joint energy projects and proposals. Obviously OAPEC members also are major participants in the OPEC policy-making process, but the regional body includes, in addition to the Arab OPEC states, nations such as Syria and Egypt that are not oil exporters. And OAPEC goals and policies clearly are distinct from those of OPEC, although the OAPEC charter restricts the regional organization to policies that do not contradict OPEC decisions. Finally, the orientation of OAPEC tends to be highly political, in contrast to the more narrow economic focus of the petroleum cartel.

The Organization for Economic Cooperation and Development Another important energy-related IGO is OECD, whose membership includes the major industrialized energy-consuming countries of Western Europe, North America, and Japan. As in the United States, the initial responses to the energy crisis in OECD member states emphasized independent national actions attempting to reduce import dependency. As shown in table 2.3, petroleum import dependency in most of the Western European countries far outstripped American reliance on foreign sources of oil, and the uncoordinated national emergency measures that followed the 1973 crisis generally did little to resolve this serious problem. This is not to say, however, that OECD activities have been entirely fragmented. In addition to its creation of the International Energy Agency (discussed below), the OECD performs a major role in analyzing and assessing world energy policies, and contributes to the resolution of global energy financial issues through its Financial Support Fund, which aids in the recycling of petrodollars and in easing balance of payment deficits brought on by higher oil prices.[13]

The International Energy Agency Created in 1974 by nineteen major oil-importing countries (essentially OECD members with the exception of France), the IEA provides a vehicle for cooperative oil sharing and demand restraint. The primary roles of the IEA relate to the provision of planning capabilities for the emergency sharing of oil supplies, but this mechanism's utility is highly uncertain given French refusal to participate and the divergence of views of member states. The longer-term goals of the organization are to encourage conservation, cooperative research and development programs, and the development of broader energy policy "principles." To date, conservation guidelines have been reviewed, and there has been an agreement on targeted import levels. In addition, twelve basic principles that would serve as national guidelines have been developed, and the participants have agreed that the agency should conduct regular systematic reviews of each country's energy policy. But the major contribution of the IEA may be more philosophical than programmatic. As one analyst has noted:

> Comparing the situation between the OECD countries—and even within the EEC—prior to October, 1973, with the situation that now exists, one can only conclude that the radical changes in the oil market have led to equally radical changes in the willingness of industrial countries to cooperate on energy. The emergency system has undergone substantial improvements; the basis for long-term cooperation has been established; the idea that oil consumers have common interests has made very considerable progress. One must realize, however, that the real tasks still lie ahead, and that the IEA will only be successful if member governments remain determined to achieve larger results.[14]

World Bank   Officially termed the International Bank for Reconstruction and Development or IBRD, World Bank financing of energy development projects has focused on the oil-importing LDCs, with several new roles having been defined for the Bank in recent years. Investments are now emphasizing exploration and production activities rather than the previous focus on refining and marketing. And the World Bank now directs financial assistance more toward general fossil fuel projects in contrast to its history of concern for electricity-generating facilities. At the same time the International Monetary Fund and other development assistance organizations have been strengthened with expanded resources, some of which are targeted toward energy concerns.[15] As has been noted, much of this funding comes from OPEC sources; and because the IBRD, IMF, and International Development Association are seen by many in the Third World as tools of the West, OPEC countries have established a number of independent agencies of their own. A less successful venture has been the United Nations' establishment of a Revolving Fund for Natural Resources Exploration based on voluntary contributions.

Finally, it should be noted that there are a number of IGOs that specialize in one aspect of energy policy. The European Atomic Energy Community (Euratom) and the International Atomic Energy Agency (IAEA) promote atomic power and provide for a range of technical assistance measures.

International Nongovernmental Organizations

The positions of governmental and intergovernmental actors in global energy policy making are more visible and perhaps more easily defined than is the case for other participants, but it is clear that international nongovernmental organizations play major roles as well. In fact, the activities of NGOs have been more controversial precisely because relatively less is known about their structures and functions in the international policy system. This is certainly the case with regard to the multinational energy firms and global environmental groups that are the most significant NGOs involved in energy decisions.

Multinational business enterprises   Multinational corporations (MNCs) dominated international oil policy from the earliest days of the development of petroleum resources in the United States and Middle East. The most significant of the oil MNCs are among the world's largest corporations. These "integrated majors," sometimes termed the Seven Sisters, include Exxon, Mobil, Standard of California, Texaco, Gulf (now part of Chevron), Royal Dutch Shell, and British Petroleum. Each of these business enterprises is characterized by a high level of what is called "vertical integration" (i.e., control of operations from the bottom to the top—reserves, production, refining, retailing, and transportation activities). Other advantages enjoyed by the largest MNCs and to some extent by other majors in the United States and abroad are their large capital resources, their great research and development (R&D) capabilities, and their rapid and relatively constant economic growth rates. Until recently these factors, in combination with extensive management skills, a high level of application of capital and technology to oil exploration and development, the evolution of an extensive and sophisticated logistics system, and complex but generally supportive relations with home governments, led to a situation in which the largest MNCs controlled every aspect of the world oil industry. For example, in 1952 the seven major companies produced 90 percent of the crude oil and marketed 75 percent of the oil products outside North America and the Communist world. This share of the industry declined in subsequent years, largely due to the entry of "lesser majors" based in the United States (such as Getty, Phillips, Signal, Union, Continental, Sun, Amerada Hess, Cities Service, and Marathon) and the competition of a number of international independents (Compagnie Française Petrole, for example). Nevertheless, in 1972 the Seven Sisters still produced 75 percent of the crude outside North America and the Communist bloc, and they marketed slightly more than half the petroleum products sold in that same year.[16] A good indicator of the global power wielded by

Table 2.4. America's 15 largest industrial corporations, ranked by assets in 1978

Rank	Company	Assets ($000)	Sales ($000)
1	Exxon	41,530,804	60,334,527
2	General Motors	30,598,300	63,221,100
3	Mobil	22,611,479	34,736,045
4	Ford Motor	22,101,400	42,784,100
5	IBM	20,771,374	21,076,089
6	Texaco	20,249,143	28,607,521
7	Standard of California	16,761,021	23,232,413
8	General Electric	15,036,000	19,653,800
9	Gulf	15,036,000	18,069,000
10	Standard of Indiana	15,109,264	14,961,489
11	ITT	14,034,866	15,261,178
12	Atlantic Richfield	12,060,210	12,298,403
13	U.S. Steel	10,536,300	11,049,500
14	Shell	10,453,358	11,062,883
15	Tenneco	10,134,000	8,762,000

Source: "The Fortune Directory of the 500 Largest U.S. Industrial Corporations," Fortune 99 (7 May 1979): 270–89.

the largest petroleum firms in the period immediately preceding the oil embargo is provided by table 2.4, which lists the fifteen largest U.S. manufacturing corporations ranked by assets in 1978. Nine of these were petroleum MNCs, and all five of the U.S.-based Seven Sisters (plus Shell's U.S. subsidiary) were among them.

The economic strengths of the large multinational enterprises, however, have led to fears on the part of consumers that there will be MNC manipulation of energy supplies, prices, and alternative resource developments in many of the Western industrialized societies. Thus, social regulatory policies in many developed nations have been applied to the oil industry on the grounds that petroleum firms have developed energy monopolies and have engaged in anticompetitive forms of behavior.[17] Moreover, regulatory constraints on the international oil industry also emphasize the perceived failure of these corporations to promote income distribution and to consider environmental and other externalities in their exploration, production, transportation, and marketing activities.

Even more significant for the oil MNCs than these actions on the part of consumer states has been the assertion of control over crude oil production and pricing by the producer governments. These actions have all but removed the multinationals from decisions affecting either volumes or prices of world oil. As a result, the distributional role of the MNCs has become more significant than the former emphasis on production. According to a recent study:

> From the viewpoint of the producer governments, it is the ability of "majors" to move nearly 52 percent of oil in world trade to the consumers' markets which is presently so consequential. Moreover, in a period of general oversupply, the majors can make decisions as to supply from which sources, which relieves the government from having to do so in an OPEC forum. Over time, with the universal availability of communications and data processing, consumer or producer government oil companies could move these volumes; but very few, if any, governments possess today the requisite managerial resources to cope with the complex supply arrangements inherent in oil moving in world trade. As they acquire the necessary talents, a diminishing role for the international majors would seem to be a natural consequence.[18]

In light of these trends it is not surprising that one of the most significant changes in the energy industry in recent years has been the growth of conglomerates that own multiple resources. Especially important in this new "horizontal integration" has been the acquisition in the last decade by the oil MNCs of coal and uranium resources, thereby creating the first true "energy companies." In the United States, for example, as of 1977 about sixty separate oil companies held approximately 21 percent of existing coal reserves and 17 percent of coal production capacity. At the same time petroleum firms controlled 48 percent of U.S. uranium reserves and 44 percent of uranium production. Moreover, the top five American oil companies held about 68 percent of national uranium milling (processing) capacity, and the top four petroleum firms held over 42 percent of the known uranium reserves.[19]

It must also be observed that there are additional factors that contribute to the oil multinationals' potential power as they entered the decade of the 1980s. The strength of industry associations (such as the American Petroleum Institute) and policy advisory bodies (like the United States National Petroleum Council) are not to be underestimated. In addition, there is a significant community of interest among oil firms on such political matters as the decontrol of petroleum prices, possible divestiture policy, and the use of government tax incentives and sanctions, although differences between the integrated majors and the more specialized independents have on occasion weakened this consensus.

Global interest groups   These energy policy–related groups include a number of environmental organizations like the Friends of the Earth, which have played a significant role in coordinating international resistance to such developments as the siting of nuclear power plants. Similar functions are carried out by loosely structured professional associations, such as the Union of Concerned Scientists. Most of these groups operate on limited budgets, poor professional staffing, and small memberships. As a result, international ecological interests must channel their resources in order to be able to undertake major transnational energy policy initiatives. But buoyed by the global impact of the "limits of growth" ideology promulgated by The Club of Rome and other institutions and broad public distrust of the existing energy technocracies, environmental interests have been successful in pressing for the incorporation of ecological concerns in energy decisions. Often, however, the impact of global environmental groups is indirect or even in some cases unintentional. For example, when the Australian branch of the Friends of the Earth, as part of their antinuclear campaign, provided documents to the California State Energy Commission and Public Utilities Commission regarding price fixing in the American nuclear industry, the documents actually had a greater effect on the European community because of the great influence the U.S. nuclear industry has had on community markets. In this case the transnational consequence of the environmental interest action was to force EEC investigations of uranium producers and to encourage the mobilization of environmental participants in Europe against nuclear power.[20]

National Interest Groups

Relatively few of the public interest groups active in the energy policy system operate at the international level; the majority of consumer or ecological groups are much more likely to focus their efforts at the national or subnational level. That is because of the ad hoc nature of many public interest coalitions and the shortages of funding and manpower characteristic of these kinds of organizations.

While generalizations about national interest groups are difficult to make, one recent study of several American public interest lobbies involved in energy decision making has generated some interesting conclusions. According to this analysis, Common Cause, the League of Women Voters, the Sierra Club, the Consumers Union, the Consumer Federation of America, Americans for Energy

Independence, and Ralph Nader's organizations share the following characteristics and roles: (1) their mass support is derived largely from college-educated, middle-class persons with skeptical attitudes about the present quality of American government; (2) leaders of these groups believe the function of public interest groups is to counteract the power of special interest for the benefit of the public at large; (3) these groups expect to achieve reform through ad hoc coalitions specific to particular policies and issues rather than through scientific, impartial public administration; (4) they are increasingly critical of nuclear power; (5) most of these groups oppose the traditional "development-independence" position of U.S. programs that emphasize a supply orientation and the maximization of domestic resources; (6) they will not support the deregulation of energy prices because they oppose powerful special interests, which include oil companies; (7) all of these lobbies support energy conservation and the development of solar energy and other alternative resources; and (8) these groups often serve to initiate innovative policy proposals in areas in which they have a consensus among their supporters.[21]

Similar energy consumption roles have been observed in many West European national interest groups, particularly in the context of the widespread debate about the future of nuclear power. This debate has featured the development of a number of powerful parties-at-interest in Sweden (the so-called Green Wave movement), the Netherlands (the Federation of Environmental Defense and the Foundation for Nature and the Environment), and Austria (the Naturfreunde) that have pressed for broader participation in governmental policy making.[22]

Of course, not all national interest groups are critical of the conventional approach to energy resource development. Mention has already been made of the national associations that strengthen the petroleum industry—organizations like the American Petroleum Institute (API). This and other industry associations are major avenues through which the petroleum firms exercise considerable political influence. The API, for example, comprises some 350 member companies with a 1974 budget of over $15 million, which is used for the purposes of information collection and dissemination, research, and the development and presentation of policy options at every level of American government. An estimated $10 million per year is spent by the sixty oil and gas organizations in Washington alone for lobbying purposes. The "oil lobby" has, in fact, expanded to such an extent that foreign governments have engaged their own Washington lobbyists to monitor petroleum policy developments on their behalf.[23]

Governmental Subunits

The category of governmental subunits includes subnational public sector energy producers and consumers. Examples of this category of actors would include American state and local governments. Prior to the 1973 crisis, participation in energy policy making by state governments within the United States was severely constrained by the inability of state authorities to deal with energy supply markets that were national or international in scope, the inadequacy of traditional state agencies in coping with complex nonlegal energy problems, and the absence of effective energy policy coordination mechanisms between the federal and state governments.[24] Although the scope of energy problems continues to defy easy solutions, state governments have reacted to these shortcomings by creating new energy councils, committees, and task forces to deal with energy issues and to coordinate policy.

Historically, American states have exercised extensive authority over policy decisions in areas such as the regulation of facility siting and licensing, the availability of state-owned resources for development, and the establishment of prices and rates of production for intrastate energy resources. The opportunities for greater state participation in the energy system have, in many cases, been enhanced by the energy crisis. Under general federal guidelines, states have been delegated important responsibilities for formulating and adopting water and air quality criteria to meet federal requirements, collecting data to form the basis for federal rules and regulations, and enforcing conservation standards. But a major factor constraining cooperative efforts between states has been the extreme diversity of state energy policy orientations. For example, even within a region such as the Rocky Mountain area, states with similar cultural and political histories—Colorado and Utah, for example—have vastly different energy policy objectives. And when energy-producing states are compared to energy-consuming states, these differences are amplified even further.[25]

Local governments have generally paid little attention to the need to develop institutions to cope with energy problems until very recent times. And while local control of the administration of zoning ordinances, building and health codes, and health and sanitation standards can have major impacts on energy development, the importance of these powers is often not fully appreciated. The limitations of local governments also are a consequence of a lack of technical expertise, inadequate data bases, and a long tradition of decision making that stressed accommodation with and wide discretionary authority for the private sector.[26]

Individual and subnational interest groups   Other significant subnational actors in energy policy making include ethnic groups, such as those American Indians who have increasingly taken a more active role in securing for themselves control over energy developments on their tribal lands. Through organizations such as the Council of Energy Resource Tribes (CERT), Native Americans have begun to perform a range of energy functions. And on occasion these roles take on a transnational nature, as when CERT brought in OPEC advisors in the negotiations between tribes and United States federal energy officials.

Scientific and technical elites also play important roles in the making of subnational, national, and transnational energy policies. Individuals like E. F. Schumacher, Amory Lovins, and Barry Commoner have contributed to the global energy debate by calling into question long accepted "paradigms" or bodies of thought and assumptions about the very nature of our energy past, present, and future.

Perhaps no single individual has had a greater impact on the international energy controversy than Amory Lovins. In a series of works, many of which have already become classics, Lovins outlined the different implications of pursuing what he termed the "hard" and "soft" paths to energy development. For Lovins, the hard path is an extrapolation of the recent past—rapid expansion of centralized high technologies to increase supplies of energy, and especially of electricity. The problems with this version of our energy future are the shortage of gaseous and liquid fuels, the high level of loss of energy in the conversion of conventional fuels to electricity (Lovins compares the process of generating electricity from a nuclear power plant to heat a home to "cutting butter with a chain saw"), and the extremely high capital costs of pursuing sophisticated high technologies. On the other hand, the soft path is a commitment to the efficient use of energy; the rapid development of renewable energy sources matched in scale, in energy quality, and in geographic distribution to end-use needs; and the use of special transnational fossil fuels (chiefly coal) to bridge the gap between our hard past and soft future. The types of soft technologies that constitute the soft path include solar space heating and cooling, the conversion of biomass, and wind systems.

Whether or not one agrees with Lovins's perception of the international energy future, he has successfully altered the entire debate by contrasting the differences in the two paths as follows: they represent a choice between greater centralization of political and economic control and a move toward decentralization; they provide a clear choice between higher and lower environmental risks and between higher and lower capital costs; and they demonstrate the decisions that must be faced about the international implications of energy resource development—that is, the risks associated with hard path emphasis on nuclear power and its accompanying dangers of nuclear proliferation and global conflict.[27]

Summary and Conclusion

Clearly the roles played by the various subnational, national, and transnational energy system actors reflect a variety of physical, technical, and economic factors, including the extent, chemical characteristics, geographical distribution, and price of the global energy resource base, the level and type of technological sophistication, and so on. But they also mirror the political complexities of a modern international system that is decentralized, potentially unstable, and fragmented in its policy orientations and implementation strategies. Such factors place serious limitations on any attempt to classify energy actors in a systematic fashion. As Mason Willrich has observed: "The world energy situation is thus baffling. Although energy is a vital interest of almost every nation, energy politics may well create patterns that are inconsistent with other important patterns of international relations. Nation-states form the political bedrock of the world community. But it is difficult to find a general scheme for classifying the bedrock for purposes of defining international energy relationships."[28]

This fragmented system has been constructed on a fragile basis consisting of a range of legal, administrative, and historical factors, each of which is founded on substantial ideological, attitudinal, or value elements. Thus, we must turn to the next chapter, an elaboration of the role of values in energy policy making, if we are to understand the roots of the interrelationships among these actors.

3 Energy Values

Energy actors enter the policy arena in order to achieve determinable objectives of one kind or another. Indeed, we tend to identify actors through their association with a particular set of goals. The OPEC nations meet periodically in an effort to determine new crude oil pricing and to adjust production to support those prices. The United States seeks to improve its relationship with the major oil-producing state of Saudi Arabia through the sales of military equipment. Environmental groups such as the Sierra Club or the Friends of the Earth endeavor to protect the environment by lobbying for legislation to regulate ecologically threatening activities like the strip mining of coal or the disposal of nuclear waste. Multinational corporations such as the Seven Sisters seek to increase their profits. And consumers around the world try to find the lowest price for gasoline at service station pumps. In each of these examples, the actors are pursuing valued goals that are attainable by participating in energy or energy-related activities. The nature of the goals pursued may determine the sphere of action—whether it is in governmental institutions, the marketplace, or technological research —but in each instance energy action is contingent on the motivating values. It is often disagreement among such values that leads to conflict between energy actors on a global scale.

The term "values," however, assumes many meanings as philosophers, scientists, economists, and policy makers grapple with the impetus behind individual and group behavior. In the realm of philosophy, values define the legitimate ends for human development; thus, determination of proper and just values provides the essential meaning for all conduct. In the realm of science, on the other hand, an effort is made to disregard values as irrelevant to the objectives of research, although no scientist who has ever sought an answer to a vexing problem will deny that he chose that problem instead of another because of some preference or concern. The economist introduces a financial and commodity component in defining value by focusing on determination of utility or other measures that can explain economic behavior. In a similar though distinctive way, the policy actor is primarily concerned with value as the determination of desired end-states even though not all policy actors explicitly examine their values. Values become manifest as an actor pursues policy objectives that seek to maintain an existing condition or create a new situation. The policy maker operates under the pragmatic assumption that certain steps must be taken to achieve (or maintain) outcomes that are perceived as real and tangible whether they result from formal governmental action or informal action, such as making one's home more energy efficient.

In broadest terms, energy values then motivate consumers to ensure that there are adequate supplies at a price they can afford. Suppliers in turn seek to provide those supplies while making a profit, and governments oversee this process, assuming an increasingly important role as the marketplace has become subject to intrusions from a variety of outside forces. Problems arise because the process of ensuring that the energy needs of everyone—individuals, groups, corporations, countries—are met is subject to the stresses of competition for other "valued things." All energy actors do not in fact share the same values. Those who want energy do not have enough of it. Those who have enough energy for their own consumption rely on its use as an export to obtain badly needed capital. Because of the ever-increasing imbalance between supply and demand, the process of obtaining an adequate supply comes up increasingly against the corresponding difficulty of obtaining enough at a cost, financial and otherwise, that is affordable to the consumer. The producer wishes to obtain the highest price possible and still maintain a market for the product. The consumer wishes to find the lowest possible price and still sustain incentive for continuing production. And, while energy is obtained and used, it is hoped that the buyer, the seller, and the distributor alike are able to act without creating a whole host of other problems such as polluting the environment or disrupting the economic or regional balances that support a stable market.

Because global energy actors assume different roles arising from their functional efforts as producer, distributor, or consumer, there are inherent tensions. Each role carries a potentially competing set of desires or values. Even within the functional role there may be competing interests. Established consumers in the developed nations may compete for supplies with relatively new consumers in the developing world whose differing level of industrialization calls for different energy needs, both present and future. Moreover, simple market mechanisms of supply and demand no longer operate in a vacuum. Rather, political considerations have played an increasingly important role since the early 1970s. It is an accident of geography that much of the world's proven petroleum reserves reside in a set of countries that are now at the center of one of the most volatile political controversies of our time. The conflict between Israel and the Arab nations over the Palestinian issue intrudes on whatever energy matters arise from the production and distribution of Middle Eastern oil. In that conflict, political considerations thus represent an impediment to addressing energy concerns (and, by the same token, the Arab possession of large oil reserves provides them with an instrument to affect the outcome of the political considerations in resolving the Palestinian issue). As a consequence, political goals have achieved a significant if not dominant position during the past decade.

If one then recalls the economic force of demand and supply inelasticity and the resulting cartel of the major oil producers, it is clear that valued differences are a definitive part of the global energy arena. Policy making and implementation represent the strategies for resolving conflict among these different value preferences.

Energy Values

Accordingly, we need to turn our attention to those specific values which propel energy actors in the global arena. These can vary from a few abstract and relatively widespread ideals to a narrow set of objectives characteristic of a particular situation. Depending on the situation, apparently consistent values held by a single actor may prove to be contradictory. Hence, although values may be products of established processes over a long period of action, they nonetheless remain transitory and subject to change as the result of concrete conditions.

The contemporary global system can be addressed in terms of six energy values that usefully categorize the motivations behind actor behavior:

1   Assuring reliability of energy supply in both the short and long run
2   Achieving the most advantageous cost for energy

3 Avoiding inequity
4 Safeguarding the quality of the environment
5 Maintaining the regime
6 Pursuing autonomy and self-reliance (national and corporate)

Supply Reliability

Supply reliability can be achieved by following either of two paths —the guarantee of foreign supplies, or the establishment of self-sufficiency—or by some assured combination of the two. For residents of most Western industrialized countries, the Arab oil embargo of 1973 to 1974 brought the value of assuring reliability of energy supply from obscurity to the forefront. It continues to dominate energy values today in two specific dimensions: (1) sufficient volume, and (2) continuous supply. Prior to the oil embargo (which, it should be remembered, arose in part as a consequence of the political turmoil surrounding the October 1973 Arab-Israeli war), the notion that energy would always be available prevailed throughout the Western industrial world. Reliability of supply was simply not a matter of concern. With the shock of interrupted energy supply from the major Arab producers, however, all of that was changed. "Energy self-sufficiency" became the cry, because it was seen as the only guaranteed route to the supply reliability previously obtained without concern from imported oil. Industrial nations, which had not had to address such issues, now began to contemplate the trade-off between long-term and short-term requirements, to consider the implications of the direction of economic growth and development, and to focus on paths to establish and implement conservation measures.

Supply reliability, for many nations, grows out of the larger value of national autonomy and self-reliance. There has always been concern for the security requirements of the nation. The United States has always had some form of strategic petroleum reserve for the exigencies of military conflict. The same concept is applied now to provide security against any form of interruption in supply whether military, political, or economic. While this may be a valid contingency strategy, the overall path of supply reliability through national energy self-sufficiency is viewed by some as shortsighted. Advocacy of policies to attain supply reliability for one nation by accelerated usage of its own nonrenewable resources (e.g., better oil extraction or additional pipelines) may well benefit that single nation for a while. However, such continued use of exhaustible resources may be at the expense of *world* supply reliability or may even threaten that nation's own longer-term supply reliability. In short, a nation's accelerated use of its own finite resources does not bode well for either the total world stock of energy sources or the specific nation's future stock. If, on the other hand, accelerated use of domestic nonrenewable resources is accompanied by development of alternative energy sources, long-term and global supply reliability need not be compromised.

Nations of both the industrialized North and developing South must make choices between alternative economic and social paths. Reliability of energy supplies is crucial to many such options. Even discounting the energy requirements of proposed industrial development in the Third World, one encounters problems of supply reliability. For instance, the Green Revolution—to produce high yield crops for food deficit nations—requires extensive use of petrochemical fertilizers. Interruption of the supply of oil from which those fertilizers are made would debilitate that agricultural option. Similarly, efforts by countries of the North to sustain already high levels of economic output depend upon reliability of energy supply. In the industrialized countries of the North, efforts to improve or sustain already high levels of food production are heavily energy dependent (and much of the world's exported food—as well as the petrochemicals exported to the Third World countries for their own food production—comes from those nations). The direction of "development" for either type of country, then, depends upon energy supply reliability.

Conservation can be one step in the direction of long-range supply reliability. If consumption and therefore demand are diminished through conservation, the supply needs are less, thus extending resource availability. Conservation occurs as a consequence of cutting back on activities requiring energy or as a result of more efficient use of energy for the same set of activities. The comparison was made earlier between usage patterns in Sweden and the United States.[1] The major difference in the consumption patterns of these two countries is found in process heating, space heating, and transportation. With respect to the latter, for example, while the Swedes travel less than Americans, 60 percent of the total mileage, they also consume only 60 percent as much fuel *per passenger* mile.

Conservation itself or the further shift to renewable energy sources may not create supply security, particularly in the short run. This view is reinforced when one carefully examines public pronouncements by policy makers concerning self-sufficiency. President Ford in his 1975 State of the Union Address, for example, viewed energy independence as occurring in three stages: "First, we must reduce oil imports by 1 million barrels per day by the end of this year and by 2 million barrels by the end of 1977. Second, we must end vulnerability to economic disruption by foreign suppliers by 1985. Third, we must develop an energy technology and resources so that the United States has the ability to supply a significant share of the energy needs of the free world by the end of this century."[2] While the second and third stages stress self-sufficiency, the first clearly acknowledges the continuing role of imported supplies as a part of the overall strategy of maintaining reliable energy resources. The government thus uses two strategies to provide a secure supply of energy. One is an attempt to "stretch" domestic energy by increasing available sources or by slowing down the demand, and the other is an effort to cover the difference between energy needs and domestic contributions by arranging for guaranteed imports. However, the third stage of self-sufficiency—developing U.S. energy technology to meet "the energy needs of the free world"—has not been pursued seriously since the 1975 statement.

Hence, while governments adopt a variety of internal measures such as subsidizing energy production by absorbing the risk of research and development or becoming the prime contractor for incremental energy supplies, they prefer to maintain the quota of external energy without disruption and they act accordingly. This may be accomplished by reinforcing existing sources of supply. The United States, for example, has undertaken a significant shift in its Middle Eastern policy in order to improve relations with Arab oil-producing states. With the fall of the Shah of Iran and subsequent turmoil there in 1979 to 1980, this shift has focused particularly on Saudi Arabia. In 1980, despite considerable domestic resistance, the United States concluded a package of military sales to the Saudis involving Airborne Warning and Control Systems (AWACS) aircraft, F-15 fighter planes, and related hardware/software. This action can certainly be attributed, at least in part, to efforts to maintain favorable conditions for uninterrupted oil shipments by the leading world producer.

The other side of the problem, should original distribution lines be cut, is to ensure that alternative external sources are found. Nineteen market-economy countries of Western Europe, Japan, New Zealand, Canada, and the United States, which now constitute the International Energy Agency (IEA), have thus agreed that energy resources will be pooled if one or more members suffers severe supply disruptions. The focus of IEA was to establish an institutional means to achieve coordinated policies for supply reliability. In the first phase this approach was to concentrate on procedures to acquire and distribute energy reserves provided by strategic stockpiling. Later IEA was to coordinate consumption policies to reduce the member nations' demand for imported oil and then, on that basis, establish a negotiated framework with the oil-producing nations to stabilize the energy market. IEA arrangements now appear to be able to handle short-term disruptions, should they arise again.

But the projected longer-term availability of supply presents another situation for European importers if the current levels of oil dependency continue. The problem of European supply may arise from weaknesses within the oil-exporting nations that are themselves less economically advanced. In an analysis of Europe's major suppliers one author has concluded that there are both temporary constraints such as lack of infrastructure and shortages of skilled personnel, and permanent constraints such as a lack of raw materials, land, water, or manpower that may interrupt or stop altogether the oil shipments on which nations depend.[3] In other words, the political or economic stability of the supplier is an integral part of the reliability of supply. Hence, efforts to establish stable consumer-supplier relationships may be a critical part of a nation's energy strategy. Such an effort is evident in both the motivation and controversy surrounding the construction of the gas pipeline between Western Europe and the Soviet Union. For some, such reliance on a potential adversary like the Soviet Union places Western European energy needs at a greater risk. However, this kind of government-to-government arrangement appears to many to hold greater potential than agreements between private oil companies and exporters in politically volatile areas.

Until now, discussion of supply reliability has focused on oil, as the primary energy resource of the industrialized nations. Less developed countries, however, have an even greater difficulty ensuring an adequate supply of energy. For them the cost of oil set by demand and supply factors among the major industrial consumers and leading petroleum exporters far outstrips their own capacity to accumulate new capital. By necessity, these countries then seek other energy sources. Table 3.1 summarizes present and future world consumption for renewable energy, most of which will occur in countries for which increased oil consumption represents a dwindling option.

A number of countries have adapted to these new sources. Brazil has taken the lead among the rapidly developing nations in moving toward a sustainable energy economy through three basic strategies: the development of its enormous hydroelectric potential, the use of wood as both a residential and industrial fuel, and the development of an agriculturally based alcohol fuels program.[4] China, the Phillipines, and even Sweden have adopted similar strategies. For those countries outside the industrialized networks of Western Europe, North America, and Japan, supply reliability may well be obtained only through such alternative sources, particularly those, unlike solar and nuclear, requiring low start-up costs. But the consequences of the failure of these countries to ensure reliable supply are no less severe, and perhaps more so, than those for the heavy consumers of imported energy.

Advantageous Cost

The second major energy value is the attainment of the most *advantageous cost* for energy. Of course, the term "advantageous" has opposing meaning for producers and consumers. The producer, it is assumed, seeks as high a price as the market will bear (or even

Table 3.1. World consumption of energy from renewable sources, 1980, with projections to 2000

Source	1980	1985	1990	1995	2000
	Million metric tons coal equivalent				
Wood	1,015	1,110	1,220	1,410	1,640
Hydroelectric	600	710	850	1,020	1,200
Wind	3	5	17	90	200
Crop residues	100	110	110	100	100
Waste (methane)	4	10	30	53	90
Waste (electric and steam)	10	12	15	20	25
Geothermal	13	27	52	87	140
Energy crops	3	16	30	45	55
Solar collectors	1	5	18	49	100
Cow dung	57	60	60	55	45
Photovoltaics	1	1	2	20	40
Total	1,807	2,056	2,404	2,949	3,635

Note: Electricity from all sources calculated in terms of coal required to produce the equivalent amount.

Source: Lester R. Brown, *Building a Sustainable Society* (New York: W.W. Norton, 1981), p. 243.

higher than the market can withstand in some recent instances).
But this assumption oversimplifies the case. Low-income exporting
countries such as Indonesia, Mexico, Nigeria, and Algeria—the
"high absorbers" mentioned in chapter 2—have consistently sought
to maximize income from oil exports.[5] In contrast, the more af-
fluent among OPEC members—the "low absorbers"—seek to stabilize revenue and, hence, tend to take into account the effects of
sudden price increases on the major Western industrialized countries where these same OPEC countries have significant levels of
investment.

Consumers are concerned, on the other hand, with achieving as
low a cost for energy as feasible. It is this effort to minimize energy
cost which has characterized the activity of this value in the energy
marketplace of the 1970s and early 1980s. Achieving the lowest
possible cost for energy is certainly not a new value, but it has
taken on new urgency in recent years, as energy costs have risen.
Although oil is far from the only energy source, its price changes
have stimulated much of the discussion of energy cost reduction.
The direction of these changes, with the exception of the constant
dollar cost during 1978, has been one of continuous increase. The
most dramatic increases came in 1979 and 1980 (although by 1982
there was evidence that oil prices had begun to stabilize around $35
per barrel).

These and similar increases have had identifiable effects on both
the North and South. The effects in the North have been highly
publicized. Rising prices of oil imports have contributed to a balance of trade deficit and to inflation in most countries, especially
in North America and Western Europe. Economies have become
less stable, and individuals have experienced rising prices at the
gasoline pumps and at the store for petrochemical products and for
foods for which energy-related production costs have risen. One
illustration of the way in which supply reliability and cost have
come into conflict is the case of strategic petroleum reserves. As
Northern nations such as the United States attempt to set aside
some oil in a strategic petroleum reserve in order to increase supply
reliability, oil-producing nations respond by increasing the price of
oil. This is partially a market mechanism —the law of supply and
demand—but even more important, it is a manifestation of the
realization by petroleum-exporting nations that it is not in their
best interest to allow substantial reserves to be accumulated by
large oil-consuming nations.

In the nations of the South, increases in energy costs have the potential to be seriously debilitating. Since the market price for oil is presently determined by the interaction between the major industrial consumers (the United States itself, remember, consumes nearly one-third of all the world's energy) and the major producers seeking to maximize profit, the lesser developed countries—with neither the industrial base, the available export earnings for trade, nor the domestic economic wealth to compete in this interaction —can be effectively shut out of market determinations. They must pay the going rate. Under these conditions recurrent price fluctuations are a detrimental factor. Since the economies of these nations are smaller than those of the industrialized North, a dramatic increase in the price of energy cannot be absorbed as easily. Just as with supply reliability, cost increases can close options in the developing world, ranging from industrialization to the Green Revolution, since both of these rely on heavy energy use.

Another aspect of the total cost of energy relates to the *level of efficiency* for energy consumption. In earlier days when energy was cheap, consumers did not worry about using it in a less than optimal fashion. Societies were industrialized under an energy model where increased energy consumption was assumed to be a necessary by-product of advances in economic growth. And because energy was plentiful and cheap, little research and development addressed the goal of optimal efficiency. Citizens were constantly exposed to direct and indirect pleas through the media to engage in life-styles that required high and rather inefficient energy consumption. Not so long ago, for example, gasoline companies in the United States competed for retail business by giving away glassware, dishes, footballs, or by employing other gimmicks. Automobile advertisements emphasized speed and power. It is particularly instructive to contrast these strategies with contemporary energy company commercials on television, which tend to stress conservation, responsible resource management, and efficient consumption.

This same transformation is occurring in even broader areas of energy-related cost considerations. The prevailing trend of disposable containers and planned obsolescence — "the throw-away society"—required replacement products that needlessly consume additional energy.[6] The energy-induced awareness of the cost impact of this needless consumption has led to efforts in a number of countries to reverse this trend. Sweden now requires waste paper to be separated from garbage, while the remaining organic materials are placed in a compost heap, thus lessening the need for energy-based fertilizers. In Cairo most garbage is recycled. A set of common container sizes has been established in Denmark to expedite recycling. The Japanese even recycle American cars in the form of scrap to produce new Japanese cars.

Many countries also have returned to energy systems of the past in order to make more efficient use of energy in terms of cost. Since 1973 one of the most prevalent developments in this regard has been the return to wood as fuel in many parts of the globe. In the United States, for example, the number of wood-burning stoves stood at almost 7 million in 1980, contrasted with only 160,000 eight years earlier.[7] The Canadian government has created incentives for those industries burning wood wastes, and Finland is moving in the same direction. Fast-growing trees in the tropics are being heavily exploited. In the United States, coal consumption as well as the practice of reopening oil fields abandoned as marginal (in terms of cost extraction) have both increased in the last several years after decades of declining use. Energy from waste, from crops, and from falling water, wind, and the earth's heat are strategies adopted in various parts of the globe. It is clear that the same considerations of cost that attracted consumers to oil as a cheap, efficient fuel in the postwar period and that resulted in the world's oil dependency are now working to turn consumers away from oil as a fuel because its high cost has placed a premium on other forms of energy.

Equity

Defining equity is a difficult task. As one observer notes, in commenting on equity in the context of scarce global resources: "Everyone knows its meaning, and everyone's meaning is different."[8] In this context equity might be thought of as a substantial degree of fairness or justice in the allocation of resources. Or as President Carter defined it in his National Energy Plan: "Our solutions must ask equal sacrifices from every region, every class of people, every interest group."[9]

Trying to avoid economic inequities because of energy activities is especially difficult because a system of unequal distribution of wealth and resources already exists throughout the globe: between rich and poor nations, between rich and poor individuals within specific nations, between traders of primary products and manufactured goods (the relationship known as the "terms of trade"), between those who control the international economy and those who must participate in it without controlling influence, and between holders of large reservoirs of raw materials and those without such commodities but in need of them. In the post–World War II era the gap between the haves and the have-nots for each of these inequitable situations has widened. This process was in full stride prior to the dramatic increase in the cost of energy during the last decade. Thus, avoiding inequities—or more accurately, preventing a further erosion of already inequitable situations—is tremendously difficult when dealing with energy. As already noted, energy demands, particularly for imported oil, and the ability to pay for such energy without creating a myriad of other problems within a country differ greatly among the nations of the globe, whether they are developing or already developed. In chapter 1 we saw the delayed effects of the 1973 oil export slowdown and subsequent price increases on both the heavy importers of the industrialized world and the new class of consumers from the developing sector. And this process simultaneously produced the so-called petrodollar problem; that is, how can the oil-exporting countries most effectively use the vast hard currency profits from petroleum to maximize national goals?

The costs borne by the lesser developed countries have been particularly severe because of tremendous energy needs characteristic of the early decades of industrialization as well as the large increases in energy requirements arising during the last fifteen years from the shift to energy-intensive approaches to achieve greater agricultural production quickly. This outcome has been a blow to Third World expectations. Past patterns of economic development have been translated into industrial growth, with the developed nations of the North setting the standard. Industrial growth increases energy demand. Hence, the less developed countries, in formulating their development objectives, anticipate and feel that they have a legitimate claim to energy resources, yet those resources have not been readily available. Badly needed capital was diverted from the urban industrial sector (or at least was not stretched as far in that sector) as a consequence of higher energy prices worldwide, producing either slowdowns in the industrial process, increased accumulation of debt or both. Some OPEC countries attempted to mitigate against this disparity by creating a two-tiered pricing system, in effect advancing aid to poorer countries. These programs were essentially short lived, however, and where still in existence fall far short of earlier promises rendered. In summary, then, energy price increases have tended to widen the gap between rich and poor nations.

Questions of cost may also have continuing political implications. In a number of countries already experiencing economic problems—for example, Great Britain, Portugal, and India—the high cost of oil in the 1970s reduced the ability to withstand domestic political pressure.[10] Governments in these countries have had to face the inflationary consequences of the high cost of energy as a key ingredient in their survival.

In OPEC countries it has been the opposite problem of the just distribution of profit. The notion of a trickle-down effect—new wealth will filter down from the top throughout all segments of society and thus everyone will benefit—is simply not operating or at least not operating well. Broad international distribution of oil profits is fiction rather than fact. For example, in Kuwait, which has the highest GNP per capita in the world, some twenty families control the bulk of the nation's income, as did some forty families in the days of the Shah in Iran, and as does the royal family of Saudi Arabia.[11] Even the existence of military regimes in so-called socialist societies does little to redistribute wealth.

On a much larger scale an interesting argument has been made that recent staggering profit making by oil-rich countries really represents a movement toward a more equitable distribution of wealth. This argument suggests that the terms-of-trade relationship, in which profits rise more slowly for exporters of primary commodities than for those exporting manufactured products, may be reversing itself. Because of the rather successful pricing operation of the oil cartel, the gap between industrialized and certain segments of nonindustrialized society has decreased. This is obviously true to a point, but the debate over the legitimacy of this argument will grow more intense as oil profits outpace inflation.

Another aspect of equity relates to the question of meeting basic human needs in the pursuit of a standard for minimal living conditions. Those energy actors who try to assure energy subsistence levels for all seek fulfillment of such standards. For instance, in the United States, as the cost of electricity, natural gas, and heating oil have increased, many utility companies have seen growing numbers of customers who are unable to pay their energy bills. This condition has elicited the establishment of governmental (and a few nongovernmental) programs to assure winter heat to the homes of those unable to pay. Such programs have been justified on the grounds that to do otherwise would be to deprive citizens of basic human needs.

A final aspect of equity addresses the right of actors to play a role in determining energy outcomes that affect their energy futures.

This right of participation affects such issues as the quest for appropriate energy technologies. What is "appropriate" in one region or for one community—the largest output or most advanced technology —may not be what is determined as best for all. Large-scale nuclear plants, for example, may be quite efficient and may, in fact, be appropriate for an urban, industrialized nation. But for less developed, predominantly agrarian societies, where there are effective local energy resources such as wind or wood, such plants may not be appropriate. The point argued with regard to equity is that communities or individuals affected by such decisions should be afforded the opportunity to address those choices and play a role in determining the outcome.

Environmental Safeguards

In the early days of energy consumption environmental concerns did not occupy much of policy makers' time. And where it was a problem the issue tended to be local in nature. One reason for this low level of concern related to the lack of understanding about immediate and long-term environmental consequences on land, water, and air from activities associated with energy production and consumption. Another reason for the failure of policy makers to act can be found in the trade-offs of such behavior. Environmental protection costs money and in the early days of industrialization the tremendous start-up costs of the process overrode any concern for safeguards. Thus, some have argued that there is a relationship between the wealth of a country and its inclination to allocate resources for protecting the environment.[12] Protecting the environment requires wealth. Consequently, it should not be surprising that many Third World countries—now in the early stages of industrialization—argue that they simply cannot afford environmental protection.

Production and environment The production of energy as well as its consumption creates a number of problems.[13] In crude oil and natural gas production, natural pressure may lead to fire on land and the pollution of water surfaces and shorelines from offshore drilling. The transportation of oil, whether by supertanker in the Atlantic or by pipeline in the Arctic, is a procedure fraught with danger to the surrounding flora and fauna.

However, environmental problems arising from the mining of coal caught the world's attention first, particularly as strip mining became more pronounced. This technique is still practiced on a large scale in West Germany, Australia, and the United States, and on a smaller scale in Great Britain, Canada, Ireland, and Greece.[14] If the mining is carried out in flat country with proper land reclamation, little environmental damage follows. But if it is done without any steps undertaken to protect the environment, then not only is land left scarred but streams are polluted from the resultant acid mine drainage. Mountainous strip mining (contour mining) creates a greater potential for a wider range of problems. Deep shaft mining leads to yet another set of problems. Acid water can leach out into streams and endanger both human and animal life some distance away. Water seeping down from the surface can lead to cave-ins.[15]

Another production problem is the siting of large energy facilities, representing major decision making on the part of the industrial giants who own them. In a 1977 OECD study it was estimated that its members need 250 new large-scale power plants in the next ten years, half of them nuclear. An additional fifteen to thirty oil refineries will be required.[16] Environmental concerns are heightened as the possibility of problems is enhanced. But this endeavor has not involved many groups concerned with the environment until the last decade. Now, however, throughout the industrialized North, one finds many groups involving themselves in a variety of ways in each step of the decision-making process.

One final set of concerns about energy production relates to catastrophic threats.[17] These threats are highly uncertain and of low probability but have the potential for severe damage. Nuclear reactor accidents, once thought virtually impossible, now concern most citizens as a consequence of the Three Mile Island incident a few years ago in Pennsylvania.

Consumption and environment   There also are many problems associated with the consumption of energy.[18] Burning coal emits particulates (fine pieces of ash, the most visible smoke), sulfur dioxide, and oxides of nitrogen. Particulates can be controlled, although the cost increases more rapidly for higher levels of control.[19] Preventing sulfur dioxide from entering the atmosphere is a more difficult and costly venture. The technique currently used, scrubbers, is fraught with controversy over its cost and effectiveness. It is a technique that itself uses energy. The problem of nitrogen oxides is related to particular design configurations of boilers, and apparently it is not feasible to change them solely to control these gases. While comparatively fewer problems exist with the burning of oil, automobile pollution is another matter. Pollutants from automobile exhausts include hydrocarbons, carbon monoxide, oxides of nitrogen, and sometimes lead. Automobile emission standards work in the cases of hydrocarbons and carbon monoxide but are less successful with the other emissions.

Nuclear power use leads to a variety of problems, most of which are too little understood. No adequate measures have yet been devised to dispose of radioactive wastes produced from power-generating reactors. That waste, still accumulating, is transported and collected in designated disposal sites. Waste heat also becomes a problem in nuclear energy (as it does for all fossil fuel burning). It is estimated that at least sixty-five percent of the heat value of the fuel is wasted, that is, it is discharged into the environment.[20] Substantial increases in water temperature can occur, particularly if the volume of the water body relative to that of the wastewater is low. The problems of thermal pollution created by consumption of all forms of fossil fuel energy may prove catastrophic in nature because of an increase in global temperatures.[21] Climate modification is a real possibility as a consequence of increased carbon dioxide levels brought on by increased burning of fossil fuels, particularly coal. Acid rain is now recognized as a source of a variety of environmental problems.

As can be observed, the potential set of environmental problems arising out of energy production and consumption is substantial. But because environmental integrity represents a relatively new goal as a carefully articulated policy, the institutional mechanisms do not yet appear to have the necessary foundation to deal with the issue effectively. A part of this problem arises from the requirement for sacrifice. In the United States, for example, a recent poll showed that Americans had an intense interest in protecting the environment for the future. Sixty-seven percent of those polled favored strict environmental laws at the sacrifice of present economic growth. However, when specific environmental issues were measured against those of energy availability, the majority shifted. An equal percentage (45 percent) favored extracting oil and natural gas, as opposed to preserving wilderness lands; and 61 percent favored oil and natural gas development as opposed to enforcing strict laws to control offshore oil spills. In short, in hard trade-offs environmental integrity tends to diminish in importance.[22]

Regime Maintenance

The fifth energy value, *regime maintenance*, refers to the strong effort by those operating within a prevailing system to retain that system. "Regime" is a broad concept encompassing the overall norms, processes, and structures that characterize the many systems, such as the international system, currently operating for the production, distribution, and consumption of global energy. In that context a relatively well-accepted distinction is made in international relations between the center and periphery nations of the world—roughly equivalent to North and South—and centers and peripheries within individual countries. The latter distinction refers to the influential elite in a country that controls the economic and political systems—the center—as opposed to the masses who have no serious influence on economic and political decisions—the periphery. Regime maintenance is therefore pertinent as an expression of the desire of the center within nations or within systems to continue to stay in power and, thereby, control the economic and political processes.

Energy is an area in which regime maintenance manifests itself quite frequently. Tax decisions in the North and nationalization decisions in the South are examples of energy issues in which the regime maintenance value surfaces. In many Western democracies the issue of gasoline taxes has been controversial. A few policy analysts and a very small number of politicians in such countries have argued that dramatic gasoline price increases would help lower demand and enhance long-term supply reliability. The argument may seem sound, but it has seldom been adopted. One of the major reasons for its failure to be accepted is that in order to be enacted elected officials would have to support it publicly. In most systems where officials are elected, short-term economic or pocketbook considerations are among the major factors that individuals consider in casting their votes. Dramatic gasoline price increases may bolster long-term supply reliability, but it is likely to have negative short-term economic effects, and therefore, it is unlikely to help politicians get elected. Since getting reelected—one form of regime maintenance—is a crucial value at work here, the future of dramatic gasoline tax increases in many democracies does not appear bright until such time as the perception of voters being motivated by short-term economics changes. Some political scientists and economists would go a step further and argue that an additional reason, and perhaps a more important reason, for reducing the likelihood of such tax increases is that the prevailing regime in most center nations is so tied in with "big business" that they would not want to take any steps that might hurt profits. Regime maintenance is thus doubly relevant since the argument is made that withdrawal of political support by big business would spell doom for those in power.

In some nations of the South that possess petroleum or other energy reserves nationalization has been a major issue. Should the government take over private corporations that are extracting raw energy materials? Arguments on both sides have involved regime maintenance. Some who have argued in favor of nationalization have made the point that nationalization is usually a very popular idea in most Southern nations, and any regime that moves in the direction of nationalization is likely to stay in the good graces of the citizenry. One argument against nationalization is that such a step would close off foreign investment in virtually all areas because corporations would assess the political risk as being too high. In many Southern countries the withdrawal of foreign investment can lead to economic chaos, a situation not conducive to regime maintenance. Another argument builds upon the latter one and adds that some of the corporations with the foreign investments will help prop up the regime in power through monetary payoffs and contributions to internal suppression. In return for helping maintain the regime they ask for protection from nationalization.

Nongovernmental actors also seek to maintain the prevailing "regime," that is, the structure and systems for energy that allow them to follow their own interests. Multinational corporations, for example, could not be expected to pursue strategies that adversely affect their ability to price their products and to obtain desired supplies. These corporations have dominated the prevailing energy regime through the vertically integrated control over every aspect of petroleum development from the wellhead to the service station pump. In most industrialized nations the multinationals have significant levels of political influence and play major roles in the pricing and control of supplies. While nationalization has reduced some of the production roles for these multinational corporations, they still operate in the oil fields of such countries as Libya and Saudi Arabia under licensing arrangements. And, while major oil producers are now entering the "downstream" aspects of the distribution and consumption functions, the major oil corporations still clearly dominate the refining and marketing of oil. These corporations, particularly the Seven Sisters, are based in the major industrialized consuming nations, are staffed at the top with personnel of those nations, and are composed largely of stockholders from those nations. Hence, the interests of multinational corporations in maintaining the prevailing global energy regime tend to coincide with the interests of producing and consuming nations that use their services. Recently, the strategy of multinationals to use excess profits to gain control of other energy-producing structures has been viewed as a clear expression of maintaining and enhancing their regime.

The other side of this picture is represented by those countries in the world that are disadvantaged by the prevailing energy regime. The lesser developed nations that are effectively priced out of the energy marketplace now call for a new regime to provide for a more equitable distribution of energy resources. This approach is consistent with the broader efforts toward establishment of a New International Economic Order, which, in turn, is manifested in a number of other issues. World lending institutions—such as the World Bank and International Monetary Fund—supported through funding from nations that compose the prevailing political and economic regime, make efforts to accommodate such demands without threatening that regime. Nonetheless, contemplation of further developments in the global energy system must be attentive to these challenges to the present political and economic regime.

Autonomy and Self-Reliance

Autonomy and self-reliance constitute a pair of related values that underlie many actions in the energy sphere from both the national and corporate perspective.

National autonomy From a national perspective the notion of "self-reliance" is most commonly associated with the efforts of the lesser developed nations of the South to break the cycle of dominance by the developed world. However, the phrase "energy independence" has been used frequently in the United States in a similar way, signifying the American desire to break the pattern of dependence on foreign oil. In both cases the quest for autonomy is to assure the ability of an individual nation to make decisions independent of the influences of other countries. One of the most common manifestations of this value is the call for reduction of energy imports. Another expression of autonomy is the nationalization of oil fields in the Middle East and elsewhere. And national autonomy has motivated several additional recent initiatives such as construction of the Alaskan pipeline by the United States and the efforts on the part of some of the oil-producing countries to control the "downstream" operations of shipping, refining, and marketing their oil.

Corporate autonomy The quest for corporate autonomy and self-reliance also has a strong impact in the energy arena. One clear expression of this value is in the pursuit of profit and growth or accumulation, the fundamental goals of a business enterprise. Profit is one of the factors that leads many energy-related multinational corporations to pursue strategies that seek to minimize risk and produce stability (as seen also in the value of regime maintenance). Supply security and economic efficiency often appear therefore as interim corporate goals in the pursuit of profit. A large oil corporation, for example, can be expected to decry governmental interference with its ability to price its products or to obtain the supplies it wishes (where it wishes).

Incompatibility among Values

We have now described six basic energy values sought by the dominant actors of the global energy system. In summary, these include supply reliability, advantageous cost, economic and regional equity, safe environment, regime maintenance, and both national and corporate autonomy.

It is evident from examining the six individual energy values that they are not all compatible with one another. Since, as noted at the outset, values are what cause actors to enter the energy arena, competing values represent competitive action. In the actors' effort to realize their values, they clash with other actors attempting to realize theirs. Hence, a full understanding of the force of values in the energy area must recognize the tensions or incompatibilities among them. Those incompatibilities may take two forms, the competition among two or more individual energy values, or the impact of a nonenergy value, such as national security, on energy values. Let us consider the former group first.

Competition among Energy Values

Reliability vs. cost The tensions between supply reliability and cost represent a basic dilemma for policy makers. It is the argument between strong advocates of national interest and those who adhere to the principle of comparative advantage. The latter principle would dictate that each individual or country ought to make those products that it can make at the lowest cost relative to other products and buy those items that it cannot produce efficiently. Applied to energy in an era of oil dependency, this vulnerability—in the eyes of national interest adherents—directly hurts national power and restricts the ability to make foreign policy decisions potentially free of external influences. "Project Independence," for example, became the rallying cry of the United States in 1973 after OPEC began to interfere with the regular flow of its oil. The United States found itself in a position of vulnerability because it had turned to cheap energy from abroad in ever-increasing volume, even though the potential for threats to supply reliability increased. This process evolved over a long period. The United States began importing oil in 1947 but remained under strict import controls, especially after 1959 when import quotas were set not to exceed 12 percent of total consumption (although those quotas were in fact exceeded). That quota system was imposed to prevent the threat of dependency to national security in a time when domestic oil was plentiful, but nineteen times more costly to extract than foreign oil. By 1970, however, availability of domestic oil had been sharply reduced. Imported oil began to expand as a share of total consumption as the increasing cost of domestic oil (even though prices became controlled) dictated a shift to foreign sources. Dependency increased, and the stage was set for the "energy crisis" of the 1970s.

But an irony emerged during that decade. As a consequence of the 1,100 percent increase in OPEC oil prices, consuming nations now have a clearer choice in the debate between supply reliability and cost minimization. Whereas in the past cheap OPEC oil created a dilemma, now in many instances domestic oil and other energy sources are becoming the most inexpensive source, thus reducing the tension between these two basic energy values. Nevertheless, until renewable sources become a viable option for all consumers, the basic dilemma will remain.

Cost vs. environment   The tension between lower prices and a clean environment represents a second major dilemma for energy users. While few actors who deal with the energy issue would disclaim either value if all other things were equal, all other things are seldom equal. Earlier we briefly described the various procedures in combating environmental problems arising from energy production and consumption. All of these cost money, and the cost typically rises exponentially as the percentage of environmental damage being eliminated is increased. As already indicated, trade-offs force difficult choices. Solar energy advocates argue that when the two values come into conflict, safeguarding the environment should take precedence. Nuclear energy advocates do not mind safeguarding the environment, except when it severely threatens the value of lowering energy costs.

Reliability vs. cost vs. environment   In another energy option —high sulfur coal—one can see the tensions among three values: reliability, cost, and safeguarding the environment. For countries that possess large coal deposits, energy supply reliability can obviously be considerably improved by mining and burning coal. However, much of that coal will have a high sulfur content and when burned will produce high levels of pollution unless steps are taken to prevent it, such as investing in the development of new technology or employing the existing technology such as scrubbers, which remove the pollutants from coal exhaust systems. Both of the latter are costly, however, raising the cost of coal to the producer and therefore to the consumer. All three values cannot be satisfied completely, and hence trade-offs among them will be necessary in considering coal as an energy source.

Other Value dilemmas   Although the supply reliability versus cost and cost versus environment debates represent two major dilemmas confronting energy actors, there are other less prominent value tensions that also create problems for decision making. Many analysts argue, for example, that economic efficiency cannot be achieved if there is to be a global redistribution of wealth to provide a more equitable allocation of resources, no matter how this redistribution is to be effected.[23] Within the industrial West the oil companies have used this argument as a justification for what others term windfall profits. The latter argue that equity demands that no one group shall benefit at the expense of other groups, particularly during conditions of crisis. This argument suggests an inherent tension between the values of equity and regime maintenance. Finally, regime maintenance strategies obviously allow little time for focusing on the creation of equity for all energy actors, and thus the pursuit of the former typically comes in conflict with the latter.

Nonenergy Values

In addition to tensions among energy values, there exist difficulties trying to achieve one or more energy goals in the face of related *nonenergy values*. Perhaps the most significant nonenergy value is summarized by the phrase "national security." In the period of high oil costs and increased dependency upon energy from the volatile political and economic region of the Middle East, for example, American security and foreign policy interests became closely related to energy needs. Those latter interests, however, were not always compatible with efforts to achieve reliable, stable-priced oil. Among its policy interests, the United States has a commitment to preserving the stability and strength of its allies. A recent report on "energy security" noted that because the American economy and "international objectives are intertwined with the economic and geopolitical postures of other free world nations . . . security in energy supplies is an international challenge."[24] However, the United States also carries a commitment to preserve a defensible Israel and promote settlement of the Palestinian issue. These commitments have often been activated by political tension in the region and have complicated achievement of pure energy values. Additional complications have risen by the interest and presence of the Soviet Union in the Middle East, giving the region a heightened security profile.

As concern for the interruption of oil supplies increases, the potential for military involvement also has increased. At the height of the crisis of the 1970s Secretary of State Kissinger stated that the United States would not permit itself to be "strangulated" and implied clearly that military intervention was a consideration. A research study was conducted at the time at the request of Congress to determine the feasibility of seizing the Middle East oil fields if forced to do so in an emergency (concluding that it was infeasible).[25] When the Soviet Union invaded Afghanistan in 1979 similar concerns were expressed, and the United States made its commitment to preventing disruption of Persian Gulf oil flows explicit in the Carter Doctrine and established a military force structure—the Rapid Deployment Joint Task Force (now the Central Command)—to meet such an emergency. Even local conflicts, like the Iran-Iraq war of the 1980s, have evoked similar suggestions of military responses.

The threat or presence of external military forces, however, may destabilize rather than stabilize the political conditions for energy availability. Similar sets of concerns have motivated American resistance to completion of a Soviet–West European natural gas pipeline, even though such a pipeline would ensure a reliable supply of relatively low cost energy. American concern is that the Soviet Union could use that pipeline as leverage to achieve political ends.

Table 3.2. Value-Actor relationships

Specific energy values	Profits for Actors		
	Producer	Distributor	Consumer
Supply reliability	High	High	High—short term for some (e.g., United States) Low—long term
Cost	Low	Varies	High
Equity	Low	Medium: sometimes necessary to keep a market	Varies
Environment	Low	Low	Varies
Regime maintenance	High for centers of nation-states*	High*	High for most*
Autonomy:			
National	High*	Medium to High*	High (at least in short term)*
Corporate	Medium	High	Low

*For established energy sources (e.g., petroleum).

Value-Actor Relationships

Although the six energy values described in this chapter serve as guiding principles throughout the global energy system, each value is viewed differently by various energy actors. That is, different actors have diverging priorities among these values, and the priorities of some actors are incompatible with those of others. Table 3.2 summarizes the strength of the six specific values for producers, distributors, and consumers. The discussion that follows addresses highlights of that table.

Reliability of supply is generally a high-priority value for producers and consumers. In such energy sources as fossil fuels, however, producer supply reliability is only geologically based: can more of the energy source be extracted? Some have argued that certain multinational corporation distributors in such high-demand energy sources as petroleum do not value supply reliability as much as they might, since erratic supply in the short run could push up profits in the long run. This is clearly the exception rather than the rule, however, because stable market conditions are more highly valued than short-term profit taking. The highest and most obvious salience for supply reliability is of course exhibited by consumers. Energy self-sufficiency is a clear manifestion of supply reliability; it ensures national control over necessary energy resources. While this reflects the value of supply reliability in the short run, however, it may go counter to supply reliability in the long run. Building a pipeline to tap Alaskan oil is an example. Since oil is a nonrenewable resource, it can be argued that by using up United States oil more quickly, the Alaska oil pipeline represents a high short-term value on supply reliability and a low long-term value. This would not be the case if the Alaska pipeline were coupled with a strong alternative energy source research program. In many societies (like the United States) that consume much energy, such programs are not now present but are being actively pursued.

With respect to the value of lowering cost, consumers again have an obvious high interest. In energy sources with low supply and demand elasticity (i.e., oil), producer cost has little effect on producer profit, and therefore the value is low. Only if supply elasticity were to diminish and vertical integration decrease would lowering cost become a more important producer value. Nonetheless, as we have seen, there are factors that may diminish the salience of cost minimization even for consumers. In the United States accumulation of strategic petroleum reserves and pursuit of energy independence have in fact increased the cost of energy. But that increase has had the salutary effect of creating a sharp advance in energy conservation, including the natural force of conservation elected by cost-conscious consumers.

For the values of economic and regional equity as well as safeguarding the environment, only a subset of consumer actors (seldom any producers or distributors) rank the values high. In the case of equity, however, consumers who benefit from inequitable arrangements will not push for equity. Similarly, safeguarding the environment is irrelevant to some energy consumers.

Regime maintenance is valued quite highly by most energy actors, especially producers and distributors. This is because most producer and distributor contracts and other arrangements are predicated upon those in power remaining in power. The challenge to regime maintenance tends to come from actors involved with non-established energy sources.

The salience of the value of national and corporate autonomy also varies with respect to energy source. For established sources such as petroleum, virtually all actors value autonomy highly, at least for the short term. That is the mark of the prevailing role that oil plays globally as an energy resource. With nations dominating the production and consumption of petroleum, the world market reflects the continuing effort toward national autonomy. However, such efforts toward self-reliance produce a competitive dynamic: producers often undermine the long-term national autonomy of consumer nations; distributors recognize the value of autonomy only insofar as it contributes to stability; and consumers seem ambivalent, tending to favor reliability to autonomy when supplies are limited. With nonestablished energy resources, the general tendency to place a high value on national autonomy does not hold. At the present time efforts to develop most of the nonfossil fuel energy resources are not tied to national decision making structures, and there is certainly little national competition globally over such emerging energy resources.

In the case of corporate autonomy the highest level of salience is exhibited by distributors. That is because virtually every significant energy source that is marketed today is distributed to corporations (predominantly the vertically integrated multinational oil corporations). Other actors tend to view this situation as negative. Consumers in particular are prone to view corporate autonomy as an obstacle to lowering the cost of energy.

These examples demonstrate that various levels of salience for selected energy values serve to create still another layer of tensions among actors. But it is clear that a lack of agreement on values among the players of the three basic roles—producer, distributor, and consumer—does little to help resolve basic problems subsumed under the global energy issue. What is more, it is clear that those values that are regarded as highly salient by the most influential energy actors—supply reliability, cost minimization, regime maintenance, and autonomy—are self-interested values, showing little concern for basic human needs. The remaining values—equity and protecting the environment—tend to display low salience for most actors. That fact suggests that additional problems arising from the broad linkages between energy and other global issues like development and environment may yet have to be faced.

Summary

In this chapter we have suggested that energy issues arise and policies to resolve these issues emerge because actors are propelled by certain value preferences. Specifically, we suggested that six basic energy values seem to dominate: supply reliability, advantageous cost, economic and regional equities, environmental safeguards, regime maintenance, and national and corporate autonomy.

Seeking one or more of these goals, however, may lessen the likelihood that some remaining value will be achieved. This is particularly true when the decision is one of enhancing the reliability of supply or lowering cost, or between lowering cost and safeguarding the environment. Tensions also exist between energy values and other foreign and domestic policy goals. Chief among these is the nonenergy value of national security.

Finally, tensions arise because individual energy values are not equally sought by energy actors. Some are considered essential, others important, still others unimportant. Most differences can be explained by the role played by the actor in the global energy system.

As a consequence of these various sets of tensions, policy making in the energy arena becomes extremely difficult. When there is disagreement over desired end-states and over policies designed to achieve them, and when policy resolution and implementation must take place in a world where power is not distributed vertically —that is, no one actor enjoys a monopoly on the means of coercion —then resolving the global energy issue becomes difficult. And thus the study of policy making becomes the essential task for students of energy.

4 Energy Policy

The previous three chapters have provided ample evidence that the study of global energy issues involves understanding a number of factors. Not only must the various categories of actors be taken into account, but the values of those actors add another complex set of factors to the energy equation. In this chapter, we are concerned with yet another complicated aspect of the international energy situation—the policies that are pursued by the range of global actors, each of whom operates on the basis of a unique set of values and norms. By energy *policy* we mean the process of making decisions, and responding to and modifying actions in the light of their consequences. This takes us back to the basic energy functions of production, distribution, and consumption.

Approaches to Policy Making

Three approaches to the resolution of the problems raised by these functions appear to be most significant for the study of energy policy: *political, economic,* and *technical.* These approaches will be described and then applied to the problems of production, distribution, and consumption in both the short and long term.

The Political Approach

The most broadly defined strategy views energy issues in terms of the political process. A political solution to energy issues might suggest changing the manner in which actors identify problems (through modifications in the processes of individual or group perception and problem identification, for example), or it might propose alternative ways to develop specific programs, different means of justifying such programs to interested parties, or various options for funding these programs. Similarly, a political strategy could emphasize the need to change administrative or bureaucratic mechanisms, organizational structures, or other formal or legal bodies that control policy outcomes and impacts.

A good example of a political approach to energy issues is the development of new institutions to provide for greater citizen access to and involvement in energy decisions made by nation-states. Throughout the world, but especially in the nations of the industrialized West, one of the central issues of the coming decades appears to be the overall distrust of existing consent procedures, planning mechanisms, and decision-making structures in the energy policy system. These procedures, mechanisms, and structures are perceived by some to be closed, ruled by an elite "technocracy" that has its own narrow set of cultural orientations and values. This elite is then seen as insensitive to the negative impacts of large projects and unresponsive to the desires of the society as a whole.[1] Since the mid-1960s perhaps no single factor has been so important in national energy policy making as the uncertainty that has resulted from growing alienation and lack of faith in the established institutions on the part of the general public and from the rising demand for a more open energy policy-making system.

As the public in developed nations (and increasingly in less developed countries as well) has been made aware of the social, economic, and political consequences of the decisions to implement huge, complex energy projections, such as nuclear power plants, the role of the affected citizens in the policy process has become a sensitive political issue. As a result, a number of Western societies have initiated political approaches and strategies in an effort to enhance the level and the quality of citizen involvement in their energy policies. Essentially, four general types of participatory options have been tried: those that merely exchange information; those that provide new institutions or make modifications in old ones to allow citizens and their government representatives to interact in a meaningful way; those that develop avenues for the general public actually to make the final energy decisions themselves; and those that provide financial, legal, and technical support for the representatives of the general public so that they might participate on a relatively equal footing with the agents of more specialized interest groups.[2]

The most innovative experiments have been developed in Europe, where the political approach has combined elements from each of the four types of policies outlined above. For example, in Austria the spread of opposition to nuclear power generated a policy response that included the Nuclear Energy Information Campaign. This involved organized national debates focusing on specific nuclear energy problems and issues. Scientists and other technical experts were organized on both sides of each issue (safety, risk evaluation, etc.), and technical information was disseminated in the form of pamphlets and dictionaries. The debates themselves were televised, and questions from the public were encouraged and were forthcoming. Finally, a referendum on the subject was held.[3]

Similarly, in Sweden the government initiated "study circles" when it became obvious in 1975 that about half the population was opposed to any new nuclear power plants. The study circles were managed by the major national sociopolitical organizations (unions and political parties, for example) and were financed by the government. These small study groups ultimately involved more than 80,000 people in questions ranging from safety to the level of acceptable risk of nuclear energy resource development. Public hearings, polls, and referenda were implemented in the wake of these meetings and information exchanges.

In the Netherlands the government undertook a participation strategy termed the "structured scheme" by which a method of distributing all government plans and objectives in a systematic manner to localities was implemented. These "policy intentions" provided data about the impacts of nuclear technologies to communities through the use of television, lectures, and discussion groups. The government also sponsored "information evenings" to facilitate the communication of public reactions to these data to an Advisory Physical Planning Council. This body, composed of representatives of unions, local governments, industry, and housing associations, was charged with conducting hearings and making recommendations based on public input. Moreover, the Dutch government has gone beyond these initial reforms to create "science shops." These organizations were established at five universities to attempt to link the research of the educational establishment to societal needs and to provide client groups with technical data and support. Staffed for the most part with university faculty and students, the science shops are the technical equivalent of "storefront" legal services.[4]

Although little is known about the full range of consequences of efforts to use these innovative participation schemes, it does not appear as if they have entirely resolved political conflicts over such issues as the future role of nuclear power. There is evidence, for example, that in the Swedish nuclear debate the provision of alternative interpretations of the costs and benefits of atomic energy did not significantly alter public attitudes and actually may have served to legitimize existing biases and positions by providing information to support these attitudes.[5] Nevertheless, this kind of political approach is gaining widespread acceptance by nation-states determined to respond to the rising public expectations of participation.

The Economic Approach

Unlike the political orientation to energy issues, which views problem solving in terms of value conflicts, organizational change, and modifications in power relationships, the economic approach treats energy as a commodity. That is: "Exchange takes place when energy is transferred from one party to another and some valuable good, usually money, is transferred in the opposite direction. Energy is principally used as an input to an economic process and as an intermediate good. When energy is exchanged, it has a price, in dollars per unit."[6]

The economic approach thus is concerned with the use of various sanctions and incentives, such as prices and taxes, and a range of trade, investment, and other financial methods to govern the transfer of this scarce resource, energy, within the global marketplace. Crucial to this strategy is an overriding concern with the efficiency of energy production, distribution, and consumption. In other words, the basic economic question is: How can the world community develop, allocate, and use energy resources in the least costly way? In economic terms, therefore, efficiency equates with costs and an economic approach to policy making attempts to minimize these costs while maximizing the benefits of energy resource development.

The best example of the economic tendency to treat energy as a commodity is provided by the recent efforts of the global financial community (including nation-states, intergovernmental organizations, nongovernmental organizations, and national interest groups) to respond to the problems of the recycling of petrodollars (i.e., oil-exporting nations' using the dollars earned from the sale of oil to invest in other economic ventures within the countries that purchased the oil) and the accompanying threat to global economic development. As we have already noted, the success of OPEC's pricing policy has led to the accumulation of vast financial surpluses by many of the oil-producing countries, a reduction in the rate of global economic growth, and the expansion of trade deficits in most oil-consuming nations. The problem has been serious across the board but has become especially acute for the less developed countries, many of which have borrowed heavily to postpone paying higher energy bills and now face the prospect of having their economic development strategies frustrated by dramatically changing patterns of investment and world economic financial flows as a result of the burden of higher energy prices.

In the wake of the 1973 to 1974 OPEC price hikes many observers of the global economy had serious concerns about the possibility of an international financial collapse triggered by what at that time seemed to be the "unmanageable, open-ended consequences" of the costs of petroleum. And although the doomsday predictions soon subsided, there was a growing awareness that these difficulties were both great and urgent.[7] Most significant, major changes in the international economic structure were almost revolutionary in their implications for the international system. One author has suggested: "The governments of the oil-exporting countries today in effect control not only prices but, by extension, the economic adjustments to these prices—the low elasticity of demand makes the producing countries the final arbiters of economic policies in the West. For when alternatives to a critical industrial commodity are not commercially available, the sellers' policies determine the buyers' reactions."[8]

Thus, the first responses to OPEC's policies were attempts by the oil-consuming nations to free themselves from these new economic relationships. Most of those nations who were net importers of energy immediately took steps to increase investments in substitute forms of energy (by encouraging, for example, coal resource development in ways that could replace oil use) and energy conservation (by substantially raising energy prices and taxes as well as adopting such devices as incentives for home insulation), as well as making an effort to expand their export industries.[9] Soon these unilateral responses were followed by multilateral ones. In the period between the 1973 oil embargo and 1977 the International Energy Agency was created and its OECD member states agreed to constrain their consumption of energy, to share available oil supplies, and to draw down emergency petroleum stocks in the event of supply shortfalls.[10] At the same time the International Monetary Fund established its special oil facility to provide credit for short-term economic adjustment problems, and the World Bank expanded its borrowing and lending operations in the energy area. Moreover,

OPEC countries themselves began to accelerate their efforts to mobilize surplus revenues for the purposes of aiding the less developed countries. An OPEC Special Fund was created, and a number of member states established their own independent aid mechanisms. Also one should not ignore the very important role of the international banking community (i.e., the private sector) in these policy actions. Taken together, these economic measures represented the first comprehensive response of nation-states and international organizations to the global energy economic crisis, and they were adequate to deal with some short-term balance of payments difficulties. They did not, however, resolve the longer-term problems of debt accumulation and disruption of economic growth prospects in the Third World. Nor did they address the broader issue of managing the transition away from oil and toward the higher cost energy sources of the future.[11]

Since 1977 the efforts of the world financial community have increased dramatically as the long-term challenges posed by ever higher petroleum prices have become more obvious. One indicator of the threat caused by higher petroleum costs was the recent IMF estimate that approximately $150 billion was needed to finance non-oil-producing LDC cumulative deficits in 1980–81 alone (as compared to an annual current account deficit of about $10 billion prior to 1974). In response the IMF has substantially enlarged the amounts that members can borrow in relation to their quotas, and the time during which members are expected to restore their external payments position to a sound economic footing has been extended. At the same time the World Bank has accelerated its program for fossil fuel development and has undertaken the financing of exploration as well as production activities. The Bank's lending for the generation, transmission, and distribution of electric power more than doubled in 1980 from its level in the previous two years. Looking to the future, the Bank is considering establishing a new affiliate or facility with substantial resources of its own to finance energy resource development. Such a facility might expand the Bank's energy lending program from its 1980 level of $13.2 billion to more than $25 billion by 1985.[12]

The Technical Approach

The third strategy for resolving energy issues is to implement a technological "fix." This approach involves bringing scientific and engineering expertise to bear on energy problems. It is a highly complex effort to take energy technologies through the initial idea stage, to the more elaborate construction of models and the testing of prototypes, to the development of experimental and then commercial processes, procedures, and techniques. Thus, energy technologies such as synthetic fuels (synfuels)—the conversion of coal or oil shale to liquids or gases—must proceed through an elaborate series of steps in this "innovative process," from "basic" research (the search for knowledge), to "applied" research (the search for ways to put this knowledge to practical use), to engineering design (the first attempts to test technical models), to production and marketing activities.

The response of most industrialized societies (and not a few underdeveloped ones) to the energy crisis through technological fixes is a well-established pattern which recognizes that the resolution of these problems by other methods (by, for example, altering human attitudes or behavior patterns) is extremely difficult and that technical solutions may resolve public policy issues without having to face the complex political choices that are implicit in other strategies. And while technical solutions may not focus on the basic sociological problems underlying energy issues, they at least have the short-term effect of responding to the difficulties at hand.[13] For most countries, as well as international organizations, nongovernmental organizations, and subnational interest groups, it is politically more desirable to use technology to produce energy from new sources than it is to require the adoption of life-styles that consume less energy—as in the political approach—or to modify the production, distribution, and consumption of the energy commodity—as in the economic strategy.

Technological fixes may be applied at every stage of the innovative process, but by far the most consistent technical approach used by nation-states and many IGOS and MNCS as well has been research and development (R&D) policy. The most striking indicator of the increased emphasis on R&D as a nation-state problem-solving approach is the U.S., Japanese, and Western European consolidation of national responsibilities and programs and the growth of R&D budgets since the oil embargo. The energy R&D expenditures of IEA member governments in the period 1974 through 1977 expanded by as much as 180 percent (in the United States), and the IEA average percent change was about 89 percent.[14]

International organizations and multinational business enterprises also have opted for the technological fix of energy R&D. Typical of this tendency is the IEA's agreement to place stronger emphasis on R&D as part of its set of "principles," which its member states would agree to follow in the conduct of energy policy. As a consequence the IEA has sponsored energy R&D actions that range from conventional alternatives such as coal technology to the pursuit of renewable sources from ocean energy systems or biomass conversion. And the private sector has also been active in pursuing the energy R&D alternative. For example, in 1972 American industries spent an estimated $1.4 billion on energy R&D activities; the expenditures of oil firms alone was estimated to be in excess of $700 million.[15] And while the growth rates in industrial energy R&D are difficult to monitor and predict, chiefly because few companies track their precise spending on "energy-oriented" programs, many corporate energy R&D budgets have doubled since 1972, and most have at least increased in real terms.

In large part the focus on technological fixes to the energy crisis reflects the absence of any powerful, entrenched political interests that resist R&D as a policy tool. Everyone seems to favor spending more money on R&D activities. In fact, the entire bureaucratic/technocratic structure of most advanced industrial nations has been strongly supportive of R&D as an element of what the Ford Foundation's Energy Policy Project called "historical growth" and what Amory Lovins termed the "hard path" to energy development—an emphasis on the rapid deployment of large, centralized technologies to increase the supplies of nonrenewable forms of energy, especially the supplies of electricity from coal and nuclear energy sources. But there are other advantages to the use of R&D as a response to the energy dilemma. For one thing, energy R&D programs may be structured to respond to almost every possible energy policy objective. Among the goals toward which energy R&D efforts have been directed are reducing the cost of energy; providing flexibility of supply; providing customers with a choice of energy systems; promoting competition; expanding knowledge; increasing energy availability; exploiting indigenous resources; promoting self-sufficiency; promoting environmental quality; and providing a market for foreign producers.[16] In other words, the technical approach emphasizing R&D is equally applicable to production, distribution, and consumption activities.

Perhaps as important as the flexibility of R&D is its ability to respond to the tendency of policy-making elites in most highly industrialized nations to be optimistic about technological solutions. The rhetoric of the energy crisis in America, for example, has featured constant calls for "massive spending," "crash programs," or "another Manhattan Project."[17] But there are some characteristics of R&D that serve to limit the applicability of this particular technological fix to every energy policy problem. Most important, energy R&D is characterized by long lead times, especially when highly sophisticated technological innovations are involved. The kinds of uncertainties associated with many energy technologies require substantial time commitments before they have even a remote chance of being resolved; between ten and twenty years may be needed to bring a technology to the point of commercial use so that it makes an impact on the energy supply-allocation-demand situation. Also R&D options involve great uncertainty about the ultimate output of the technological process; costs, benefits, and time frames for various competing R&D efforts may lead to breakthroughs that attain or modify objectives quite unexpectedly. Finally, the high costs of many R&D alternatives are legendary, and cost may be a substantial barrier to the use of energy R&D policies even in industrialized societies.

In theory these problems associated with technological fixes should encourage international R&D programs as well. And, in fact, most nation-states have expanded their bilateral and multilateral commitments to cooperative R&D activities. In the United States, for example, the 1977 commitment included nine different IEA programs, an extensive nuclear program within the International Atomic Energy Agency and the OECD's Nuclear Energy Agency, and several energy conservation and alternative energy resource development projects within the North Atlantic Treaty Organization's Committee on the Challenges of Modern Society.[18] These policies are undertaken on the assumption that no nation alone could cope with the many-faceted problems of global resource shortfalls and price inflation, and that isolated responses only make the crisis worse. Moreover, because energy R&D is so expensive, duplication among the nations of the world has been spotlighted as an approach to be avoided at all costs. Finally, since no single nation has a monopoly on scientific ingenuity, there has been a growing awareness that cooperation, joint projects, and the exchange of scientific information make sense.[19]

But despite these obvious advantages, cooperative energy R&D has been blocked to a great extent by national rivalries, commercial interests, and the linking of R&D policy to other energy issues. Thus, in spite of the creation of the IEA, accelerated efforts by the OECD, and the first attempts of other international bodies to become involved in these activities, the primary areas of cooperation are those where there is not already a vested interest and consequently little apparent prospect for success. In a recent Ford Foundation report the authors caution against relying on joint energy R&D efforts involving several governments because there have been few successful examples of joint development programs.[20] Responding to this problem, the Trilateral Commission, a cooperative association of private individuals—scholars, businessmen, governmental figures, and the like—from Western Europe, Japan, and North America, has proposed that each of the major Western powers focus its R&D effort on those areas that currently offer the most significant potential payoff and that the Trilateral countries should set an agreed-upon target for energy R&D expenditures based on a combination of factors like growth in the gross national product, import dependency, domestic economic production, and energy resource base.[21]

In the above discussion we have highlighted three distinct approaches to energy policy making. Policy can also be distinguished according to the part of the global energy system being emphasized. That is, policy making is usually directed toward one of the three functional parts of the system: production, distribution and consumption. Combining both factors—approach and function—we can represent energy policy making in a 3 × 3 matrix, as shown in Figure 4.1.

Figure 4.1.   Approaches to energy policy

Function Approach	Production	Distribution	Consumption
Political			
Economic			
Technical			

Short-Term versus Long-Term Strategies

As this discussion has indicated, each of the major approaches to resolving energy issues varies widely according to the time frame in which results are expected. That is, some policies may be implemented in order to have an impact on the global energy production-distribution-consumption situation in the relatively short term (the next decade or so), while others are carried out on the basis of longer-term expectations (the next twenty years or more). Thus, a political approach might emphasize a participatory strategy which sought to provide citizens with instant access to the policy making levers, by means of a referendum on the use of certain energy technologies, or such an approach might take a longer-term view by undertaking an educational or information exchange effort that might not show significant results (in terms of changing the attitudes or behavior of the general public) for a number of years. Similarly, an economic approach could attempt to solve the petrodollar recycling issues by short-term national strategies emphasizing energy substitution or conservation, or by focusing on longer-term efforts like the modification of global financial institutions such as the IMF or World Bank. And a technical approach can be oriented toward short-run "fixes" in the way existing technologies are produced or used, or it can support R&D or other strategies slanted toward the need to develop new and better technological options for the distant future. Therefore, it is important to make some basic distinctions between these short- and long-term characteristics of international energy policy.

Short-Term Policies

Many policies are undertaken with the goal of having a payoff by the end of the decade of the 1980s. Most global energy actors have emphasized short-term policies because the energy crisis is perceived to pose immediate and urgent needs. Moreover, many of the short-term obstacles to achieving a better energy supply-demand balance serve as constraints for the later time periods.[22] For example, we need better information about the environmental impact of almost every energy option, and such data would help policy makers make crucial decisions today and in the near future. But systematic analyses of such impacts would also provide critical "baseline" data upon which to build for that eventual time when current technologies are modified and new ones become commercially viable.

Long-Term Policies

Actions taken to influence the energy situation in the year 2000 are of necessity more speculative and may not respond to one or another of the various detailed descriptions of the global energy future. Moreover, long-term policies must be initiated in an atmosphere in which there is tremendous disagreement among the major energy actors (and even widespread ignorance) about many fundamental facts, and there is no clear consensus on what major long-term policy gains and objectives should be. These difficulties help explain the relatively shortsighted outlook of most global actors, for, in the words of the recent report of the U.S. National Energy Strategies Project: "All of us are reluctant to make sacrifices at any time (whether these represent higher prices, lower profits, less comfort, more inconvenience, or any other sort of personal penalty) unless we know where energy policy is taking us and agree that we are satisfied with that ultimate destination."[23]

In the sections that follow, the production, distribution, and consumption actions of the participants in the global energy arena are examined in some detail, and it becomes obvious that energy policy may take us in many directions. Generally, however, most short-term policies are *reactive* in nature (that is, they respond to identified problems), while long-term actions take a more *anticipatory* stance (attempting to predict problems before they actually appear on the political agenda). And it should also be noted that short-term policies tend to focus more on incremental responses, while longer-term ones are, at least in appearance, more systematic and comprehensive in their makeup. Finally, short-term actions generally attempt only to modify the functions of energy actors, while long-term policies may undertake more far-reaching modifications, involving changes in the actual structure of the actors.

Energy Production Policy

We have already defined energy production as the series of stages of energy resource development required to convert a physical resource base to a usable energy source. And we have said these stages usually involve exploration, extraction, and processing activities. Thus, energy production policies are concerned with maximizing the supply of available resources and, as we have observed in previous chapters, global energy actors have tended to focus on the supply side of energy issues. The "energy syndrome" as Leon Lindberg has described it, is very much a consequence of the tendency of all actors, but especially the industrialized nation-states, to adopt uncritically the perspective of energy producers. This orientation has in turn led to an emphasis on highly complex projects, the almost total concentration on nonrenewable (fossil fuel and nuclear power) resources, and a high degree of influence of the values of an industrial technocracy in the formulation and implementation of production policies.[24] And the supply orientation has also meant that policy has tended to be made in a fragmented uncoordinated fashion. In the early American response to the crisis, for example:

> Program formulation in energy was characterized by widespread participation among many departments, agencies, and committees; inadequate and unreliable information about the problems; premature announcement of broad-scale proposals with impossible goals; and, as a consequence of the foregoing, little or no credibility for any one set of formulations. In short, the scene was one of confusion bordering on chaos. More analytically speaking, what we witnessed was not all that unfamiliar in American politics —that is our particular brand of crisis decision-making made more dramatic by a major political upheaval.[25]

The crisis mentality associated with supply motivations has thus meant that most production policies have been carried out in an incremental, piecemeal manner as each actor has attempted to respond to change in the global energy situation, especially in the dynamic petroleum setting. With every price fluctuation announced by OPEC and with every forecast of impending oil shortfalls or "oil glut," actors are forced to redefine the energy problem and to restructure their own production policy responses. Table 4.1 summarizes the production segment of policy responses in both the short-term and long-term and, in turn, provides the framework for the discussion which follows.

Short-Term Production Policies

Nation-states that are net importers of energy have responded to energy issues with short-term production policies based on a set of goals and objectives that emphasize the need to achieve supply security and energy self-sufficiency. In order to reduce their perceived vulnerability caused by import dependency, these nations have emphasized political and economic approaches in the short-

Table 4.1.   Energy production policies

Function / Approach	Production policies	
	Short term (1990)	Long term (2000)
Political	Import guarantees, strategic stockpiles	Multilateral control of global resources (seabed)
Economic	Price supports for producers, pricing decontrol, windfall profits tax	Strengthened global financial bodies to recycle petrodollars
Technical	"Nonhardware" R&D on on resource availability, environmental impacts of production	"Hardware" R&D on radioactive waste disposal, synfuels

term. The primary reliance has been placed on political strategies to decrease supply interruptions and to strengthen guarantees of foreign sources of supplies, and economic approaches to maximize indigenous energy resource development. Thus, oil-importing states have undertaken efforts to build stronger bilateral energy trade relationships with the OPEC countries and with those non-OPEC states that have either existing or potential petroleum-exporting capabilities. The American–Saudi Arabian "special relationship" is perhaps the best example of this political approach in action. This relationship is based on American military and national security commitments to the Saudis, and it has been held to be at least partially responsible for the moderate stance of the Saudi regime in OPEC pricing decisions and in their willingness to expand oil production capacity. But it must be emphasized that no policy maker regards such import guarantees as more than an interim solution to the energy supply problem. Political instability, particularly in the volatile Middle East, is always an obstacle to long-term import agreements, and oil-exporting states have consistently linked energy decisions to other controversial concerns such as economic development and national security. Thus, even the most concrete import guarantees must be viewed as only a short-term production option.

Strategic stockpiling has been another attractive alternative for the net importing countries. Stockpiling has obvious advantages for the nation worried about potential interruptions of supplies, and an emergency storage capability is not only an edge against energy shortfalls, but it may also help to prevent severe price fluctuations.[26] However, strategic storage is expensive and it provides only a limited period of protection for the import-dependent state. No stockpiling effort is capable of withstanding a long-term interruption in supplies, but the potential benefits of such a reserve have largely been seen as worth the costs, so the policy has become a central component of the IEA's International Energy Program.

Pricing reform has been the major short-term economic approach for oil-importing nations seeking an effective and efficient response to energy issues. These policies may take many forms, but the most common have been the provision of price guarantees or other supports for production activities, and the removal of price controls thus allowing the price of energy to rise to world market levels. Either of these options may be used to encourage the expanded development of existing resources, or to enhance the diversification of energy supplies. Price supports (sometimes used in conjunction with loan guarantees or other special incentives) can be especially valuable in the development of nonconventional or renewable sources such as solar or geothermal energy; and price decontrol is a clear incentive for accelerated exploration and extraction activities not only in conventional fossil fuel and atomic energy, but also in those areas, such as synthetic fuels, where the high costs of development have always been prohibitive. Unfortunately, price reform has some substantial problems, including the addition of severe inflationary pressures to the global economic system and major alterations in the way income is distributed in a society. Both of these problems raise significant equity issues—upward changes in the price of energy generally have negative consequences for the poor who spend a disproportionate amount of their income on energy, and those same increases can quickly result in windfall profits for the owners of energy resources. As a result, various schemes for taxing these increases in wealth have been implemented for the purposes (not always stated explicitly) of redistributing income throughout the society.[27]

Purely technical responses to short-term energy problems have not played a large role, primarily because, as we have observed, technological fixes are generally more suited to the resolution of longer-term supply, allocation, and demand difficulties. But research and development of a "nonhardware" type have proved to be useful for reacting to some shorter-run problems and issues. By nonhardware R&D we mean the problem-oriented activities of the so-called soft sciences—life science, social science, and related interdisciplinary ventures—that seek to provide descriptions and conceptual understanding of the social, economic, and physical environment in which energy technologies will be used.[28] Research of this type is useful because it can provide additional "baseline" data about the physical, biological, or social consequences of pursuing any particular energy production option. As the Ford Foundation has concluded:

> Basic research in physics, chemistry, health sciences, and earth sciences directed toward understanding the processes of combustion, and impacts of pollutants on health, the effects of carbon dioxide on climate, and so on is essential. Social science research to identify and explore policy options and their impacts and general information programs informing people what individual options they have and what the costs and benefits might be are as important as the hard science and engineering research.[29]

Of course, these short-term political, economic, and technical measures generally have not been implemented in isolation from one another. Rather, the reactive policies of most of the oil-consuming countries have reflected a sense of urgency surrounding an atmosphere of energy crisis and the need to "do something" even if such actions sometimes work at cross purposes or if they have primarily symbolic value and little impact on the energy supply picture. Thus, many of the programs put into operation by the import-dependent nations have an ad hoc flavor and something of a shotgun appearance. But most oil-importing nations have learned from their initial emergency efforts and more coherent, comprehensive policies have emerged over the last half decade.

The Canadian experience provides a good example of this incremental learning process. Immediately following the 1973 embargo, Canada's government began to phase domestic oil prices toward the world level to reduce the flow of Canadian wealth to the oil-exporting countries and to encourage petroleum resource development and pipeline construction in Canada's frontier regions. But along with this policy of gradual decontrol, the provincial governments were allowed to increase their royalties in order to preserve profits for all Canadians. These two policies had the effect of largely neutralizing each other and very little increased petroleum resource development took place. Thereafter, despite some intensive debate about the proper federal-provincial relationship in energy policy, and particularly some dramatic intergovernment disputes over the pricing, taxation, production, and distribution of energy supplies, an uneasy compromise has been worked out by which the provinces have been able to increase their rents on energy projects, industry has been provided added incentives to expand domestic supply (including an expanded role for Petrocan, the government-owned national oil company), and the national goal of achieving energy self-sufficiency has been brought closer to realization.[30] As in Canada, the harsh realities of petroleum dependency have forced most net importing countries to forge compromises among the competing goals of economic growth and industrialization, resource diversification and energy substitution, and the redistribution of wealth.

Net exporting countries have had to deal with many of these same issues, but from a different perspective. The OPEC member-states have been primarily concerned with economic development and national security in the context of gaining clear and unrestricted sovereignty over their energy resources (an orientation that generally leads to policies that try to secure freedom from perceived multinational business interference in resource development decisions) and attaining guaranteed access to markets in oil-importing countries (and here the emphasis is on the development of greater interdependency, through military and other security arrangements).[31] But real divisions exist within OPEC, based on the need to absorb the profits from oil sales for internal development, and these divisions color the cartel's approach not only to pricing policy and the availability of petroleum on the world market, but also to the overall approach to economic development:

These divisions have pitted "high absorbers" against "low absorbers"—that is, countries that also possess nonpetroleum assets and have relatively low per capita incomes from petroleum against countries with small populations, few petroleum assets, and large foreign exchange reserves. The former are eager for additional income for development, but the latter are primarily interested in preserving the value of their existing foreign assets rather than in raising prices to add to their monetary accumulations. The principle "high absorbers"—Indonesia, Algeria, Venezuela, Nigeria, and until the 1979 revolution, Iran—have been producing near capacity and have generally advocated large price rises. The "low absorbers"—chiefly Saudi Arabia—have considerable spare capacity and hence have favored modest price increases or even periodic price declines in real terms. Although Libya and Kuwait are "low absorbers," they have for ideological and domestic political reasons, respectively, sided with the "high absorbers" in advocating large price increases.[32]

Other intergovernmental organizations have had much less important roles than OPEC in the formulation and implementation of short-term production policies. The OECD and IEA, as well as other IGOS, have performed valuable functions by acting as places where supply issues could be addressed and various policy positions stated, but other than facilitating some agreement on broad policy guidelines, these organizations have been secondary actors. This is not the case, however, with the performance of the multinational energy firms.

Petroleum MNCS, as we have noted, are significant economic and political forces because of their high level of involvement in every stage of oil resource development, "from the wellhead to the pump" (vertical integration), and their participation in the exploitation of other energy sources in addition to petroleum (horizontal integration). They are major technical actors due to their dominance of virtually every high technology sector, and their significance as vehicles for the international transfer of technology. And while the role of MNCS in global energy production has been eroded somewhat by the success of OPEC as a supply and pricing body, the highly integrated "majors" are still important producers and, perhaps more significant, they support active and powerful lobbies that advocate such policies as pricing reform and import guarantees. Although a subject of controversy in almost every society because of their strength as a vested interest group, the oil MNCS have not only encouraged higher prices and diversified energy resource development, but they have also successfully resisted efforts of some opponents who press for the horizontal or vertical "divestiture" of the largest companies. Divestiture policy, as proposed in the United States and elsewhere, generally would force corporations to divest themselves of certain vertical or horizontal functions, for the express purpose of increasing the competitiveness of the energy industry.[33] However, the events of the last few years clearly indicate that this policy option has been either eliminated or at least postponed for the immediate future in the major industrialized countries.

National and subnational interest groups have joined the energy policy debate from almost every conceivable position. Environmental and consumer interests, for example, have been particularly active in focusing on the equity issues raised by production scenarios that require higher prices, for example, massive development projects. Potentially widespread international opposition to nuclear power, rooted in concerns about reactor safety and the risks of radioactive waste disposal, has been mobilized around the "small is beautiful" and "limits of growth" ideas. These groups tend to propose policies that in their extreme form often approach a "zero energy growth" orientation but that more typically favor some decentralization of bureaucratic control of energy decisions, greater reliance on alternative energy sources (and especially on solar power), and more attention to the ecological consequences of large power facilities.[34]

On the other side of the debate, industry, professional associations, scientific and technical elites, and energy-producing subnational governments often line up in support of strategies that maximize supply. But like IGOS and NGOS, the national and subnational groups play primarily a reactive role, and their input into the policy process is constrained by the overall goals and objectives that are developed at the national government level within nation-states.

Long-Term Production Policies

The first point that must be made about long-range production policies (or, for that matter, about distribution and consumption policies) is that they are dramatically affected by and linked to short-term actions. That is, in energy matters, "current decisions about location, investments, and designs have such a strong influence on the long-run future and are so strongly influenced by expectations about that future that short-term and long-term policies cannot be made independently."[35] And second, long-range policy making in any particular substantive arena, such as energy, simply does not proceed independently of efforts to resolve other global issues. This point is clearly made by the *Global 2000 Report to the President*: "The time has passed when population (or energy, or food, or clean air, or public health, or employment) can be considered in isolation. In establishing a foundation for longer-range analysis and planning, ways must be found to better understand the linkages and interactions among these important elements of the world system."[36]

With these serious reservations in mind, however, it is possible to identify a number of long-term, energy-oriented policies that have been pursued by global actors. The most significant approach for resolving long-run energy production issues is the technological fix, and especially the rapid expansion of energy R&D capabilities by nation-states, IGOS and MNCs. Most energy R&D policy has a dominant supply focus, a heavy reliance on the development of nuclear energy options within this production orientation, and a high pri-

Table 4.2.   International comparisons of public energy R&D, 1973

Energy technologies	Percentage of total funding				
	United Kingdom	United States	Germany	France	Netherlands
Nuclear fusion power	67.7	60.9	82.0	62.7	82.3
Developing indigenous fossil fuels	5.8	4.1	2.4	13.4	1.1
Substitute fuels (synthetic fuels from coal, oil shale, etc.)	0.6	7.1	6.9	0.5	0.8
New primary energy sources (solar, geothermal, etc.)	4.3	12.4	7.6	4.4	7.0
Energy utilization	12.8	4.8	0.1	7.7	3.6
Other	8.8	10.7	1.0	11.3	5.2
Total	100.0	100.0	100.0	100.0	100.0
$ million	183.8	671.9	240.1	250.2	35.5

Source: John Surrey and William Walker, "Energy R&D: A UK Perspective," *Energy Policy 3* (June 1975): 92.

ority attached to the search for liquid and gas substitutes for petroleum and natural gas. These general emphases are illustrated in table 4.2, which presents international comparisons of public sector energy R&D across several categories of energy technologies at the time of the energy crisis of 1973.

The R&D program promulgated in the United Kingdom in 1976 is fairly typical of these technological fixes, which have been pursued not only in the industrialized West, but also in the socialist bloc countries and in the more advanced LDCs (such as Brazil). The British program attached high priorities to most primary energy technologies (production options), but was especially oriented toward the role of nuclear power as a solution to possible future "energy gaps." Coal and oil R&D were placed in something of an intermediate postition in this scheme, while alternative sources, such as solar and geothermal energy options, were clearly viewed as being of limited long-term importance. Moreover, other than the case of offshore petroleum exploration and recovery—remember that the United Kingdom has significant North Sea resources— there was little indication that the British policy anticipated a significant role for international cooperative R&D efforts. On all these points, the United Kingdom orientation is typical of the responses of industrialized societies. And one should not be surprised at the absence of global or even bilateral cooperation in the R&D area. An overall strategy emphasizing cooperation has not evolved even within the OECD, the organization most likely to foster such efforts given the interests and capabilities of its member-states.[37]

International cooperative policies have been equally difficult to carry out in other, nontechnical approaches to long-term production issues. We have mentioned the limited success of global economic attempts to deal with the complex petrodollar recycling problem, and similar efforts have been undertaken with regard to continuing a global dialogue between the developed nations of the West and the lesser developed Third World through various conferences (such as the International Fuel Cycle Evaluation designed to explore areas of the nuclear energy resource development process that might provide opportunities for reducing the risk of weapons proliferation as nuclear technologies are adopted by increasing numbers of countries). Attempts also have been made to induce the communist countries, and especially the Soviet Union and China, to expand their production by transferring critical technology and providing technical expertise and investment capital.

On the political front, long-term production policies have emphasized the need for the creation of new global resource management regimes, such as a controversial international seabed authority or some other institution to control the development of energy and mineral resources beyond the continental margins of nation-states. As the world oil industry has expanded its operations toward economically marginal deposits, so have exploration and extraction activities been introduced into high-cost, high-risk "frontier" regions such as the outer continental shelf (OCS). But pressures for oil and gas development thus far have encouraged unilateral "ocean grabs" on the OCS and the creation of a series of 200-mile national resources zones that have frustrated ideas of a seabed authority to manage the oceans for the benefit of all mankind.[38]

Energy Distribution Policy

The distribution of energy encompasses not only its movements among the stages of production, but also the transportation of these products to users (whether this transport involves local, regional, national, or global mechanisms), and the final apportionment of energy in all its end-use forms to consumers. Because issues of distribution are so closely linked to questions of equity, policy making in this area has been somewhat controversial; there is no accepted means of determining who will win and who will lose

Table 4.3.   Energy distribution policies

Function / Approach	Distribution policies	
	Short term (1990)	Long term (2000)
Political	Allocation controls, nationalization of MNCs	New regional trade structures (U.S.-Mexico-Canada energy trade)
Economic	Rationing, changes in freight rates	Encourage "downstream" (refining, transport) activities of LDCs, MNCs
Technical	"Nonhardware" R&D on the transformation losses of energy distribution	"Hardware" R&D on LNG tankers and ports, slurry pipelines

when the scarce resources and the related costs and benefits are claimed by the many global actors who compete to impose their own conception of policy "fairness":

> Concerns about fairness have interfered with implementing policies which would lead to efficient energy outcomes; and we suggest multiple reasons for this. First, people do not believe that the real cost of energy has risen. They feel cheated when they are forced to pay higher prices. Second, people do not believe that general instruments of social policy will rebalance equities once a change has occurred in the energy sector. Hence, they resist every loss of welfare related to energy, regardless of its positive impact on society as a whole. Finally, the political process responds to *categories* of people—to interest groups or to regions, rather than to individuals. This interferes with compromises that could be accepted as fair by individuals, and leads instead to conflict. In a phrase, there is no "constituency" for overall fairness.[39]

Table 4.3 presents the energy distribution segment of the basic policy matrix for both short term and long term, and serves as the framework for the following discussion.

Short-Term Distribution Policies

The major short-term responses to distribution problems by nation-states, whether they are importers or exporters, have been political and economic in nature and have employed either allocation controls or rationing schemes. Both allocation and rationing policies seek to channel energy to specific geographical regions, to particular sectors of the economy (industry, transportation, commercial, or residential, for example), or to targeted groups within the general population (the poor or elderly, etc.). And both policies employ a system of priorities for access to energy sources and products and a heavy reliance on centralized administration to oversee the distribution process.

In the United States the federal government reacted to the 1973 oil embargo by establishing the Federal Energy Administration (later incorporated into the Department of Energy as the Economic Regulatory Administration) and passing the Emergency Petroleum Allocation Act. These allocation regulations were organized around two programs: crude oil and refined petroleum products. The years 1972 and 1973, chosen because they represented the most recent periods of petroleum abundance in the United States, provided a base period for these programs, that is, a standard upon which allocation decisions would be based. In general, the regulations provided that a purchaser had to buy from the same supplier or suppliers as he did during the base period. For example, the crude oil rules specified a "freeze date" identifying all supplier-purchaser contractual relationships as of 1 December 1973, and then based the allocations to refiners on the amount of crude oil refined during the preceding year, 1972. Allocation levels were determined by the actual availability of a particular product, and distribution levels were determined either as a percentage of requirements or as a percentage of prior use during the base period. For essential public services and critical industries (agricultural production or national defense were regarded as essential) the levels were mandated at 100 percent of use during the base period, but the specific priorities for less crucial activities varied. Thus gasoline priorities were highest for such users as passenger transportation services, while residual fuel oil was allocated to such high-priority users as manufacturers of drugs.[40] This brief outline of only a small portion of the American allocation rules gives an indication of the major problem associated with such policies—the regulations were extremely complex, requiring a substantial regulatory apparatus and an entirely new bureaucracy, and they tended to hamper the efficient performance of the petroleum industry.[41]

Rationing policies, which have been promulgated for such items as gasoline, suffer from similar difficulties. The use of gas coupons or gas stamps, or other means of distributing this or any other refined product (as requested in the U.S. National Energy Plan), require an enormous bureaucratic system to allocate fuel equitably and efficiently to the millions of users in any industrialized society. More experts agree that any such system of rationing must by definition be "crude, arbitrary, awkward, and imperfect."[42] But these widely recognized obstacles have not kept national governments from implementing rationing and allocation policies, often used in conjunction with each other and in addition to other production and consumption policies.

One such example is Japan's response to the energy crisis. Voluntary measures were inadequate, so two laws were enacted in December 1973. These allowed the government to declare a state of emergency and establish a period of mandatory controls on energy consumption by large users. One law, the People's Life Stabilization Law, allowed the government to recommend pricing levels for daily necessities, production, stockpiling, importation, and sales of goods in short supply and to make emergency commodities available. With prior notification of the legislature, the government could also impose short-term rationing, quotas, and bans on the use of certain goods. The government had the authority to suspend construction in order to restrain investment, ask firms to report their costs and profits, and conduct spot checks of inventories. A separate resolution also permitted the government to confiscate unusually large profits received through the sale of goods at prices above the suggested ceiling levels. After six months the government had to inform the legislature concerning the enforcement of the law, which itself would be reviewed by the latter body after one year. The second law, the Petroleum Supply Adjustment Law, required oil dealers to report their levels of production, sales, and imports plans to the Ministry of International Trade and Industry (MITI). The latter could determine the quantities of oil that could be used by larger consumers. Finally, MITI could order gasoline stations to curtail their business hours.[43]

Other nation-states followed parallel, though quite often not as comprehensive, approaches to distribution as they sought to develop policies more equitable and more politically acceptable than outright price increases. This last point is significant because, at least in the United States, there is considerable evidence to indicate that almost any distribution policy was for some time more popular with the general public than price increases.[44]

Political acceptability has also been a driving force behind other short-term national distribution efforts that have focused on exerting a greater measure of control over the multinational energy firms. The oil MNCs have found themselves increasingly restricted at both ends of the petroleum resource development spectrum by the greater production control now exercised by OPEC states and other oil exporters and the rise of the power of private independent oil companies and government petroleum firms, as well as by the forceful actions of many consumer nations to restrict corporate freedom at the consumption end of the process by imposing rules requiring the disclosure of pricing, profits, and planning data. However, the large integrated majors still are virtually irreplaceable as managers of the global movements of crude oil. Even though producing countries have been able to reduce the oil they can provide to the major corporations and even though the majors can, therefore, no longer provide quite the level and type of service to third parties that was once possible (as more and more of the oil is sold directly, or often through trading companies), the tanker fleets, refineries, and huge markets of the MNCS continue to provide them with decision making power regarding the complex supply arrangements inherent in petroleum trade.[45] Richard Barnet describes why the critical power of the MNC to manage distribution is extensive:

> No country can match Exxon's global monitoring and marketing system. On the twenty-fourth floor of the company's international headquarters is a row of TV screens linked to giant computers and terminals in Houston, London, and Tokyo. This "Logistics Information and Communication Systems" (LOGICS) records the daily movement of 500 Exxon ships from 155 loading ports to 270 destinations, carrying 160 different kinds of Exxon oil between 65 countries. This sort of competitive advantage convinced the oil-producing countries that they could not compete in such "downstream" operations as retail marketing and transportation.[46]

But a number of nation-states have attempted to reduce further the power of MNCS by pursuing policies that range from the creation of competitive national energy marketing or transport organizations, through requiring divestiture of MNC distribution functions (pipelines, tankers, trucks, etc.), to the actual nationalization of private sector corporate actors.

From the point of view of the MNCS themselves, the current situation demands policies that allow them either to hold their present positions or to diversify into other activities related to energy distribution or falling outside the energy sector altogether.

The major short term technical response to distribution issues for all significant actors, including IGOS and subnational interest groups, has been to concentrate on nonhardware research and development. Most participants in the global energy policy system, for example, have favored undertaking studies of the losses incurred for various energy distribution techniques. An analyses of the environmental and health impacts of such transportation technologies as high-voltage power lines or LNG tankers also has ranked high on the agendas of a number of global actors.

Long-Term Distribution Policies

By the year 2000 most nation-states hope to be able to resolve major uncertainties in the area of energy storage, waste heat utilization, and electricity generation peak loads through the use of a technical emphasis on hardware R&D. The United Kingdom's technological fix strategy, discussed earlier, incorporated these and other energy conversion and distribution responses as relatively high priorities, giving a clear indication of how industrial societies have formulated long-term energy distribution policies.

Nontechnical approaches to such policies have focused on efforts to work out new patterns of international energy trade. These economic and political policies generally have involved two sets of actions. One has been to create new distribution roles for the MNCs or the oil-producing LDCs by encouraging them, for instance, to accelerate "downstream" refining, transportation, and marketing in new regions, new energy sources, or new product lines. The second has been to move toward new trade relationships that promise more efficient or "secure" energy transactions. An example of new distribution roles would be the ongoing international endeavor to develop export capabilities among natural gas resource holding states in the Middle East and Africa as well as efforts to link USSR gas to potential importing states. (The Soviet pipeline to Western Europe is an example.) In each of these regions the natural gas reserves are sufficient to meet the major importing countries' demands, but the key policy issue is developing ways to move the gas to markets.

The effort to pursue new trade relationships is exemplified by American actions to formulate new energy agreements with Canada and Mexico in order to restructure United States' imports toward more reliable Western Hemisphere sources. Over the last half of the 1970s there was a dramatic shift toward these so-called secure sources of foreign oil (Canada, Venezuela, and Caribbean nations) from less reliable eastern hemisphere producers (OPEC countries in particular). Thus, some policy makers have concluded that Mexico's potentially large oil reserves are the only relatively secure and reliable source of imports for the United States over the next decade and that American government actions should press for rapid, short-term integration of the two national energy economies. But Mexican nationalism and more realistic assessments of that country's petroleum reserves, resources, and production and transmission possibilities appear to indicate a more moderate level of interaction and a long-term strategy, which might be based on the following concepts: (1) a special comprehensive energy agreement between the United States and Mexico; (2) a North American energy common market including the United States, Mexico, and Canada; and (3) a western hemisphere agreement that would include Venezuela and the Caribbean refinery nations along with the North American nations.[47] Such regime changes are only in the preliminary stages of negotiation, but regional energy distribution networks of the Canada–United States–Mexico type appear to be reasonable long-term energy policy options.

Energy Consumption Policy

The neglect of the consumption phase of energy resource development by nation-states, IGOs, and most other global energy actors can be explained by several factors. First, when energy in the form of crude oil and refined petroleum products was cheap, there was little incentive for policy makers to focus on anything but the supply stage of resource development. Second, most energy experts accepted until very recently the "conventional wisdom" that an almost one-to-one relationship existed between the consumption of energy and economic output. That is, global actors of all types were convinced that there were sound, proven reasons for believing that energy input and economic output were unalterably linked and, therefore, that there were few if any policy alternatives available to reduce energy use per unit of product in the economies of nation-states. Third, unlike the production or distribution phases of energy resource development, a focus on consumption for making policy modifications requires the participation of literally millions of energy actors. The actual end-users of energy in all its forms in each of the major economic sectors (industrial, commercial, transportation, and residential) must be somehow persuaded or forced to alter their energy demand patterns. And fourth, as we have observed in previous chapters, few energy policy-making elites have demonstrated anything but the strong ideological orientation toward technological fixes on the supply side of the energy equation. An emphasis on making energy decisions in order to reduce demand (through the use of conservation techniques, for example) has not surfaced among international energy elites with the notable exception of Sweden's energy establishment, where a balanced orientation toward the production-distribution-consumption policies has been in evidence since at least the mid-1950s.

Each of these points of resistance has begun to erode over the last decade as energy prices have dramatically increased, as considerable evidence has accumulated indicating that there are widely different degrees of increase of economic output per unit of energy consumption, as new consumption policy alternatives have been developed, and as the ideological assumptions of "small is beautiful" and the "soft path" energy future have become more generally disseminated and discussed. But energy demand policies clearly remain a secondary concern of most nation-states, IGOS, MNCS, and subnational interest groups and individuals. In part, the obstacles to implementing policies to reduce consumption, such as conservation actions, are symbolic in nature.

Slowly this perception of conservation as curtailment of industrial activities or a massive overhaul of the existing economic system has begun to shift, however, to a view that also incorporates the idea of adjustment or "productive conservation." This viewpoint stresses the role of conservation as an energy resource in itself. Reducing demand, therefore, increasingly is seen in terms of a "barrel saved is a barrel earned." Reducing demand, whether in

Table 4.4. Energy consumption policies

Function Approach	Consumption policies	
	Short term (1990)	Long term (2000)
Political	Fuel efficiency and insulation standards, changes in zoning or building codes	Citizen participation options, public education programs
Economic	Price increases or taxes to reduce demand, negative income tax for poor	Modifying ownership structures and power generation prices to encourage cogeneration
Technical	"Nonhardware" R&D on "noncommercial" energy sources (wood, animal wastes)	"Hardware" R&D on electric automobiles, battery storage

the short- or long-term future, takes at least three policy directions: (1) there can be a shift to less energy intensive processes (such as substituting labor for capital, or substituting renewable materials for nonrenewable ones); (2) efforts may be undertaken to reduce energy-consuming activities (by changing to new methods of heating and cooling residential and commercial space, for example); and (3) improvements may be made in the efficiency of existing energy-consuming activities (by modifying automobile performance characteristics, or by recycling materials). New ecological concerns, more progressive notions of corporate responsibility, and a growing future orientation among all types of global policy makers are just a few of the forces that appear to be acting to press many societies in the direction of such substitutions and policy changes.[48] The final segment of the basic policy matrix, focusing on consumption policies in the short-term and long-term, is shown in table 4.4.

Short-Term Consumption Policies

Earlier we noted that an examination of the energy and GNP information for the most industrialized countries indicates a large variation for countries like Sweden and the United States in the amount of energy expended to produce one unit of GNP. According to one recent study, the U.S. transport sector uses more than twice as much energy for each dollar of output as the transport sector in European societies, chiefly because of disparities in passenger travel (more miles per capita, more travel by auto and less by mass transit, the use of heavier autos, and less energy-efficient engines). Similar differences may be noted in the residential and commercial sectors, where artificially cheaper electricity has encouraged more U.S. consumption, and in the industrial sector, where America has not made very efficient use of waste heat.[49] These striking differences may be affected by a range of factors, but *policy* clearly has played a large role in shaping consumption patterns throughout the industrialized West. In the Swedish case we said that policies such as tougher building codes and higher taxes on gasoline appeared to account for much of the disparity in energy use when comparisons were made with the United States. And similar policy-generated consumption variations may be noted across the board. For example, transportation end-use seems to be significantly affected by the tax structures with regard to gasoline pricing; U.S. taxes in 1973 made up only 21 percent of the total gasoline price at the pump, whereas in Italy at that time they were 65 percent and in France 61 percent. That is, European governments have modified transport consumption because they have tended to treat gasoline as a revenue raiser.

To respond to such issues requires overcoming private sector uncertainty about the future availability and cost of financing. Industry has not invested in conversion options because scarce funds are reserved for essential business activities. Therefore, government incentives and/or sanctions are required in most nation-states to encourage energy conservation options. These incentives and sanctions represent the majority of the short-term consumption policies that have been generated to date. The range of possible short-run policy options is illustrated in a proposal for an American "Accelerated Conservation Policy" that would include the following elements:

(1) More aggressive and comprehensive enforcement of the mandatory automobile fuel economy standards already enacted by the Congress.

(2) The construction of alternative electric generation capacity in lieu of planned central station facilities—to focus, for example, on more decentralized options such as cogeneration and space heating from district plants, and a greater emphasis on the use of trash as an input into electricity generation.

(3) The establishment of efficiency goals for all energy-intensive industrial-processing equipment and systems, including refineries and chemical plants.

(4) The enactment of mandatory heating, insulation, and lighting standards for new residential and commercial construction, and making use of "passive solar" (design and architecture) options.

(5) Enacting progressively stricter efficiency standards for all major energy-consuming appliances, such as water heaters and refrigerators.

(6) The phasing out of natural gas as a fuel, either for central station electricity generation or for process steam applications in industry (because of its value in other industrial processes, many of which have no known substitute).

(7) Providing direct government loans and other economic incentives to finance the retrofitting of houses with conservation equipment such as insulation and storm windows.[50]

The controversial issues that are raised by such an aggressive political and economic approach to solving energy demand problems chiefly emphasize the potential conflicts resulting from such a dramatic restructuring of the priorities for developing energy resources. Direct government intervention of the kind envisioned in this proposal threatens many actors who are committed to the "free market approach" to energy policy. In fact, the correction of market distortions to enable energy conservation options to compete equally with other, more conventional supply alternatives is a central aim of many demand policies. Moreover, new policy analysis capabilities are demanded for such a broad-scale consumption orientation to succeed. Any society that embarks on a path of demand reduction must be able to foresee scarcity and to plan for energy shortfalls in a comprehensive manner. And it must be able to juggle the supplies of labor and capital in such a way as to fill the gaps that might be left by shortages of nonrenewable energy resources.[51]

Policy options that may cause changes in life-style also are part of the economic and political approach in the short term. Public and private incentives to change consumption behavior through car pooling, the greater use of available mass transit systems, and the use of autos for longer trips and at lower speeds are but a few of the transportation sector options available.

Short-term technical options also may be used, particularly non-hardware R&D, which assesses the utility of "noncommercial" energy resources around the world. Such R&D is especially relevant to the needs of less developed countries, many of which rely upon firewood, animal excrement, and agricultural waste for a large portion of their energy consumption. India, for example, generates about one-third of its total energy needs from such noncommercial sources. But there are few good data about such patterns of end-use for most of the Third World because LDC economies often change so rapidly that energy demand structures also change quickly (due to rapid migration, industrial modernization, etc.). Moreover, many demand models based on minimization of cost and maximization of utility simply do not apply to underdeveloped states where operating constraints or management problems may force decisions about energy consumption to be made on the basis of other standards.[52]

Long-Term Consumption Policies

Long-term efforts to alter consumption patterns have taken the form of political approaches that incorporate participation campaigns such as those "study circles" and "science shops" discussed earlier in this chapter. A related policy option is the use of energy conservation popularization programs, which place a heavy emphasis on public education. Although a minor element when compared to efficiency policies, these educational efforts have been undertaken in many industrialized democracies. The most aggressive programs have taken place in Great Britain, Canada, Italy, the Netherlands, and Sweden, where governments and energy utilities have pursued policies designed to alter long-term behavior by increasing the public's awareness of the ways in which they use energy, increasing their perceptions of the need to save energy, and actually demonstrating the ways in which such energy may be conserved. These comprehensive public education programs on energy conservation often are supplemented by more specialized efforts targeted for such personnel as architects, engineers, building contractors, supervisors, and inspectors. And most education policies combine meetings with industrial decision makers, the publication of various brochures, handbooks, and films, the provision of visiting and consulting services, a variety of seminars, and occasional demonstration projects in the industrial or commercial sectors.[53]

Economic approaches to reduce consumption have emphasized the modification of energy-pricing structures to change long-term demand behavior. Encouraging the adoption of energy-conserving practices such as cogeneration—supplementary systems used in conjunction with a central system, in this case the joint production of electricity and process steam—requires overcoming a range of ownership problems and resolving a set of issues surrounding the terms and procedures under which excess power will be distributed. Alternative policies for dealing with these issues would include incentives for utilities to construct and operate cogeneration facilities, the development of leasing arrangements under which corporations might be likely to undertake the manufacture of cogeneration equipment, and the decontrol of electricity generation prices.[54]

As was the case with production and distribution policies, research and development of a hardware nature is the major long-term technical approach to respond to consumption issues and uncertainties. The example of the United Kingdom again illustrates the type of technologies that are typical components of demand-oriented R&D programs in the industrialized world. In addition to funding conservation in buldings, industry, and transport, the United Kingdom energy utilization program has focused on such technical alternatives as heat pumps—the movement of energy through temperature differentials.

But despite the fact that energy conservation R&D has become a more significant part of the overall technological fix strategy in most developed nations, consuming as much as 30 percent of the total energy R&D budget in countries such as Sweden, there are major problems with the ways most R&D policies for the reduction of consumption have been formulated and implemented. For example, there have been extensive pressures toward demonstrating immediate payoffs for consumers, which have tended to push R&D funding into many areas in which the private sector should have already developed considerable interest. And these pressures have, therefore, in many cases actually impeded corporate investments because of the loss of market incentives. This same shortsightedness means that most consumption R&D is concentrated in projects that are not too speculative and have a tendency to ignore unusual ideas that might create new opportunities for energy savings or might actually redefine energy use in imaginative ways. To remedy these problems, some experts have suggested that "for the longer term and in the national interest, it seems that public capital (for R&D) should give priority to those situations in which the risks are so great, the time for commercialization is so long, or potential returns based on *present* energy price are so low that private investment alone cannot rationally be expected to suffice."[55]

Summary and Conclusions

In this chapter we have focused on energy policy-making strategies. Three basic approaches—political, economic, and technical— typically address one of the three basic functions—production, distribution, and consumption. In turn, these policies have sought either a short-term or a long-term payoff. Not all strategies (or cells of the policy matrix) are equally explored, however. Most energy policy is made by nation-states with the goal of maximizing energy production in the short term. But as is the case with other global issues (food, population, or the environment), energy decisions are not made and actions are not taken in a one-dimensional way. Other actors (especially IGOS and MNCS) are significant participants in the process of defining energy issues and in making certain that particular energy policy options are stated and placed on the energy policy agenda. And other energy functions (distribution and consumption) are gaining wider attention by the range of actors in the energy policy system . In fact, there is good evidence that a slow transition is taking place in which the dominant concern with the traditional supply technologies is being replaced with an entirely different set of policy priorities and criteria that incorporate growing concerns about how to reduce energy demand and how to ensure efficient and equitable global energy distribution patterns in the face of serious pressures from the Third World for a new set of international arrangements.

Among the key policy issues yet to be resolved as we enter the crucial period of transition away from the era of oil, questions about energy supply-demand imbalances in LDCs dominate. The ad hoc, reactive, and fragmented approach to energy problem solving thus far in evidence in the industrialized West and in the socialist bloc alike has not overcome most of the energy-related barriers to economic development in the Third World. Those less developed countries that are not oil producers have found themselves in a progressively worsening position since the 1973 crisis, and LDC needs of two distinct types have become evident. First, there are industrial growth requirements for conventional urban energy systems. And second, the more isolated rural areas that do not have access to power grids and fossil fuels and thus rely on noncommercial energy sources appear to be able to benefit from renewable energy options.[56] How these and other issues will be resolved is very much a function of how energy variables are defined and how forecasts of the energy future are carried out. The next chapter addresses these critical dimensions and anticipatory approaches to our energy future.

5 Energy Futures

Future Energy Characteristics

In earlier chapters we have discussed the evolution of the global energy system and the use of energy problems throughout the 1970s. We have examined the range of actors—both new and old—who are now major participants and the range of values that propels them to seek a variety of short- and long-term policies in pursuit of solutions to the global energy problem. We turn our attention now to the subject of what the world's energy future holds in store for us. Specifically, we want to examine future characteristics of the three major components of the global energy system—production, distribution, and consumption—as well as the nature of the future international system in general and specific political and organizational structures as they affect the energy system of the next decade and next century. We begin by identifying and briefly discussing the major factors of energy supply (part of the production function), energy demand (part of the consumption function), energy distribution, and political and organizational characteristics.

Energy Supply Factors

The first set of factors to be examined are those that help to determine the future supply of energy sources. Energy supply is related, but not identical, to energy production as discussed elsewhere in this book. Four aspects of supply variables will be considered: (1) geological processes, (2) currently known nonrenewable resources, (3) possible additional nonrenewable resources, (4) and the stage of development of renewable energy resources.

In the case of fossil fuels, geology is a crucial aspect of supply. The *geological processes* by which fossil fuels are created limit their availability. Oil sands, for instance, are a fossil fuel. But oil sands require a long-term geological process for them to be even potentially available as an energy source. Only in Venezuela and Canada are significant oil sands resources to be found.[1] Nature, in the form of geological processes, must therefore be considered in calculating future energy supplies.

Another determinant of energy supply is the *reserves of existing sources*. Known reserves of nonrenewable energy resources are the only reserves upon which we can rely in planning for the world's energy future, although there also may be significant *unknown reserves*. As of December 1975, for instance, one estimate showed that the proven petroleum reserves of the world were 658 billion barrels.[2] This means that forecasts of the energy future could treat 658 billion barrels as a baseline figure, i.e., the minimal amount upon which projections can be reliably based. More forecasters, however, believe that global petroleum reserves are in fact much larger. A 1978 study analyzing "recoverable resources" estimated crude oil resources to range from 1,700 to 2,300 billion barrels.[3] To forecast overall world energy supplies, equivalent figures would need to be known for all nonrenewable resources such as natural gas and fossil fuels other than petroleum. Of course, in order to provide the full range of possible energy futures, any additional unknown reserves of nonrenewable energy resources would have to be considered. Estimates from such experts as geologists would be sought in this area. Plausible guesses concerning as yet undiscovered global natural gas reserves, for instance, would be crucial to an overall estimate of energy supply. Estimates of the timing with respect to extraction would also be helpful. Table 5.1 shows current knowledge about proven and potential fossil fuel resources.

Most people reading this table for the first time would probably be struck first by the row entitled "years of consumption at current projection," which estimates the number of years left for use of an energy source based upon existing projections of future usage. While many would label this row rather optimistic, it is based on the reserves and resources figures shown in the table. Those figures are relatively consistent with the estimates cited at the beginning of this section, since one barrel of crude oil converts to approximately 5.6 million BTUs. That bottom row is also based, however, on "current projections," which are more controversial (we will discuss some of the reasons for the variance in such projections later). In addition, table 5.1 also is quite optimistic about the recoverability of such resources as oil shale. While few would quarrel with the

Table 5.1.   Resources of principal fossil fuels

	Proven reserves		Potential sources	
	United States	World	United States	World
Oil	.3	3.7	2.9	14.4
Natural gas	.3	1.0	2.5	15.8
Coal (including lignite)	15.0	95.0	30.0	170.0
Shale oil	12.0	19.0	150.0	2,000.0
Tar sands	—	1.8	—	1.8
Total	27.6	120.0	185.0	2,200.0
Years of world consumption at current projections	48.0	102.0	120.0	500.0

Note: All reserves and resources are measured in British Thermal Units (BTUs) 10^{18}.
Sources: Ford Foundation, The Energy Policy Project, *Exploring Energy Choices: A Preliminary Report* (Washington, D.C., 1974). D. A. Brobst and W. P. Pratt, eds., U.S. Geological Survey, *U.S. Mineral Resources* (Washington, D.C.: Government Printing Office, 1973). National Research Council, Committee on Resources and Man, *Resources and Man* (San Francisco: W. H. Freeman, 1969). Overall source: Herman Kahn, William Brown, and Leon Martel, *The Next 200 Years* (New York: William Morrow, 1976), p. 63.

notion that there is a great deal of shale that contains oil, most would disagree with table 5.1's contention that such a large amount (2000 × 10^{18} BTUs) can be recovered (indeed, many oil corporations have withdrawn from efforts to exploit this source). The important point to remember about this table is that we can count on the energy amounts listed in the first two columns, the baseline for projections, while noting that there is some far less certain chance that we will also have the resources listed in the last two columns to use in the future.

Beyond the nonrenewable sources, renewable energy sources also must be considered in order to obtain a comprehensive picture of future energy supply. One way of viewing renewable sources is to look at the *process of technological innovation*. That process can be conceptualized as having the following four stages:

Stage 1:   Conception of idea (invention)
Stage 2:   Development of initial application (often a pure technical test of feasibility)
Stage 3:   Beginning of commercial development (initial commercialization)
Stage 4:   Introduction into market use

Current developments in such renewable resources presently involve hydroelectric power, solar power, wind power, and wave power.

To illustrate the application of the four stages of the innovation process, let us take the case of solar energy development.

In its crudest forms—stage one for solar power—the conception of the idea of using the sun to generate energy can be traced back to the seventh century B.C. when burning glasses were used to light fires in ancient Assyrian cities. A more recent example of stage one innovation is the 100-horsepower solar power steam engine that was invented in 1912 by Frank Shuman, a United States engineer in Egypt. Stage two, developing initial practical applications, has a number of current examples in the area of solar energy. The U.S. National Aeronautics and Space Administration and the National Science Foundation continually sponsor studies in this area, and experimental applications have been plentiful. Equipping buildings with solar collectors to provide some of their energy supply, for example, has served as a test to determine whether large-scale collectors could be developed that would collect solar energy efficiently. Additionally, experiments have been conducted with solar-powered air-conditioning by use of a technology called "absorption refrigeration." A few companies are now working on the third stage of solar power innovation. For example, early commercial development of solar-powered hot water heaters is presently under way. Although stage three and four do not usually proceed until stage two has been completed, public policy can hasten the time when the initial commercialization of stage three reaches a wider clientele, especially in the area of solar energy. Some solar panels and hot water heaters have, in fact, been marketed on an extremely small scale, the beginning of stage four of the innovation process.

Most of us would not even be aware of a potential energy source until it was at least late in stage two, and more likely not until stage three. The crucial question for our energy future, particularly in the short run, is whether there are ways of speeding the innovation process for some energy sources through the often lengthy early stages.

How soon will some of the energy sources that are presently in the innovation process progress into wide-scale commercial use? Table 5.2 estimates the future of presently available resources, and also presents estimates—generally considered to be somewhat optimistic—of the commercial feasibility dates for resources not yet available, together with overall long-term potential from each source. For instance, in this 1976 estimate, solar radiation is seen as being commercially feasible by 1980. But we now know that table 5.2's estimate was a bit optimistic. It will also be quite a

Table 5.2.   Summary of global energy resources

	Long-term potential (estimated)	1st Commercial feasibility (estimated)	Problem areas
Hydroelectric	.1 Qe/yr	Current	C
Oil and natural gas	30 Q	Current	E
Tar sands and oil shale	30-2,000 Q	1985	C,E
Coal and lignite	200 Q	Current	E
U-235 (Free World)	15 Qe	Current	E
U-235 (ocean)	3,000 Qe	Current	C,E
Uranium for breeders	10,000 Qe	1995	C,E
Li-6 (D-T fusion reactor)	320 Q	1995–2005	C,E,T
Deuterium (D-D fusion reactor)	1 billion Q	2020–2050	C,E,T
Solar radiation (1% of surface energy)	30 Q/yr	1980–2000	C,T
Ocean gradients	20 Qe/yr	2000	C,T
Organic conversion	1.2 Q/yr	1975–90	C
Geothermal-magma	1 billion Q	?	C,E,T
Hot dry rock	100,000 Qe	1990–95	C,E,T
Liquid-dominated	1,000 Qe	1980–85	C,E
Dry steam	1 Qe	Current	—

$Q = 10^{18}$ BTU; $Qe = 10^{18}$ BTUs of electrical energy.
C = Cost; E = Energy; T = Technology.
Li-6 = The lithium isotope used to breed tritium in first-generation fusion reactors. World resources might be ten times greater than shown.
Source: Herman Kahn, William Brown, and Leon Martel, *The Next 200 Years* (New York: William Morrow, 1976).

while, if ever, before such large amounts of energy (30×10^{18} BTUs) can be harvested in one year from solar radiation. The "problem areas" column is related to a number of factors which we have discussed. *T* refers to technological difficulties, i.e., the energy source has a problem at some stage of the innovation process. *C* and *E* refer to problems of cost and effects on the environment. These relate back to values that were discussed in chapter 3—achieving the lowest cost to the consuming society for energy and safeguarding the quality of the environment. Solar radiation, for example, is seen to have both a cost and a technology problem but to present no environmental difficulties.

In summary, then, determination of the current stage in the innovation process for particular energy resources is a step in the direction of forecasting energy supply. In a manner similar to what we have presented here in the case of solar technology, such technologies as fission and fusion of nuclear energy or even fossil fuel technology can be traced through the innovation process.

Energy Demand Factors

The next logical set of determinants of future energy paths is global energy demand factors. Just as energy supply is similar to but not identical with production, energy demand is quite similar to energy consumption, as discussed elsewhere in this book. Three factors of energy demand need to be considered: (1) the present use of each individual energy source, (2) the degree of conservation, and (3) the interchangeability of energy sources.

To be most helpful, consideration of the *present use of an individual energy source* would have to account both for absolute amounts of world energy usage over time and for the distribution of that usage throughout various regions of the world. Separation into regions would allow for more careful forecasts, given the differing likelihoods of converting one energy source into another between regions. An estimate of what world energy consumption would look like for approximately the next two centuries can be found in table 5.3. The values in this table have been obtained by an optimistic assumption that technology combined with a new awareness will increase energy efficiency.

The table assumes that even as world population grows, the wealth (gross world product) of the world will grow much faster. But it also projects that the relative overall efficiency of production, conversion, and utilization of energy will improve dramatically.

Table 5.3. Estimates of world energy consumption

Year	Population (billions)	Gross world product ($ trillions)	Gross world product per capita	Annual consumption (unit-10^{18} BTU)	Cumulative consumption (from 1975) (unit-10^{18} BTU)
1975	4.0	5.2	1,300	.25	—
1985	5.0	8.5	1,700	.35	3
2000	6.6	17.2	2,600	.60	10
2025	9.3	52.0	5,600	1.20	30
2076	14.6	152.0	10,400	2.40	115
2126	15.0	228.0	15,200	3.20	240
2176	15.0	300.0	20,000	3.60	400

Source: Herman Kahn, William Brown, and Leon Martel, *The Next 200 Years* (New York: William Morrow), p. 62.

Only if these optimistic developments come true will the world be able to accommodate the consumption increases forecast in table 5.3. The important idea to keep in mind, however, is that the rate of consumption of specific energy sources must be one of the factors considered in order to forecast future energy paths.

Degree of conservation is a second energy demand factor to be considered in forecasting the future. Since conservation dampens overall demand, it is important to consider both overall and regionalized patterns of conservation: To what degree is energy conservation growing in traditionally high demand areas? In traditionally low demand areas? Which energy sources are most seriously affected?

Interchangeability of energy sources is the third relevant demand factor. Given usage patterns, the question to be asked is: When and to what degree can one source be substituted for another? In particular, what are the prospects for the substitution of particular renewable sources, such as solar power, for such nonrenewable sources as oil? This issue is related to the concept of demand elasticity, discussed earlier.

Energy Distribution Factors

The third component of the global energy system, distribution, is more important for fossil fuels than for such energy sources as solar or nuclear. Other factors such as *energy source location* and *energy consumption rates by location* play a role here. With respect to these, the crucial point to remember is that both access to an energy source and its likely usage patterns are in large part determined by where that energy source is located. In addition to these two, there are three others worthy of discussion. They are (1) resource availability, (2) the vulnerability of ecosystems, (3) and the degree of prohibition of energy purchase created by pricing structures.

Problems of *resource availability* rest within particular countries as well as between regions and nations of the world. For instance, in dealing with distribution of coal within the United States, chemical characteristics are important. In the American West, coal is low in sulfur content, while the eastern United States contains a great deal of high-sulfur coal. Clearly, then, national energy policies will have a different impact upon their regions and their economies. Such differences also exist on a world scale and must be considered in forecasting energy futures. Capacities to develop resources, invest in energy innovation, and influence the means of energy production are distributed quite unevenly between richer and poorer regions of the world.

Vulnerability of ecosystems also is uneven in its distribution. Development of our energy resources requires some alteration of the surrounding environment. Frontier or primitive areas, as yet unaltered, are substantially more vulnerable, and, as a result, energy production facilities in such areas would be likely to have a more severe impact than such facilities in urban areas, which have already been built up and significantly changed.

Pricing structures also create energy distribution issues. An increase in gasoline prices may prohibit some potential customers, such as the poor, from affording gasoline. Other consumers, the wealthy or corporations, may feel little effect from such an increase because of a greater financial base. The impact of an alternative structure of price increases might be distributed in quite a different manner. In short, differing degrees of prohibition of energy purchase are created by differing pricing structures.

Additional Political and Organizational Factors

In addition to the factors relating to the three principal components of the global energy system, a number of political and organizational factors of the international system will help determine the nature of the world's energy future.

Institutional activities   The first factor to be considered is the role of the international and transnational institutions that make energy-related decisions. For example, the U.N. Energy Conference held in Kenya in August 1981, established a temporary organization to address alternate energy source development. These institutions determine many of the rules of the game that will endure into the future. Chapter 2, you will remember, lists such intergovernmental organizations dealing with energy. The International Energy Agency, for example, through its structure for the emergency sharing of oil supplies, may affect short-term outcomes by determining supply patterns for its member-nations in future emergencies. Three areas of decision are especially crucial, however, in terms of the potential impact of such organizations. They are energy pollution and safety issues, energy innovation strategies, and energy source investment strategies. The first two are relatively straightforward in their impact. The basic question with respect to pollution and safety issues is the extent to which decisions in those areas become explicitly tied to energy development. An international (or national) energy organization with some regulatory authority may, by attempting to enforce standards in the area of pollution and safety, alter the pattern of development. And, clearly, international organizations also may play a direct role in energy innovation by initiating, directing, or sponsoring research or development efforts. The organization's representation and communication patterns are crucial in determining the rate of success in encouraging energy innovation.

The third area of decision making—energy source investment strategies—tends to be more complex. If national governments and international and transnational organizations (including multinational corporations) use short-term payoff as their only criterion, the energy source in which investments would be made would differ substantially from those that would be emphasized if more risky, long-term payoff strategies were followed. Emphasis on the short term may lead to extensive petroleum exploration, while a long-term emphasis might concentrate on solar, or perhaps nuclear. Hence, rules and patterns governing investment strategies could play a large part in determining future energy paths. In the same way that international and transnational organizations play an important role in future energy patterns, the decision-making mechanisms of national governments also may affect the same three factors just discussed: pollution and safety, innovation, and investment.

North-South relations On a broader scale, but related to the pattern of both national and international decision making, the whole issue of North-South relations is becoming increasingly important in contemplating the global energy future. Such factors as North-South hostility, inter- and intra-group cooperation, and the extent of separate pricing structures will influence energy patterns. In many forums, nations of the North have come into conflict with the less developed nations of the South. The Group of 77 (a loose coalition of lesser developed countries, which by now numbers considerably more than seventy-seven nations), for instance, has adopted explicit policies favoring the South. Those policies, although usually reactive, often have led to friction with the more advanced countries of the North such as was demonstrated at the conference and meeting sponsored by the United Nations.

One aspect of this friction is its effect on communication. As the experience of the Conference on the Law of the Sea indicates, political leverage is one result of joint policy statements of the Group of

77. One other result is often the ability to solidify an internal group issue position and thereby exhibit little or no flexibility when discussing the issue with outside political actors. Issues are interpreted from the perspective of the group position rather than being evaluated on their individual merits. Another related issue is the potential for North-South divisions to polarize the debate around theoretical rather than substantive points. The evident lack of constructive communication could severely affect cooperation in global energy efforts.

Another effect of North-South friction is in the area of technology. Appropriate technology can be a difficult stumbling block in any endeavor related to international energy. While research on nuclear energy may be seen as quite beneficial by most highly urbanized Northern countries, the economics of large-scale nuclear reactors may make such innovation superfluous to a primarily rural Southern nation. On the other hand, wind and tar sands are energy sources in which many Southern states would see much benefit from extensive research and development. With wind power, for instance, energy can be generated on the small scale required by a population that is not highly concentrated in a few urban areas.

Awareness of the implications of particular voting and representational structures is crucial to the ability to cope with North-South constraints. For instance, while funding for research in an area is often a necessary condition, it is not a sufficient condition for progress in the innovation process. If an international governmental organization were founded on a one-nation, one-vote principle, funds would be likely to be allocated in line with the broad application of a particular technology to all nations. If, on the other hand, population were taken into account in a voting procedure, funding would again favor breadth of application, but with a likely bias toward technologies more applicable in relatively urban (although not always developed) societies, since societies that are not urbanized tend to have greater populations. If voting for research funding were to be determined on technical grounds, then still different outcomes would be expected. The present state of development of existing technology would be a likely criterion, and, therefore, such a scheme would almost assuredly favor Northern nations since they have already invested more research funds in "high" energy technologies.

Producer-consumer conflict Any attempt to deal with global energy issues, whether governmental or not, is likely to face considerable strain in dealing with the conflict of perceived interests between producers and consumers of energy. For example, nations that now produce high quantities of oil would prefer the development of new technologies to improve the discovery, recovery, and refining processes for petroleum. Areas of the world that are increasingly dependent upon the consumption of high-priced oil tend to be more interested in encouraging the development of alternative energy sources more suitable to their own situations. While not exactly a parallel situation, some lessons for coping with producer-consumer energy constraints can be learned from negotiations concerning the exploitation of seabed minerals. In that situation, a compromise was negotiated by two groups of nations, roughly approximating potential producer and consumer groups, in which supply and demand were to be monitored closely to arrive at prices for seabed mineral metals.[4] The acknowledgement of the commonality of interest within particular groups of nations and the attempt to channel their differences into constructive dialogue may be a clear lesson for any international energy organization. The Conference on the Law of the Sea illustrated that the lesson may have not yet been learned by energy actors, including the United States.

Emphasizing a long-term similarity of interest between present energy producers and present energy consumers is another approach to the problem. Given the nonrenewable nature of many energy sources on which the world presently relies heavily, it is not at all clear that producer nations will remain producers in the distant future. The same may be true with many consumer nations and areas of the world. Depending upon how energy innovation is channeled and where it succeeds, the present producer-consumer distinctions may be altered substantially. Acknowledgment and communication of this message may help dull the edge of potential producer-consumer constraints. If this does not happen and producer-consumer conflict predominates over the potential for cooperation, a rather different energy future is likely to emerge.

Can We Forecast Energy Futures?

We can find widely differing forecasts for the future of energy. Table 5.3 forecasts that cumulative world energy consumption from 1975 through the year 2050 will be relatively moderate (less than 70×10^{18} BTUS). According to another forecast shown in table 5.4, however, cumulative world energy consumption for roughly the same period will be much larger (159.65×10^{18} BTUS). The second forecast is more than twice as large as the first forecast. Whether or

Table 5.4.   World energy consumption

Assuming 5 percent annual increase in the demand rate:	
Cumulative consumption during	Units = 10^{18} BTU
1st doubling period (1977–1990)	5.15
2nd doubling period (1991–2004)	10.30
3rd doubling period (2005–2018)	20.60
4th doubling period (2019–2032)	41.20
5th doubling period (2033–2046)	82.40
Total 1977–2046 (70 years)	159.65

Source: Council on Environmental Quality and the Department of State, *The Global 2000 Report to the President,* vol. 2. (Washington, D.C.: Government Printing Office, 1980).

not we can anticipate that the world will run out of energy may therefore well depend upon which forecast (if either) is right. How can we account for these differences?

Few areas of study witness as many forecasts as does the energy domain. Like the two above, such forecasts are often at great variance with one another. As "consumers" of these forecasts, all of us who study energy should therefore be able to evaluate them in terms of their appropriateness. The first step in doing so is to understand what is entailed in different forecasting techniques. Let us consider three technical approaches to forecasting: *expert-based, single variable extrapolation,* and *statistical models.* Each approach will be briefly evaluated for its appropriateness with respect to: (1) short- versus long-term forecasts, (2) information requirements, and (3) the ability to trace alternative policies. These criteria have been chosen because they are important factors to keep in mind when trying to understand whether a forecasting approach is being used appropriately. Only by understanding how forecasts are made can we intelligently choose among them. In an absolute sense it is virtually always easier to forecast accurately in the short term than in the long term. There is simply greater uncertainty further into the future. However, some forecasting approaches are able to cope with that uncertainty better than others. As a result forecasting approaches can be differentiated, relative to each other, in terms of short- versus long-term forecasting capabilities.

Expert-Based Forecasts

A range of techniques are included in the expert-based approaches category. At one end are assertions by experts that a particular future state of affairs will exist. A journalist familiar with energy may write an article forecasting a particular pattern of energy demand for Western industrialized nations. That journalist may, for instance, expect the countries in question to slash their demand within five years. Reasons for expecting the decreased demand may or may not be given. More sophisticated techniques, such as Delphi forecasts, are at the other end of the spectrum of expert forecasts. Such techniques take statements of expert opinion as input, and through minimal statistical procedures and usually a number of separate analytical steps produce summary forecasts. For instance, a group of energy experts might be brought together for the purpose of producing a Delphi forecast on the subject of energy demand in Western industrialized countries. Each would write out his forecast, state his reasoning, and submit the forecast anonymously to a Delphi administrator who would distribute all such statements to each expert. Participants would then have the opportunity to revise their forecasts and to respond to the reasoning of other experts. This procedure would be repeated a number of times until as much consensus as seemed intellectually feasible was reached. A statement of group opinion on the prospects of decreasing Western energy "appetites," perhaps including summary statistics, would then conclude this Delphi forecast. The crucial similarity between all expert-based forecasting approaches is that each has as its basic element the judgments of individuals who are substantively familiar with the problem.

Expert-based forecasts have relative advantages in long-term forecasts. That is because such sources of long-term uncertainty in energy forecasting as technological innovation and policy shifts might be taken into account in expert-based forecasts. With regard to the second criterion, information requirements, experts need not specify the base for their forecasts. Hence, information requirements do not pose a tremendous stumbling block. Finally, the third criterion—ability to trace alternative policies—obviously depends upon the expert in question. There is no prior reason why an expert-based forecast cannot trace through policy consequences. On at least the last two criteria, then, expert-based forecasts are highly variable and may well lack precision.

Extrapolations

Extrapolations are trend projections where the factor being forecast is the only one considered. When extrapolations are made, therefore, they assume that any conditions affecting the factor or variable that is the subject of the forecast will remain constant. In much international energy forecasting, however, ignoring such factors, such as the possibility of technological change and/or innovation, can cause serious error. Changes in policy also are generally overlooked in extrapolations, thereby creating another important source of bias. Extrapolations, often without stating or perhaps even realizing it, assume either that governmental, business, and other policies *cannot* alter variables being forecast or that they *will* not. For instance, a trend projection of energy resource usage rate that ignored the issue of policy effects would make little sense. Clearly, both government and industry in most countries have the ability to alter such trends. Many extrapolations cannot cope with this fact, however.

There also are problems with extrapolation inherent in the method itself. If one plots a set of "data points"—that is, known pieces of information for the variable selected—two ways of projecting the information are possible. Assume, for example, that one has three points as shown in figure 5.1, with the value of the variable on the vertical axis and time represented by the horizontal axis. One possible interpretation is to take those points as indicative of a general trend and therefore plot a line which approximates

Figure 5.1.   Three data points

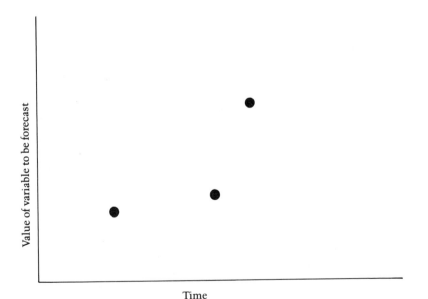

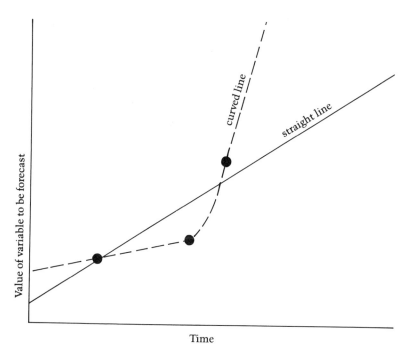

Figure 5.2.   Extrapolation (trend projection): Straight line vs. curved line

that trend. This is termed "straight-line" trend analysis and is illustrated by the solid line in figure 5.2. A second interpretation would be to take each of the points literally and therefore plot a line that traces the path between them exactly. This projection—the broken line in figure 5.2—is called "curved-line" or "curvilinear" trend analysis and obviously leads to a markedly different forecast based on the same data. Such variation may not be so extreme when using actual data, but the potential for differing interpretation by using straight-line or curved-line analysis remains present.

In turning to our three criteria for evaluating forecasting approaches, extrapolations, like expert-based analyses, tend to forecast more accurately in the short term than in the long term. The issues of technological innovation and policy change substantially reduce the potential for long-term accuracy. Figure 5.3 illustrates this vulnerability, which, as you can observe, increases over time. A policy change or technological innovation in two years may significantly alter the direction of energy developments. Since extrapolations focus on only one variable, long-term forecasts are especially vulnerable to inaccuracy due to such changes. For the same reason —the use of data over time for just one variable—extrapolation has less stringent information requirements than other approaches. As we have seen, accuracy can suffer because of the lack of information base. Finally, with respect to the ability to trace alternative policies, extrapolations fail. Again, since they only consider one variable, they are not able to deal with any policy changes.

Statistical Procedures

Statistical procedures use a set of explicit factors (more than one) in forecasting future values. The technique takes a problem and then produces the most likely possible outcomes for the variables being forecast. One might, for example, seek a statistical method to show the relationship between the number of automobiles per capita and energy consumption per capita. In that case the reasoning behind performing the statistical procedure might be as follows. First, it is known that automobiles use much fuel. Second, automobiles tend to be present in large numbers in societies that are quite industrial-

Figure 5.3.   Potential long-term inaccuracy of extrapolation

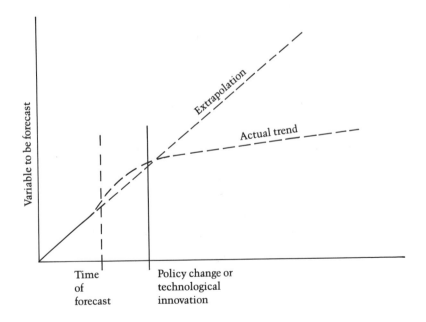

ized. Third, industrial societies should, as a consequence, use much fuel. Consequently, there should be a strong positive relationship between the number of automobiles per capita and energy consumption per capita. Energy consumption per capita would be seen to depend upon automobiles per capita. Hence, if an energy forecaster had the ability to project what the number of automobiles per capita would be in a particular nation at a given point in time, he or she also could make a good guess as to what the nation's energy consumption would be.

Evaluating statistical-forecasting approaches In terms of our three criteria for evaluation, statistical procedures are likely, first, to be more accurate for long-term forecasts than extrapolations. This is because by including more than one variable, "surprises" like policy change and technological innovation could conceivably be incorporated as additional factors in the statistical approach. Of course, such variables may not have been incorporated, and future trends would not then be anticipated. Compared to extrapolations, however, there is a greater chance of capturing such long-term trends. Information requirements for statistical approaches increase as the number of variables and the sophistication of the technique increase. Information requirements are consequently more severe for statistical approaches than for extrapolations. But, because the requirements are higher, statistical approaches frequently cannot be used because of unavailable information. It is possible, but unlikely, that statistical approaches would be employed to trace alternative policies. If policies could be translated into sets of variables represented in numerical form, for instance, separate analyses could be performed for each of the alternative policy options. However, statistical approaches are seldom used this way.

The relative advantages of the three forecasting approaches are summarized in table 5.5. As this table illustrates, expert-based forecasts have relative advantages in long-term forecasts, information requirements are inexplicit, and the ability to trace alternative policies depends upon the expert in question. Extrapolations tend to forecast more accurately in the short term, require data over time on only one variable, and do not themselves have the ability to trace alternative policies over time. The accuracy of statistical procedures is likely to decrease less for long-term forecasts than does that of extrapolations. Also, statistical procedures have more severe information requirements than does extrapolation. It is possible but infrequent that statistical approaches are employed to trace alternative policies. Comparing strengths and weaknesses as we

Table 5.5.   Criteria for using energy forecasting approaches

Forecasting approach	Short/Long term	Information requirement	Ability to trace alternative policies
Expert-based	Long	Unexplicit	Depends upon expert
Extrapolations	Short	Require data over time on only one variable	Not themselves
Statistical procedures	Better at long than extrapolations	More severe than extrapolations	Possible but unlikely

have just done allows us to judge the appropriateness of a forecasting approach, and therefore which forecast to believe when they disagree.

Alternative Energy Paths

Thus far we have studied global energy actors, values, policies, and the variables and forecasting approaches that are crucial to understanding our energy future. Let us turn our attention to the three scenarios of alternative global energy paths. The first, decentralized solar energy, is a typical "soft path" approach. The second, high coal emphasis, exemplifies a middle-level solution. And the third, nuclear energy, represents the "hard path" to the energy future. Each scenario will be briefly outlined and then described in terms of supply, demand, distribution, and the political and organizational factors that were introduced at the beginning of this chapter.

Decentralized Solar Future

Advocates of solar energy tend to reject the notion that a small elite in either a national government or a multinational corporation could determine for large numbers of people the forms of energy to be emphasized. Their primary aim is for energy decisions to be decentralized, allowing local communities throughout the world to determine their own energy paths. They argue that the issue should not be decided de facto by having options limited by those outside the community. Advocates of this path feel that it is both likely and desirable to expand the use of solar energy to widespread areas. A decentralized solar scenario would place strong emphasis on limiting the total amount of energy that is consumed. Some advocates of paths similar to this also advocate a limit on energy growth (termed zero energy growth).[5] If the decentralized solar future were to begin, rooftop solar collectors would become a more common sight in the near future, supplying much of the energy for space heating, water heating, and cooling. In the slightly longer range, this scenario anticipates many regional or community stations for solar power to provide electricity. In communities throughout the world where solar energy seems impractical, such energy sources as wind power would be likely alternatives.

Supply factors   Since the notion of appropriate technology predominates in the decentralized solar scenario, only those energy sources that could be supplied on a relatively small scale would be seen as attractive. It is likely therefore that there would be substantially less exporting and importing of energy sources. Advocates of solar energy point out: "Each year the world's solar energy income at ground level is about 500,000 billion barrels oil equivalent— about 1,000 times the energy of the known reserves of oil. . . ."[6] Critics note, however, that present technology does not allow for efficient collection. In addition to water and space heating, other direct uses include conversion of solar energy into electricity through ground and space systems (called photovoltaic conversion) and through the use of mirrors collecting the sun's heat to produce steam for power stations. The latter use assumes that a community opts for such stations. Studies have indicated that climates in at least North America, Europe, and Japan have enough solar energy falling on the average house roof to supply all of its energy needs.[7] This can be done at the present time, given that all the direct individual house applications are now feasible.

In the case of indirect applications, solar energy would use wind, waves, and temperature differences between surface and deep waters in the oceans. Among the ways of using wind power is modern windmill technology, which concentrates on blade dynamics and engine control. Researchers in Great Britain have been working on harnessing wave power. Energy from ocean waves would obviously be more applicable in some locations than in others. This feature is consistent with a decentralized energy supply picture. As a result, the fact that the overall amount of energy stored in waves is not great, even when compared with other forms of solar energy, would not eliminate wave power from consideration by advocates of scenario one. Ocean thermal systems might be especially applicable in the tropics, where temperature differences between upper and lower ocean layers are greatest. The use of such differences to generate electricity is one more part of a decentralized solar supply picture.

Demand factors   Demand factors would play a central role in the decentralized solar future. In order to strive for stringent limits on overall energy growth, conservation must play a crucial part. Extrapolations of world energy demand trends presently indicate a substantial increase in future energy consumption. That would be changed significantly in a downward direction by the decentralized solar path.

Table 5.6 and figure 5.4 both illustrate the point that most energy consumption is by the industrialized countries of the North. The burden of energy conservation, therefore, then falls most heavily upon these countries. It is plausible that future industrialization of Third World countries may produce a consumption picture like the right half of figure 5.4. In this forecast for the year 2000, note that consumption in the developing countries increases from 15 to 25 percent of the world's share, primarily due to industrialization. Nevertheless, the fact remains that disproportionate consumption in the North leads one to envision the need for a substantial curtailment in demand in the industrialized countries of that region.

Table 5.6 World energy consumption by region, 1960, 1970, 1980, and 1990

	1960		1970		1980		1990	
	Quad. BTUs[a]	Percentages	Quad. BTUs[a]	Percentages	Quad. BTUs[a]	Percentages	Quad. BTUs[a]	Percentages
United States	44.6	33.9	67.0	30.9	86.3	29.1	121.9	29.3
Western Europe	26.4	20.1	46.0	21.2	62.6	21.1	87.2	20.9
Japan	3.7	2.8	12.0	5.5	20.4	6.9	34.0	8.2
Centrally planned economies[b]	39.0	29.6	58.3	26.9	82.0	27.7	109.0	26.2
Rest of world	18.0	13.7	33.6	15.5	45.0	15.2	64.4	15.4
Total	131.7	100.0	216.9	100.0	296.3	100.0	416.5	100.0

[a]British Thermal Unit. One quadrillion BTUs is equivalent to 500,000 barrels of petroleum per day for a year; 40 million tons of bituminous coal; 1 trillion cubic feet of natural gas; or 100 billion kilowatt hours.
[b]USSR, Eastern Europe, People's Republic of China, Cuba.
Source: Based on U.S. Department of the Interior, *Energy Perspectives: A Presentation of Major Energy and Energy Related Data* (Washington, D.C.: Government Printing Office, February 1975), p. 6.

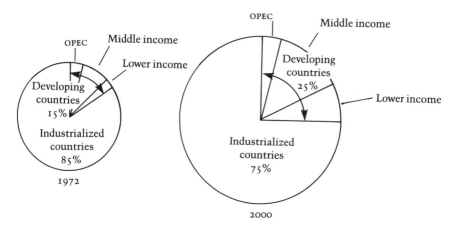

Figure 5.4.   Energy consumption (regional shares: 1972 and 2000). *Source:* Workshop on Alternative Energy Strategies, *Energy: Global Prospects, 1985–2000* (New York: McGraw-Hill, 1977), p. 97.

A decentralized solar scenario sees demand being diminished or leveled off in a number of ways. Each community and society would take measures to limit energy consumption, including the tightening of building codes, increasing automobile gas mileage, development of short- and long-range alternative means of transportation (both public and private), and strongly encouraging innovation in both energy sources and energy demand limitation. Advocates of a decentralized solar path note that a tremendous amount of energy is wasted through homes, offices, and public buildings that have been constructed without expenditure of energy in mind. Adopting building codes that mandate increased energy efficiency is new, and perhaps even existing physical structures would be a part of community response in scenario one. Even in the decentralized solar vision of the future, automobiles will continue to exist, but "gas guzzlers" will not. A variety of tax and legal incentives would be undertaken throughout the world to help bring about more efficient cars measured in terms of miles per gallon. Automobiles powered by more efficient forms of energy would also be part of the future. Alternatives to the automobile would also be emphasized in a decentralized solar future. Mass transit systems, bikeways, and rail service would play a much more central role. Individual communities would proceed with such measures as building subway systems, making traffic regulations more favorable to bicycles and less favorable to cars, and creating high-speed rail networks within small regions. Finally, communities and societies would encourage through financial and other means, research on such topics as limiting residential heat loss and energy-efficient recreation.

Distribution factors   With solar energy as the primary source, energy distribution questions would take on an entirely different cast. Recall the three distributional variables discussed earlier: location of energy sources, energy consumption rates by location, and degree of prohibition of energy purchase created by pricing structures.

Even in what students of energy consider to be the long term, the earth and sun are unlikely to change their positions relative to each other. As a result, certain areas of our planet—those closer to the equator—are likely to continue to have the capability of generating more direct solar energy for the foreseeable future. A quick look at a map will tell you that the countries around the equator are not those that control most of the present energy sources. The new patterns would also differ substantially from North-South distinctions. In general, the fact that communities would develop their own energy paths would lead to less overall concern with the location of energy sources.

As illustrated in table 5.6 and figure 5.4, energy consumption rates differ markedly by location and type of country. A decentralized solar scenario sees those differences shrinking. To the degree that local communities become more self-sufficient in energy, the disparities between consumption rates by location would follow one of two patterns. They would either diminish or would be allowed to exist only because a high-consuming area found a way (e.g., the direct and indirect solar energy applications mentioned earlier) to produce more energy.

Most advocates of solar energy support tax measures that would affect the degree to which energy purchase could be restricted by pricing structures. One such measure in the U.S. context is an energy sales tax. Supporters argue:

> Tax would be imposed gradually, on a predetermined schedule, so that purchasers of energy-consuming equipment could plan accordingly. The tax would begin in 1985 at 3 percent of the retail price of energy, and increase a fraction of 1 percent each year to about 15 percent in the year 2000. The tax would raise the price of energy intensive goods and services relative to nonenergy intensive activities and thus would use traditional market mechanisms to reduce energy consumption.

Imposed independently of other policies, such an energy sales tax would be both regressive in its impact on consumers (i.e., its impact felt more by lower income groups than by the rich) and a restraining influence on economic growth. Other policies would have to be adopted to offset these effects. A reduction of other federal taxes, or increases in federal payments, especially for lower income citizens, would be an obvious part of such an energy tax proposal. Some of the funds brought into the treasury could be directed toward public services that would facilitate and enhance zero energy growth.[8]

Note that care is taken in this proposal to ease the effects upon lower income groups. Hence, a laissez-faire market mechanism which would be likely to cut energy demand at the expense of such groups is clearly rejected.

Additional political and organizational factors The key political and organizational notion in the solar option is decentralization. Energy decisions would not be made on an international or even national level, but would often be made on subnational and/or small transnational bases. Central national energy control would either not exist or would be diminished. This can be demonstrated by looking at such issues as pollution and safety, energy innovation strategies, and energy source investment strategies.

Pollution and safety issues, for example, represent one of the fundamental differences between the decentralized solar and the "hard path" nuclear future. Antipollution requirements would be quite stringent in a decentralized solar world, and laws attempting to guarantee safety of energy systems would also be in force. Local communities would monitor both pollution and safety performance of businesses and residences. One of the main avenues for limiting pollution would, of course, be solar energy. Similarly, halting expansion of nuclear facilities would diminish a major safety issue.

A decentralized solar scenario would also include local structures designed to encourage and channel energy innovation. Both energy sources and energy demand limitations would be addressed. In terms of energy sources, two steps would be followed. First, where a community or group of communities could identify an area of research in which an innovation would be helpful (e.g., solar-powered vehicular transportation), financial incentives would be used to induce researchers to investigate this possibility, and, where possible, follow it through. Second, the same organizational mechanism could evaluate projects that were in any given stage of the innovation process (e.g., the initial application had just been developed) and judge which projects to fund through to market use. Energy demand limitation ideas could be treated in the same two ways, with the difference being that ideas containing such suggestions as education, indoctrination, and advertising—which are not technically innovations—would not be eliminated because of that "definitional" consideration.

Strategies for investment in energy sources would be made with such ideas in mind as potential for local control and application, and for safety and pollution. Grass-roots participation in organizations deciding on such strategies would combine with explicit evaluation of potential investments in terms of safety and pollution to ensure this course of action. Short-term economic considerations would clearly not dominate this aspect of a decentralized solar energy scenario.

A "High Coal" Future

A second scenario to be considered is identified as the high coal option. This option emphasizes the role of coal as the major energy resource for the future. Coal consists of carbon, hydrogen, and oxygen, with some small quantities of nitrogen and sulphur. It is mined from the ground and can be used to produce a wide variety of

Table 5.7 World coal resources and reserves by major coal-producing countries

	Geological resources*	Technically and economically recoverable reserves
Australia	600,000	32,800
Canada	323,036	4,242
People's Republic of China	1,438,045	98,883
India	81,019	12,427
Poland	139,750	59,600
Republic of South Africa	72,000	43,000
United Kingdom	190,000	45,000
United States	2,570,398	166,950
Soviet Union	4,860,000	109,900
West Germany	246,800	34,419
Other countries	229,164	55,711
Total world	10,750,212	662,932

*Units = millions of metric tons of coal equivalent
Source: World Coal Study, Coal: Bridge to the Future (Cambridge, Mass.: Ballinger, 1980). p. 160.

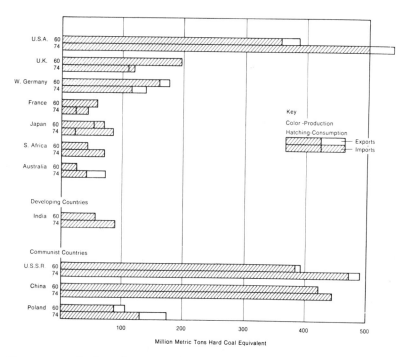

Figure 5.5. Coal production and consumption: 1960–74. *Source:* Workshop on Alternative Energy Strategies, *Energy: Global Prospects, 1985–2000* (New York: McGraw-Hill, 1977), p. 168.

products including electricity, metallurgical coke, activated carbon, gaseous and liquid fuels, and chemical feedstocks. Many of the technologies for using coal have improved at a greatly increased rate in recent years (e.g., its transformation into liquids and gases). One transnational study group, the World Coal Group, in advocating a high coal path, argued for increased international cooperation in developing new technologies for coal usage, greater emphasis on research to control the environmental impact of coal as an energy source, and adoption of a specific action program to reflect a global emphasis on coal.

Supply factors   The issue of supply is the key factor to which advocates of a high coal scenario point when building their argument. Based on 1977 data, current coal reserves—those reserves that are technically and economically recoverable now—amount to 660 billion metric tons.[9] To put that number in perspective, it is

250 times higher than actual world coal production in 1977. All known world coal reserves, not just those that are recoverable, are fifteen times higher than current recoverable reserves. These data are presented in table 5.7, together with the worldwide distribution of reserves. Thus, the supply of coal in the world is great, and the purposes for which it is supplied are expanding.

Demand factors In discussing demand for coal in a high coal scenario, one needs to examine present demand, and then focus on potential future demand. Figure 5.5 reports coal consumption figures from 1960 to 1974, and table 5.8 records 1978 figures. A number of points are worth nothing. First, coal accounts for approximately 20 percent of energy consumption throughout the industrialized world with only a small variation (from 16 percent in Japan to 20 percent in OECD Europe). Second, figure 5.5 shows us that there is relatively little importing and exporting of coal; the vast majority of coal is presently consumed in the same country where it is mined. Third, there has been virtually no drastic change in the coal production and consumption within any nation of the world. The graphs for 1960 and 1974 look relatively similar.

Table 5.9 adds to our picture of present coal demand by presenting profiles of coal uses. As the reader can see, the greatest single use of coal is to generate electricity; its use in industry is a clear second. Gas manufacture and rail transport also depend heavily on coal, but it is used indirectly and the volume consumed is small. Domestic uses of coal lag far behind on all counts.

A high coal scenario would increase virtually all the coal amounts and percentages in table 5.7, table 5.9, and figure 5.5. Trade barriers would be eliminated so that imports and exports would become more common. Those countries now heavily dependent upon oil would move quickly to coal, and all the uses in table 5.9 would see an increasing move toward coal supply. Figures 5.6 and 5.7 illustrate these export and net energy potentials, according to high coal sce-

Table 5.8.   Coal consumption, 1975 *

	North America	OECD Europe	Japan	Rest of WOCA	Total WOCA
Coal consumption	6.4	4.7	1.1	3.0	15.2
Total primary energy	37.4	23.7	6.8	15.3	83.2
Coal's share of primary energy	17.0%	20.0%	16.0%	20.0%	18.0%

*Unit = millions of barrels a day of oil equivalent.
WOCA = world outside communist areas.
Source: World Coal Study, *Coal: Bridge to the Future* (Cambridge, Mass.: Ballinger, 1980), p. 169.

Table 5.9. Markets for coal, 1975 (for world outside communist areas)

	Rail transport	Industry	Domestic	Electricity generation*	Gas manufacture*
Total energy	1.0	19.8	17.6	22.7	1.0
Coal	0.3	5.2	1.2	7.5	0.8
Coal share	35.0%	26.0%	7.0%	33.0%	76.0%

*Input

Note: millions of barrels per day of oil equivalent.

Source: Workshop on Alternative Energy Strategies, *Energy: Global Prospects, 1985–2000* (New York: McGraw-Hill, 1977), p. 169.

nario advocates. The potential central role of coal can be seen in projections for such countries as Australia and the United States. Hence, in summary, a high coal scenario would dramatically increase the moderate coal usage that presently prevails throughout much of the world.

Distribution factors   Three countries of the world presently dominate coal production. Figures 5.8 and 5.9 and table 5.10 illustrate that as of 1977–1978, approximately 60 percent of all world coal production and more than 80 percent of geological coal resources are in either the Soviet Union, the United States, or the People's Republic of China. This pattern leads to a very asymmetrical picture of the future. Not unlike present petroleum production, a few countries would emerge in a dominant position if a high coal scenario were to be followed. The identity of oil-dominant countries and coal-dominant countries is different, of course. So it is understandable that China, the United States, and the Soviet Union would look with more interest on a high coal scenario than would many other countries with less abundant coal resources.

Table 5.10 raises the issue of North-South relations by illustrating possible trade patterns in a high coal scenario. As that table indicates, the South (Africa, Latin America, and Asia, excluding Japan) would import substantial amounts of coal in this scenario. None would export coal, and, for these three areas, a total of 317 million tons of coal equivalent would be imported each year. In short, the nations of the South and Western Europe would be likely to develop a coal dependence on Australia, the United States, South Africa, and Canada. This might be seen as desirable for the exporter nations. Even many Western Europeans might view the scenario as preferable to present arrangements because of present friendly political relations with most coal exporters. However, the South would obviously be reluctant to add another element of potential dependence to future North-South relations.

Other political and organization factors   Pollution is a crucial variable to be studied in a high coal scenario, with *acid rain* and the *production of carbon dioxide* (the greenhouse effect) warranting special attention. Opponents of a high coal scenario focus a substantial portion of their objections upon the probable negative environmental impact of such a path. Figure 5.10 illustrates an array of environmental disturbances from coal. While such factors as dust and noise cannot be ignored, they are basically localized environmental factors, which affect those working in or living near coal mines. Some technology advances would be needed to omit

Figure 5.6.   Coal exporter potentials, year 2000. *Source:* World Coal Study, *Coal: Bridge to the Future* (Cambridge, Mass.: Ballinger, 1980), p. 110.

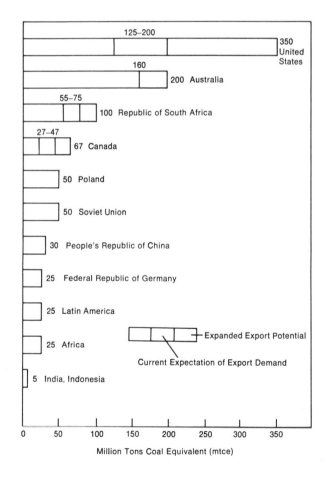

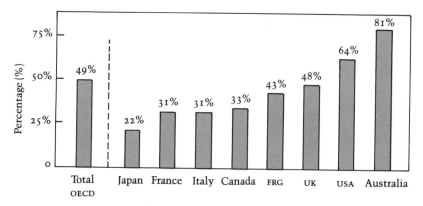

Figure 5.7. Coal's potential share in meeting the increase in energy needs (total OECD and selected countries, 1978–2000). *Note:* Figures are for Case B. Corresponding figures for Case A are OECD, 37%; Japan, 14%; France, 2%; Italy, 13%; Canada, 27%; Federal Republic of Germany, 25%; United Kingdom, 44%; the United States, 65%; Australia, 65%. *Source:* World Coal Study, *Coal: Bridge to the Future* (Cambridge, Mass.: Ballinger, 1980), p. 104.

noise and dust from a list of high coal scenario problems.

Neither noise, dust, nor any other such disturbance would be as potentially serious as the effects of acid rain or carbon dioxide production. A variety of materials ranging from automobile finishes to crops and fisheries are adversely affected by the corrosive impact of acid rain. Sulfur and nitrogen oxide emissions contribute to acid rain, and both sulfur and nitrogen oxides would be likely to increase markedly in a high coal scenario, especially since an increasing amount of high-sulfur coal would be burned in such a future. Acid rain can also create political conflict between nations. If pollution from coal burned in one nation were to create acid rain in a nearby or even distant nation, the recipient would be quite unappreciative. Thus, in a hard coal scenario, acid rain could affect not only the society burning the coal, but others as well.

However, the most serious potential ramification of a high coal scenario is the greenhouse effect. Carbon dioxide is emitted from the coal-burning process. Such emissions can influence the environment, despite their relatively small concentration, by reducing the rate of surface cooling of the earth and thereby increasing the earth's temperature. This increase is what is known as the greenhouse effect, which may change climatic patterns, thus altering a wide variety of factors around the globe. Droughts, poor harvests, and unstable weather are often pointed out as possible results of these changes. Interest in high coal paths has thus sparked further investigation by scientists and policy makers of a potential greenhouse effect. A recent U.S. government report, for instance, has warned of this very real danger from possible sharp increases in world coal usage.

Therefore, although the amount of coal available in the world seems to argue for exploration of a high coal scenario, such factors as unequal coal distribution patterns, acid rain, and the greenhouse effect argue for further study before there is significant commitment to the high coal path.

A Nuclear Future

Many aspects of the nuclear energy scenario appear to respond to what one might extrapolate from present-day energy trends. Energy demand will not be significantly curbed. A shortfall will arise from the combination of that demand increase and diminishing nonrenewable resources. Most of that shortfall will be made up by nuclear energy, which will be produced at large-scale nuclear-generating plants.

Supply factors   Let us begin by tracing the role that nuclear energy has played through the world in the past. As can be seen

Figure 5.8.   Geological coal resources of the world (as of 1978–1980). *Note:* The unit is 10^9 tons of coal equivalent. *Source:* World Coal Study, *Coal: Bridge to the Future* (Cambridge, Mass.: Ballinger, 1980), p. 160.

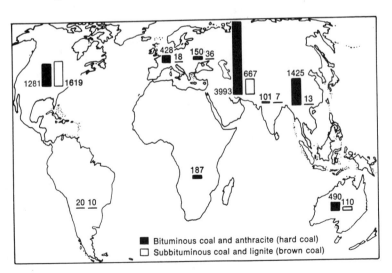

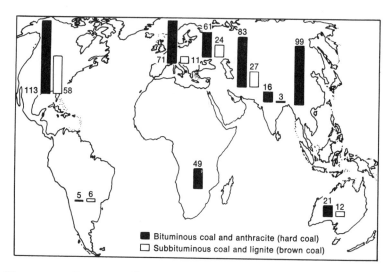

Figure 5.9. Economically recoverable coal reserves of the world (as of 1978–1980). *Note:* The unit is 10^9 tons of coal equivalent. *Source:* World Coal Study, *Coal: Bridge to the Future* (Cambridge, Mass.: Ballinger, 1980), p. 160.

from table 5.12, less than 3 percent of the energy produced in the world is hydro- and nuclear electricity. Advocates of nuclear power see that changing substantially. With rising energy prices and high economic growth as part of a nuclear future, table 5.13 illustrates how much some scholars think that the contribution of nuclear energy could be increased by the year 2000.

To accomplish this magnitude of increase in nuclear capacity, large-scale nuclear-generating facilities would have to be increased greatly. Nuclear energy supply would come from a full array of generating plants, from light water to heavy water to fast breeder. In sharp contrast to the decentralization of solar power, centralization would be the order of the day in order to enhance economic efficiency, thus raising questions about the role of developing states in a nuclear future. Those issues, however, are more appropriately addressed under the topic of distribution factors.

Demand factors We see from examining historical demand for nuclear energy in the context of world energy (table 5.14) that consumption of nuclear energy is growing at an even faster rate worldwide than is overall energy consumption. A comparison of table 5.14 with table 5.12 suggests that nuclear energy is virtually always consumed where it is produced. Therefore, while the nuclear future described here envisions larger-scale and more centralized energy production than does a solar future, they are alike insofar as future demand is met largely by production in the region of the demand.

While conservation plays such an integral role in solar energy, it is not emphasized in nuclear. The general attitude of nuclear power toward demand is laissez-faire. In other words, if excess demand becomes a problem, the "free" market mechanism, through the law

Table 5.10. World coal production by country and region (1977 and 2000)

	Production (mtce/yr)		% of world total	
	1977	2000	1977	2000
Canada	23	159	0.9	2.3
United States	560	1,883	22.9	27.8
North America	583	2,042	23.8	30.1
Denmark	—	<1	<0.1	<0.1
Finland	—	—	—	—
France	21	10	0.9	<0.1
Italy	<1	3	<0.1	<0.1
Netherlands	—	—	—	—
Sweden	—	—	—	—
United Kingdom	108	162	4.4	2.4
West Germany	120	150	4.9	2.2
Other Western Europe	38	101	1.6	1.5
OECD Europe	287	426	11.7	6.3
Japan	18	18	0.7	0.3
Australia	76	326	3.1	4.8
Total OECD	964	2,813	39.3	41.5
Republic of South Africa	73	228	3.0	3.4
India	72	285	2.9	4.2
Indonesia	<1	20	<0.1	0.3
East and other Asian countries	15	11	0.6	0.1
Africa and Latin America	25	180	1.0	2.7
People's Republic of China	373	1,450	15.2	21.4
Poland	167	313	6.8	4.6
Soviet Union	510	1,100	20.3	16.2
Other centrally planned economies	250	375	10.2	5.5
Total other regions	1,485	3,965	60.6	58.4
Total world	2,450	6,780	100.0	100.0

Note: MTCE = millions of tons of coal equivalent.
Source: World Coal Study, *Coal: Bridge to the Future* (Cambridge, Mass.: Ballinger, 1980), p. 163.

Table 5.11. Hypothetical trading preferences for sources of coal supply, year 2000

Importer country/ region	Australia	United States	South Africa	Poland	Canada	People's Republic of China	Other	Total sources
Denmark	2	2	6	5	2	1	3	21
Finland	1	2	—	5	2	1	2	13
France	28	24	20	7	19	1	16	115
Italy	16	9	12	8	—	3	10	58
Netherlands	10	5	10	11	1	—	1	38
Sweden	7	3	—	6	5	1	4	26
United Kingdom	12	—	—	5	—	—	—	17
West Germany	12	10	5	4	2	4	3	40
Other Western Europe	18	13	12	11	6	2	12	74
OECD Europe	106	68	65	62	37	13	51	400
Canada	—	9	—	—	—	—	—	9
Japan	78	66	6	1	25	16	14	206
East and Other Asia	86	52	33	—	48	—	8	227
Africa	12	10	—	—	5	—	3	30
Latin America	18	13	—	6	6	—	17	60
Centrally planned economies	—	—	—	25	—	—	25	50
Total world*	300	215	105	95	120	30	115	980

*Totals are rounded.

Note: MTCE = million tons of coal equivalent. Totals under "Total sources" are rounded.

Source: World Coal Study, Coal: Bridge to the Future (Cambridge, Mass.: Ballinger, 1980). p. 113.

of supply and demand, will lower the demand by raising the price. When the demand pushes the price up high enough, energy sources that are presently thought of as being impractical to use because of their high cost will be used. Either corporations or governments will, when the price of all energy is high enough, begin to market those sources to saturate demand. This picture is quite different from that in the decentralized solar scenario.

Distribution factors Population density is the first factor that we shall consider in discussing distribution aspects of a nuclear future. The kinds of generating facilities that are part of nuclear energy are quite large scale. This means they are designed for and operate more efficiently in densely populated areas. Accordingly, tables 5.12 and 5.14 showed that the preponderance of nuclear energy is produced and consumed in developed market economies.

Table 5.12.   Primary production of nuclear and total energy, by groups
of countries, 1960, 1970, and 1975 (millions of barrels oil equivalent)

| | Developed Market Economies | | | | |
	North America	Europe[1]	Japan	Other[2]	Total
Hydro and nuclear electricity					
1960	151.1	131.2	34.9	6.0	323.2
1970	254.3	211.5	49.9	13.5	529.2
1975	408.6	280.3	65.8	19.9	774.6
Total					
1960	7,267.3	2,641.9	291.3	146.4	10,346.9
1970	11,428.0	2,574.9	263.0	348.9	14,614.8
1975	11,064.5	2.963.3	179.7	555.6	14,763.1

[1] Austria, Belgium, Denmark, Finland, France, Iceland, Ireland, Italy, Luxembourg,
the Netherlands, Norway, Spain, Sweden, Switzerland, West Germany, and the
United Kingdom.
[2] Australia, New Zealand, and Puerto Rico.
[3] Primarily the USSR; also Bulgaria, Czechoslovakia, East Germany, Hungary, and Poland.

Since these countries are rather densely populated, large-scale
nuclear-generating facilities are quite appropriate and efficient.
Many countries or areas of the world, however, have largely rural
and consequently less dense populations. Some of those countries,
as well as others, also have physical features, such as mountainous
terrain, that compound the picture even more by making large-
scale nuclear-generating plants less practical.

Most of those who have advocated a nuclear path have not supported the kind of redistributive taxing schemes described for solar
energy. As a result, the implications for poorer countries and individuals are unclear. The combination of a laissez-faire economic
attitude and the issue of appropriateness of nuclear technology
leaves two choices. One choice is a large-scale effort, seemingly
only possible by national governments or an authoritative international body, to be undertaken in order to (1) help boost energy
production in the massive way necessary and (2) underwrite the
cost, creating prices such that all income groups can afford it. The
other choice seems to be to exclude lower income individuals and
perhaps countries from meeting their historically growing energy
demands.

Additional political and organizational factors   Institutions

Developed centrally planned economies[3]	Asian centrally planned[4]	Developing countries			World
		OPEC	Non-OPEC	Total	
33.5	11.9	0.9	38.9	51.7	408.4
81.1	23.1	5.5	101.8	130.4	704.7
90.2	31.8	11.2	155.2	198.3	1,063.1
4,539.4	2,127.3	3,170.0	1,312.9	6,610.2	21,496.5
7,712.8	2,152.1	8,515.7	2,622.5	13,290.2	35,617.9
9,814.2	3,093.9	10,083.1	3,308.7	16,485.6	41,062.9

[4]Primarily the People's Republic of China; also the Democratic Republic of Korea, Mongolia, and the former Democratic Republic of Vietnam.
Note: This table includes only commercial forms of energy. Noncommercial forms of energy such as draft animals, crop wastes, firewood, and dung are not included.
Source: McLaughlin, pp. 196–97.

making energy decisions would be much larger for nuclear energy than for solar. Nuclear power is centralized in terms of energy production, but is not predicated upon strong central governmental authority. Corporations accomplish most of the energy centralization.

Unlike solar energy, it is also possible, because of the distributional aspects of a nuclear future that have been discussed that North-South tensions would be exacerbated. This is due to the fact that most of the countries that had characteristics less suited for nuclear energy were those of the South, while most of those that were more suited were of the North. Any relatively large-scale scheme that had as its central focus nuclear energy would run the risk of alienating the South. Transfer of technology from North to South would be handled almost exclusively by multinational corporations in the scenario. This, too, would be unlikely to be greeted favorably in the South.

Energy safety and pollution issues would be treated quite differently in nuclear scenarios than in solar energy. To keep up with the increase in energy demand of nuclear power, stringent monitoring of safety and pollution would have to be sacrificed. Delaying the licensing of a nuclear power plant for a long period of time because of fears for its safety could not be tolerated if the kind of historical energy growth curve anticipation were to be taking place. Similarly,

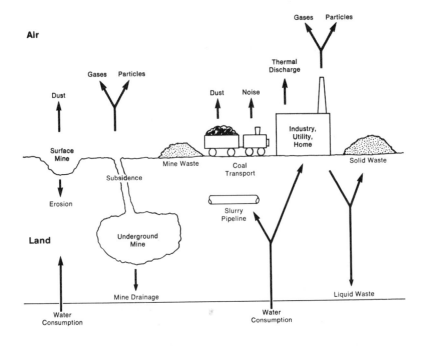

Figure 5.10. Environmental disturbances from coal-related activities. *Source:* World Coal Study, *Coal: Bridge to the Future* (Cambridge, Mass.: Ballinger, 1980), p. 138.

concerns for pollution characteristic of the burning of high sulfur coal would not be part of nuclear energy. The energy from the nuclear power plant would be necessary to meet the relatively uncurbed demand. Any mechanism for dealing with pollution and safety issues, then, would have little enforcement authority. An informal or advisory board might keep track of pollution and safety levels but they would only inform and advise. This is an example of a lack of central *governmental* authority.

Energy innovation would be the responsibility of the marketplace in the nuclear scenario. If an energy idea showed promise for corporate profit, it would be adopted. Seldom, if ever, would a potential energy innovation draw any serious attention (i.e., funding) unless it was well along in the innovation process. In other words, any

Table 5.13. WAES "Maximum Nuclear" scenario estimates of
future-installed nuclear capacity (as of October 1976)
GW(e) of installed nuclear capacity

Region or country	1974 installed capacity	1985	2000
Denmark	0.0	1.0	5.0
Finland	0.0	3.2	16.2
France	2.9	45.0	140.0
Germany	4.0	33.0	120.0
Italy	0.6	9.4	60.0
The Netherlands	0.5	2.5	16.0
Norway	0.0	0.0	4.0
Sweden	2.6	7.4	20.0
United Kingdom	5.8	15.0	58.0
Non-WAES Europe	2.5	31.0	94.0
Total Europe	18.9	147.5	533.2
Canada	2.5	12.0	74.0
United States	40.4	166.0	620.0
Total North America	42.9	178.0	694.0
Japan	3.9	40.0	120.0
Rest of WOCA	1.2	47.0	425.0
(including Mexico)	0.0	(3).0	(80).0
Total world excluding communist areas	66.9	412.5	1,772.2

Note: Non-WAES Europe includes Belgium, Luxembourg, Ireland, Austria, Greece,
Yugoslavia, Portugal, Spain, and Switzerland.
Source: From the Atlantic Council, "Nuclear Policy," as revised for WAES countries.
Quoted in Workshop on Alternative Energy Strategies, *Energy: Global Prospects,
1985–2000* (New York: McGraw-Hill, 1977), p. 203.

potential innovation that had the status of either a recently conceived idea or one in which the initial application had just been
(noncommercially) developed would be highly unlikely to garner
attention in a marketplace dominated by nuclear power. Systematic
recruitment and channeling of innovation would be far less likely
for nuclear power because of its commercial characteristics. Where
the market mechanism is the primary determinant of whether one
follows up an innovation, those with only long-term payoffs are at a
severe disadvantage. In terms of the nature of likely innovations,
high technology energy generation ideas would be most common.
Because the nuclear scenario contains such elements as steadily
increasing demand and dependence on the market mechanism for
innovations, the most highly valued innovations would be those

Table 5.14.   Consumption of nuclear and total energy, by groups of countries and typ of energy, 1960, 1970, and 1975 (millions of barrels oil equivalent)

| | Developed Market Economies | | | | |
	North America	Europe[1]	Japan	Other[2]	Total
Hydro and nuclear electricity					
1960	150.8	131.5	34.9	6.0	323.2
1970	254.2	212.2	49.9	13.5	529.8
1975	407.9	280.6	65.8	29.9	774.1
Total					
1960	7,581.5	3,870.0	524.0	233.4	12,208.9
1970	11,728.9	6,371.4	1,658.5	409.1	20,167.9
1975	12,360.6	6,711.7	1,929.0	513.8	21,515.2

[1]Austria, Belgium Denmark, Finland, France, Iceland, Ireland, Italy, Luxembourg, the Netherlands, Norway, Spain, Sweden, Switzerland, West Germany, and the United Kingdom.
[2]Australia, New Zealand, and Puerto Rico.
[3]Primarily the USSR; also Bulgaria, Czechoslovakia, East Germany, Hungary, and Poland.
[4]Primarily the People's Republic of China; also the Democratic Republic of Korea, Mongolia, and the former Democratic Republic of Vietnam.

that could meet needs quickly in societies that were both economically advanced and had large energy needs. High technology proposals for generating energy would meet those conditions. So, while overt channeling of innovation would not be a feature of nuclear power, those features of the scenario just mentioned would still channel energy innovation.

Finally, strategies for investment in nuclear energy would reside almost exclusively with corporations. Governments would make virtually no attempt to alter the investment decisions or influence the criteria used in such multinational corporate decisions. Once again, profit and short-term payoff would emerge as the key criteria. Sources that had the widest possible applicability and the greatest projected return on investment would be the likely focus of investments. High technology, particularly nuclear, investments would again emerge.

Summary and Conclusions

In this chapter we had three major emphases. First, we focused on those aspects of the global energy system that are critical to an

Developed centrally planned economies[3]	Developing countries				World
	Asian centrally planned[4]	OPEC	Non-OPEC	Total	
33.6	11.9	0.9	39.1	52.0	408.8
82.2	23.1	5.5	100.6	129.3	741.2
90.6	31.8	11.2	153.9	197.0	1,061.7
4,204.2	2,147.9	213.7	1,590.7	3,952.4	20,365.5
7,083.1	2,157.3	483.3	3,117.1	5,757.7	33,008.7
9,033.8	2,999.8	772.6	4,089.2	7,861.6	38,410.6

Note: This table includes only commercial forms of energy. Noncommercial forms of energy such as draft animals, crop wastes, firewood, and dung are not included. These noncommercial sources of energy play a major role in developing countries, generally providing most of their energy needs.

Source: Data for 1960 and 1970 are based on United Nations, Department of Economic and Social Affairs, *World Energy Supplies, 1950–1974.* From McLaughlin, pp. 198–99.

analysis of any future predictions about energy. Four characteristics of this system were addressed: supply factors (production), demand factors (consumption), distribution, and other political and organizational considerations. With respect to the supply factors, we emphasized geological processes, currently known nonrenewable resources, possible additional nonrenewable resources, and the stage of development of renewable energy sources. Demand or consumption factors highlighted were the present use of each energy source, the degree of conservation, and the interchangeability of energy sources. Distribution factors include, among others, energy source location and energy consumption rates by location. The last aspect of this system—other political and organizational factors—included the role of transnational institutions, North-South relations, and conflicts between producers and consumers.

The second focus of the chapter described three strategies or techniques for forecasting energy futures. These included expert-based forecasts, single-variable extrapolation, and statistical models. Each technique was described briefly, and three types were compared across a number of dimensions.

Finally, we described in detail three possible future energy scenarios or outcomes: a decentralized solar future, a high coal future, and a nuclear energy future. The opportunities and constraints (advantages and disadvantages) of each were outlined by focusing on those major components of the global energy system described earlier.

In summary, our purpose in this chapter was twofold. First, a number of techniques for analyzing the future were suggested. Without knowledge of the relative merits of futures analysis, we would be less likely to evaluate accurately predictions of the future. Second, we examined three possible substantive scenarios for the next century and beyond. As we continue to compare these scenarios, the techniques of futures analysis should enable us to make better judgments.

6 Global Energy: Issues and Prospects

This book began by observing that mention of an "energy crisis" had largely disappeared from public discourse. Indeed, one can easily demonstrate how conditions have changed. On 17 October 1973, meeting in Beirut, Lebanon, the members of OPEC decided to raise the price of a barrel of crude oil from just under $3 per barrel to over $5 per barrel, a 70 percent increase. Later on the same day, in order to protest support being given to Israel in the Yom Kippur War, the Arab OPEC members met separately and decided to place an embargo on the shipment of oil to the United States and parts of Western Europe. By those two dramatic decisions—one economic and one political— the significance of energy as a global issue was brought sharply to the attention of the world and especially Americans. Yet, nearly ten years later, on 25 January 1983, meeting this time in Geneva (Lebanon was now torn by political strife, civil war, and foreign military occupation), with the price of oil down to $31 per barrel, a drop of 11 percent from a 1981 high of almost $35, the same OPEC nations could not reach agreement on either pricing or production quotas. On this occasion the oil minister of Saudi Arabia, who had been instrumental in the 1973 action, would declare: "It's a total failure."[1] OPEC controls did not in fact prove to be a "total failure" (some agreement on both price and quotas was reached in March 1983), but the dominance of that organization has surely been shaken by the complex and vast interactions that had occurred in the global energy system.

The sense of urgency raised in the 1970s has been replaced in the 1980s by talk of an "oil glut," suggesting that the crisis is over and that we are now (once again) in an era of plenty. Most serious observers, however, suggest that the "glut" like the "crisis" is yet another short-term phenomenon, a "snapshot" of the true dynamic of the global energy problem. In the decade that has passed since the energy crisis was precipitated by OPEC in 1973 it has become evident that the issue of energy has deeper roots and more far-reaching global consequences than these events themselves would indicate. And today, while adjustments have been made to deal with the immediate impact of the 1973 crisis, there remain far more uncertainties in its aftermath than assurances concerning global energy. But there have been a number of changes in the conditions that define current approaches to the problem. By way of conclusion, this chapter will focus on some of those changes and on the uncertainties that accentuate the continuing importance of the energy problem for the future of a prosperous and stable world.

The most interesting shifts in energy relationships have occurred in the relative positions of the *actors*. The international petroleum market continues to provide the principal focus for those shifts. It was after all OPEC, through its exercise of market control over petroleum, the dominant energy resource, which brought energy as a global issue to such necessary prominence. But the very conditions that allowed OPEC to exercise that control have since contributed to its decline. The relative characteristics of supply and demand for petroleum have changed markedly. Whereas OPEC controlled 67 percent of the production of oil in the free world in 1977, at the height of the energy crisis, by 1982 that proportion had fallen to 48 percent (the Arab share had fallen from 55 percent to 39 percent).[2] OPEC oil production, which hit a high of 31 million barrels per day in 1979, had dropped to 18.5 million barrels per day in 1983. This last figure is noteworthy because the OPEC nations had agreed, after considerable haggling, to limit production to only 17.5 million barrels per day, i.e., some OPEC nations were cheating on their own agreed-upon production quotas.[3]

The drop in the OPEC share of the free world oil market and the evident change in the solidarity of OPEC indicated that the condition of inelasticity of supply—the unavailability to consumers of alternate suppliers—no longer obtained, or at least that some level of vital competitiveness had been returned to the marketplace. The decline in the OPEC share of the noncommunist oil market meant that other suppliers represented a larger share. Indeed, a number of nations have been able to develop as significant energy suppliers. The United States now imports more oil from Mexico than from Saudi Arabia, with Mexico's share of U.S. imports growing from 0.2 percent in September 1973, before the crisis, to 18.4 percent in September 1983 (Saudi Arabia's share declined from 17.3 percent to 13.1 percent).[4] The impetus of the energy crisis to find new oil fields (as well as alternative resources) also led to development of a number of exploitable areas outside of OPEC control, some of which were producing by the end of 1983.

Hence, OPEC found itself in a new situation and the evidence showed that in the 1980s, if there was a crisis in petroleum, it was now linked to the drop in prices and an increase in overall production, not the reverse. This trend was most evident among OPEC's "high absorbers." Nigeria, for example, had paced its development plans for the immediate future on continuation of the price rises of the 1970s, only to find those price dropping or at best stabilizing.[5] To maintain its domestic commitments to economic growth, Nigeria needed to sustain its petroleum sales. In a renewed competitive market that meant lower prices and higher rates of production. Nigeria thus became a "spoiler" in the ranks of OPEC (together with Iran, Venezuela, and Libya) and contributed to what amounted to an incipient price war among OPEC members. Although prices were stabilized in 1983 at about $29 per barrel, few analysts felt that that price could be held. As a consequence, some observers maintained, the most important aspect of the drop in prices and the weakening of OPEC solidarity was the indication of the continuing importance (and instability) of the petroleum market for the global energy system.

That condition may also be noted in the area of consumption. One evident impact of the energy crisis of the 1970s was an overall reduction in demand among the major oil consumers in the West. This reduction reflected a number of factors: slowing economic growth, increases in domestic inventories, less reliance on imported oil, conservation, etc. The decline in consumption was spurred largely by rising energy costs, providing an incentive for conservation and the search for alternative energy sources. One easy way of observing the impact of such incentives is to note the marked changes that have taken place in the United States in the nature and performance of automobiles. There is some evidence, however, that such adjustments, while extending the profile of demand, have not altered its fundamental inelasticity—i.e., the availability of alternative products to meet consumer needs. For all their economy, automobiles still run on petroleum products.

As a further part of the consumption picture, it is generally agreed that the enormous rise in the price of oil in the first half of the 1970s contributed greatly to the worldwide recession of the late 1970s and early 1980s. One analyst estimates the cost to the industrialized world alone, measured by lost economic growth, to have been $1.2 trillion.[6] The cost of energy slowed growth and thereby helped reduce consumption in the industrialized world. But that outcome proved to have a kind of countereffect for the overall energy problem. The drop in the price of oil engendered by response to the change in the characteristics of the market loosened concerns that had been generated on the demand side by the energy crisis. For example, the decline in consumption left many parts of the oil industry, which had geared itself for steady growth in demand, especially in the distribution function, with systems and equipment designed to meet a need that was substantially reduced (this outcome may be further accentuated in the West by the entry of OPEC nations, as well as other producers, into "downstream" refining and marketing operations). In the face of such losses, once demand fell off, efforts within energy industries to develop alternative sources to oil, like the search for synthetic fuels, also declined.

It appears then that the drop in prices carried its own complications for the consumption function. It cannot be said that there is agreement among experts on this matter. But there is some agreement that the short-term drop in prices has weakened the long-term approaches to resolution of the energy problem. For, in the long-term, demand must continue to grow if there is to be further economic growth, an argument that is supported by the contention noted above that the recession instigated by the oil crisis also was one of the major contributing factors to the decline in demand. Economic recovery, which has shown strong signs of development in the 1980s, could therefore be expected to reinvigorate demand.

Among those who have expressed serious concern in this regard is the International Energy Agency (IEA), created by the industrialized nations as an institutional response to the energy crisis. In its first decade IEA grew in visibility and stature as an energy actor, assuming an advocacy role by warning against the prospects for renewed demand in an environment of continuing dependence on oil. Studies prepared by IEA have maintained that the decline in the demand at the beginning of the 1980s must be viewed as a temporary phenomenon. The forecasts that it has issued tend to be pessimistic for the industrialized nations, which make up its membership. Most of these forecasts express concern for the industrialized world after 1985 when demand is projected to increase accompanied by a return to steep increases in the price of oil. The U.S. Department of Energy, for example, has forecast prices at $45 per barrel by 1990 and $60 per barrel by the year 2000.[7] With that perspective on the outcome—increased demand and higher oil prices—IEA ironically shared the same view being advanced by OPEC. With a different set of objectives, however, IEA has advocated the recommitment of the industrialized world to conservation measures and to the development of alternatives to oil as an energy source.

Other uncertainties also appear. One of those, which energy analysts address, is the future role of the Soviet Union. The fact that the USSR is the largest single producer of oil in the world is sometimes overlooked when contemplating the current energy landscape (Soviet production in 1982 was 11.8 million barrels per day compared to 6.3 million for Saudi Arabia and 8.7 million for the United States).[8] The Soviet Union has not been a major actor in the international energy market. Most of its production goes to meet its own domestic needs and over half of its exports to client states in Eastern Europe and the communist world. Nonetheless, the Soviet Union has exported oil as a means to acquire hard currency for purpose of trade with the West (e.g., to purchase badly needed foreign technology). Thus, the remainder of its petroleum exports, nearly half, go to Western European states. For the Soviet Union, therefore, the drop in world oil prices has necessitated an increase in exports to maintain the same level of hard currency acquisition. Unlike other established oil producers, the Soviet Union has continued to increase production despite the decline in world prices. If exports to the free world take up a larger share of Soviet production, however, the Soviet Union also will have to face the problem of energy demand among its own industrial development plus the prospects for demand among its communist client states. Analysts have expressed doubt for some time concerning the capacity of the Soviet Union to sustain its level of production in order to meet demand (although once again there are differing and disputed views among the experts). Thus, it is suggested that the Soviet Union may have to switch from being a net exporter to being a net importer of oil and that such a switch could be yet another variable in the changing dynamic of the energy marketplace.

As this discussion has proceeded, it should be evident that the *values* that seem to be most prominent in day-to-day developments in global energy are those that have prevailed in the course of the overall development of the issue. If one were to project values upon the positions taken by various actors in the events described thus far, there has been a remarkable consistency. The so-called hard values of supply reliability, advantageous cost to society, regime maintenance and autonomy seem to have endured despite changes in the market and in the relationships among actors. The softer values—equity and safeguarding the environment—have received considerable attention, but they do not appear to have gained significant operational salience. Actors advocating such values tend to be found outside of the prevailing global energy regime.

Among the operationally salient hard values, cost has seemed to predominate, with the market characteristics of supply and demand operating as the strongest influence on energy developments at all levels. To relieve the pressure of increased energy costs, consumers at the subnational level have sought to introduce energy-efficient products to appeal to the conservation-minded consumer, from windows and wood stoves to automobiles and airplanes. At the national level, measures have been taken to provide incentives, normally financial such as investment tax credits, to induce conservation and encourage exploration and pursuit of alternative energy sources. At the broader international level, industrial nations have followed a similar pattern, seeking further to find alternative suppliers to OPEC-controlled oil and to find alternative sources of energy to insulate them from the inelasticity of the petroleum market. The consequent effect on consumption has contributed to the appearance of declining oil prices in the 1980s (as did the increase in oil inventories accumulated to ensure supply reliability).

But that phase may prove to be only one of a series of fluctuations as major actors seek to realize their competing values. Advantageous cost to society has animated OPEC's high absorbers, like Nigeria, which need to sustain export earnings provided by petroleum sales and which therefore resist production quotas or noncompetitive pricing pegged against projections of future demand. In contrast, prominent low absorbers, like Saudi Arabia, perceive their interests in holding to the longer-term value of control of the bulk of the world's proven petroleum reserves. Hence, supply reliability and regime maintenance continue to play a significant role for those producer nations who see the long-term advantage of oil reserves in a fluctuating marketplace, where dependence on oil has not yet been displaced. Lower prices for oil appear to support that view as the initiatives leading to exploration and development of alternative energy sources once again become more expensive than oil. In effect, issues of cost—reduced demand and the decline in the price of oil—may have distracted consumers away from full consideration of the alternatives. In the case of the United States, for example, nuclear power has proven to be vastly more expensive than initially thought, and many nuclear projects have been terminated for reasons of cost alone (rather than the issues surrounding safe-guarding the environment). Over 102 nuclear power plants in the United States either were shut down or construction on them was halted in the decade following the energy crisis. By the same token this experience with nuclear power has not been duplicated in other industrialized countries (such as France or Japan) where the reliability/cost trade-off has made nuclear power a viable alternative to oil. In short, in terms of prevailing values, high-cost oil may have a more favorable effect for both oil production and the search for energy alternatives than low-cost oil. And for the majority of actors, stability rather than fluctuation appears more beneficial.

The development of energy *policies* over the decade following the energy crisis also has reflected considerations of cost. As has been pointed out, the crisis emerged from short-term factors, economic and political, and occasioned short-term adjustments, also largely economic and political. It is these adjustments, not the emergence of long-term energy policies, that have brought about the fluctuations of the world petroleum market. Many of the policies selected and supported were designed to engage the characteristics of supply and demand. And it has been argued that the most successful elements of policy have been those most closely aligned with those market factors, sometimes even unconsciously so. In the United States, efforts to decontrol the domestic oil pricing structure were intended to induce conservation by allowing the cost of petroleum to rise to reflect the market. Although other policies have imposed conservation rules like the 55-mph speed limit (through the federally controlled interstate highway system), have addressed questions of equity like distribution of home heating oil to the needy in the face of increased cost, and have established institutional responses like the Department of Energy, most policies that have materially affected consumption were those that reflected the economic costs of oil in the international market.

Internationally, much of the policy action that was taken was in response to the consequences of the energy crisis, rather than to the long-term global implications of the energy problem. That is not surprising. Most policy organizations exist in a political environment, which necessarily places a higher premium on short-term distributive response than on the longer term. Policy initiatives have tended therefore to arise from the impact of the worldwide recession induced by the steep, rapid increases by OPEC in the price of oil. Efforts to deal with energy as a problem have tended to be expressed in the same economic terms with which that problem was framed. The proposed policy approaches have tended to concentrate on the same sets of energy resources that existed at the onset of the crisis and in the same proportions. And the policies that subsequently emerged have tended to effect only incremental changes in the overall balance of the energy problem, relying for the most part on the relative automaticity of the market to resolve differences in view. For this reason, as the 1980s energy picture began to take shape around the prospects of declining prices and a potentially destabilized market, there was expression of concern for the effects on the international economy as well as on the economies of individual nations. After the sharp rise of the 1970s and the adjustments that followed, some experts feared that too sharp a decline in prices would have a negative effect on planning and stability both for the developed and the developing world.

But by their very nature, considerations of the long-term resolution of the energy problem are less tractable. With the market prevailing as the principal source of incentive for action, long-term policy would need to offer incentives promising favorable return. But the uncertainties governing developments in energy make it difficult to design reliable incentives that could shape a long-term energy policy. That level of uncertainty has of course been exacerbated by the differing views of the experts advanced in the form of projections of energy trends and energy futures. Differing projections support differing proposals for resolution. Forecasting itself then becomes a competitive enterprise, and, as noted earlier, debate tends to revolve around the projections as much as around the policies advanced in response to them. In the wake of the "oil glut," for example, some analysts have adopted a generally optimistic approach in forecasting the overall availability of energy. Looking at demand and supply and the recent cycle of price fluctuation, these analysts argue in effect that demand will induce supply and no policy intervention is necessary except to assure the functioning of the market. As a policy approach, this posture dismisses a long-term energy framework in favor of a continuing series of short-term adjustments. Energy policy would then be a cumulative rather than an anticipatory product. Other analysts continue to focus their forecast on systematic problems of global energy, stressing the need for long-term systematic energy policy. Thus, while there is general agreement that conservation is critical and a shift to alternative energy resources is necessary, there is little agreement as to proper operational means to accomplish those objectives. In a real political atmosphere, sacrifice for "future generations" is one of the most difficult to achieve. Consequently, trade-offs that are attainable (usually only with great difficulty) in the short term because the market provided a reasonably certain measure for incentive and likely return are not attainable in the long run.

For the long term the fluctuations of the decade from the energy crisis to the oil glut have not substantially changed the *futures* perspective with regard to global energy prospects. It is useful to remember once again that although the energy crisis was the product of opportunistic action, it was effective only because the fundamental conditions of the energy system provided the opportunity. The basic trends since then, including the round of price fluctuations, do suggest that a turn away from oil as a principal energy resource is under way. That conclusion is consistent with the majority of long-term projections, despite disagreements about timing and relative distribution among the alternative sources. But the decade also focused attention on specific aspects of the transition from oil. First, it is likely to take some time. Events seem to indicate that the pattern of petroleum usage can be extended by the kinds of adjustments that have taken place, particularly those that occurred in the consumption sector—fuel-efficient automobiles, decentralized home heating, and other conservation measures. It also seems probable that the market forces will continue to rule the outcome for energy. Therefore, the kinds of fluctuations that have taken place may become the norm rather than the exception. And energy futures will indeed be dictated by the kind of commercialization that one or another energy resource acquires. The new resource that replaces oil as the dominant source of energy will do so when it becomes commercially more feasible. Feasibility includes not only the actual cost of the resource itself, but also the cost of the entire system associated with it. Furthermore, the resource must be tested in the commercial arena not only against the oil that it is replacing, but also against the other alternative resources. The prospects for change thus seem to favor slow, incremental adjustments dictated by market forces. In terms of the resource characteristics, the transition from oil may differ from previous transitions because it is being "pushed" by relative scarcity rather than being "pulled" by a more attractive resource. Nonetheless, there may be a different but equally potent pulling factor that is still a function of the resource and that is the relative cost among the alternatives.

It might be argued, after a decade of acute awareness of the status of global energy, that its effects are only beginning to be learned.

Indeed, despite the complex shifts within the functional components, there appears to be little fundamental change in the situation. After lengthy debate and preliminary exploration of a number
of alternatives to petroleum as the world's principal energy resource,
the dependence upon oil persists. A number of observations illustrate the significance of this dependence. In the United States, with
an early emphasis on energy independence (which lapsed in the
face of declining oil prices), development of a Strategic Petroleum
Reserve provides only ten weeks of reserves at the current rate of
demand. Beyond that period, the United States would need to look
for other sources. Even with a reduction in demand from the levels
reached at the height of the energy crisis, the United States continues to import a significant quantity of oil. In fact, although the
proportion of oil that was imported by the United States declined,
the absolute *quantity* of oil imported did not substantially change.
In 1973, before the energy crisis, the United States was importing
3.5 million barrels per day. In 1982 it imported the same amount,
although the sources shifted to achieve less dependence on OPEC
members and, in particular, on Arab OPEC members.[9]

In the face of the continuing reliance on oil it is important to
remind ourselves once again of two facts observed at the beginning
of this book. Neither the finiteness nor the uneven pattern of distribution of the world's petroleum reserves has been greatly altered
by anything that has occurred since the energy crisis. Most experts
agree that the last of the world's "giant" oil fields (more than five
billion barrels) has been discovered. Among other things this means
that the cost of recovering oil from existing fields will increase,
since only a portion of any field is easily recoverable without additional technology. As the fields become increasingly depleted, extraction of the oil will require more and more technology with
greater expense and less return. The most recent estimates by M.
King Hubbert place the cumulative world production of oil at 2,000
billion barrels of which half has been discovered and 20 percent
already consumed. Based on projections of current demand (55 million barrels per day or 20 billion barrels per year), Hubbert continues to project a peak for consumption in the early twenty-first
century (2035–2040).[10] In short, the changes in the pattern of consumption for energy based upon petroleum will extend the availability of oil, but it will still be used within that "meaningfully
short period of time" that introduced this volume.

Neither has the overall distribution of the world's reserves been
substantially altered by new discoveries. That is, OPEC still controls

the bulk of the world's major production capacity for petroleum. This observation of course raises the continuing volatility of the Middle East as a political and economic entity. By 1983 the ongoing war between Iran and Iraq, which threatened to impede the flow of oil out of the Persian Gulf area, was again intensifying, despite efforts at mediation by Japan, a nation heavily dependent on oil from this area. The continuing dispute over the Palestine issue was by no means resolved, with conflicts raging in Lebanon not only between Israel and Arab supporters of the Palestinian cause, but also among Arab states with different stakes in the outcome and therefore different approaches to the resolution. Prospects for the revolution in an oil-rich but generally conservative nation like Saudi Arabia, while not imminent, could still not be dismissed. And in the larger context of the Middle East the unsettled status of Iranian domestic and foreign affairs and the Soviet presence in Afghanistan were further problematical factors with potential impact on the production and distribution of petroleum. The prospects for peace continue to be linked to the development and stability of the global energy system.

As citizens and consumers we face an energy future that will shape our existence. In contrast to energy transitions in the past, the choices that lie ahead promise to be more deliberate and more comprehensive. This provides an opportunity and a responsibility for action. It is incumbent upon us to recognize and accept this role. Confronted with the certainty of a new energy system where the issues are complex and the stakes are high, sound decisions are essential. This book has sought to provide a foundation for understanding the nature of those choices. But the challenge for each of us is vastly more profound than this brief introduction could suggest. It is hoped that the choices that lie before us will be made in a way that is informed, dispassionate, and sensitive to the common global experience that seems certain to affect our lives and those that will follow.

Notes

1 Energy as a global issue

1 Stephen H. Stoker, Spencer L. Seager, and Robert L. Capener, *Energy: From Source to Use* (Glenville, Ill.: Scott, Foresman, 1975), p. 7.
2 David Howard Davis, *Energy Politics*, 2nd ed. (New York: St. Martin's Press, 1978), p. 20.
3 A more pessimistic view of the transition can be found in Walter J. Levy, "The Years that the Locust Hath Eaten: Oil Policy and OPEC Development Prospects," *Foreign Affairs* 57, 2 (Winter 1978–79): 287–305.
4 For a good history of oil in the United States, see Davis, *Energy Politics*.
5 Ibid., p. 71.
6 Leonard Mosely, *Power Play: Oil in the Middle East* (Baltimore: Penguin, 1974).
7 Robert Engler, *The Politics of Oil* (Chicago: University of Chicago Press, 1961), p. 194.
8 Peter R. Odell, *Oil and World Power*, 3rd ed. (Baltimore: Penguin, 1974), pp. 76–78.
9 Foreign Policy Association, *U.S. Foreign Policy 1972–1973* (New York: Macmillian, 1972), p. 37.
10 Davis, *Energy Politics*, p. 68.
11 Ibid., p. 81.
12 Denis Healey, "Oil, Money and Recession," *Foreign Affairs* 58, 2 (Winter 1979–80): 218.
13 For the following chronology, see James A. Bill and Robert W. Stookey, *Politics and Petroleum* (Brunswick, Ohio: King's Court Communications, 1975).
14 Congressional Quarterly, *Continuing Energy Crisis in America* (Washington, D.C.: Congressional Quarterly, 1975).
15 Congressional Quarterly, *Energy Policy* (Washington, D.C.: Congressional Quarterly, 1979).
16 Healey, "Oil, Money and Recession," p. 218.
17 See Gerald Garvey, *Energy, Ecology & Economy* (New York: W.W. Norton, 1972), and Sam H. Schurr, ed., *Energy, Economic Growth and the Environment* (Baltimore: Johns Hopkins University Press, 1972), for early analyses of the relationship among energy, economic growth, and the environment.
18 Levy, "Oil Policy and OPEC," p. 289.
19 Healey, "Oil, Money and Recession," p. 217.
20 W. J. Chancellor and J. R. Goss, "Balancing Energy and Food Production, 1975–

2000," *Science* 16 April 1976, p. 215.

21   Healey, "Oil, Money and Recession," p. 220.

22   *Business Week* carried a long article entitled "The Petro-Crash of the 1980s," detailing the fears, 19 November 1979, 176–90.

23   *Business Week*, 8 October 1979, 76.

24   Congressional Quarterly, *Energy Policy*, p. 95.

25   The wide use of coal can hardly be compared to the domestication of fire, but the impact was profound. Alexander Eiffel would not have been able to construct his tower in Paris in 1889 had it not been for the advances in the iron and steel industry of the nineteenth century, stemming in large part from the relatively concentrated and even heat of coal. That construction project symbolized the advances that made possible our present cities and the railroad system.

26   Congressional Quarterly, *Energy Policy*, p. 93-A.

27   E. F. Schumacher, "Intermediate Technology and the Individual," in *Appropriate Visions*, Richard C. Dorf and Yvonne L. Hunter, eds. (San Francisco: Boyd and Fraser, 1978), pp. 68–75.

2   Energy Actors

1   Robert Stobaugh and Daniel Yergin, eds., *Energy Future* (New York: Random House, 1979).

2   John W. Sawhill, Keichi Oshima, and Hanns W. Maull, *Energy: Managing the Transition* (New York: The Trilaterial Commission, 1978).

3   Don E. Kash et al., *Our Energy Future* (Norman: University of Oklahoma Press, 1976).

4   Leon N. Lindberg, *The Energy Syndrome: Comparing National Responses to the Energy Crisis* (Lexington, Mass.: D.C. Heath, ed. 1977).

5   George Lenczowski. "The Oil-Producing Countries," in *The Oil Crisis*, Raymond Vernon, ed. (New York: W.W. Norton, 1976), p. 61.

6   Stobaugh and Yergin, "After the Peak: The Threat of Hostile Oil," in *Energy Future*, pp. 34–35.

7   Lindberg, *The Energy Syndrome.*

8   Henry R. Nau, "Continuity and Change in U.S. Foreign Energy Policy," *Policy Studies Journal* 7 (Autumn 1978): 121–31.

9   Lee Schipper and A. J. Lichtenberg, "Efficient Energy Use and Well-Being: The Swedish Example," *Science* 194 (3 December 1976), 1001–12.

10   Ford Foundation, *Energy, The Next Twenty Years* (Cambridge, Mass.: Ballinger, 1979).

11   Norman L. Brown, ed., *Renewable Energy Resources and Rural Applications in the Developing World* (Boulder, Colo.: Westview Press, 1976).

12   Zuhayr Mikdashi, "Energy and Minerals: Some Developmental Issues," *Journal of Energy and Development* 1 (Spring 1976): 279–90.

13   Sawhill, Oshima, and Maull, *Energy.*

14   Ulf Lantzke, "The OECD and Its International Energy Agency," in *The Oil Crisis*, Raymond Vernon, ed. (New York: W. W. Norton, 1976), pp. 217–28.

15   Efrain Friedmann, "Financing Energy in Developing Countries," *Energy Policy* 4 (March 1976): 37–49.

16   Myra Wilkins, "The Oil Companies in Perspective," in *The Oil Crisis*, Raymond Vernon, ed. (New York: W. W. Norton, 1976), pp. 159–78.

17   John M. Blair, *The Control of Oil* (New York: Pantheon Books, 1976).

18   Melvin A. Conant and Fern R. Gold, *Geopolitics of Energy* (Washington, D.C.: Government Printing Office, 1977).

19   Robert W. Rycroft, "The United States Oil Industry," *Current History* 75 (May/June 1978): 193–97, 225–26.

20   Robert A. Black, Jr., "Western Europe: Energy and the Environment in the Nineties," in *The Energy Crisis and the Environment: An International Perspective*, Donald R. Kelley, ed. (New York: Praeger Publishers, 1977), pp. 103–58.

21   Andrew S. McFarland, *Public Interest Lobbies: Decision Making on Energy* (Washington, D.C.: American Enterprise Institute for Public Policy Research, 1976).

22   Chapter 4 discusses at length the extent of citizen participation in nuclear decision making.

23   S. David Freeman, *Energy: The New Era* (New York: Random House, 1974).

24   Joseph C. Swidler, "The Challenge to State Regulation Agencies: The Experience of New York State," *Annals of the American Academy of Political and Social Sciences* 410 (November 1973): 106–19.

25   Kash, et al, *Our Energy Future.*

26   Marc Roberts, "Is There an Energy Crisis?" *The Public Interest* 31 (Spring 1973): 17–37.

27   Amory B. Lovins, "Energy Strategy: The Road Not Taken," *Foreign Affairs* 55 (October 1976): 65–96.

28   Mason Willrich, *Energy and World Politics* (New York: Free Press, 1975).

3   Energy Values

1   Melvin Kranzberg and Timothy A. Hall, eds., *Energy and the Way We Live* (San Francisco: Boyd and Fraser, 1980), p. 181.

2   Robert B. Krueger, *The United States and International Oil* (New York: Praeger Publishers, 1975), p. 89.

3   Hanns Maull, *Europe and World Energy* (London: Butterworths, 1980), p. 179. See pages 179–99 for an analysis of the ability of each of Europe's main energy suppliers to utilize its oil revenue.

4   Lester R. Brown, *Building a Sustainable Society* (New York: W. W. Norton), p. 251.

5   Council on Environmental Quality and the Department of State, *The Global 2000 Report to the President* (Washington, D.C.: Government Printing Office, 1980), p. 166.

6   Brown, *Building a Sustainable Society*, p. 189. The examples that follow are taken from this source.

7   Ibid., p. 205.

8   Ellis Cose, ed., *Energy and Equity: Some Social Concerns* (Washington, D.C.: Joint Center for Political Studies, 1979), p. v.

9   Ibid.

10   Charles F. Doran, *Myth, Oil and Politics* (New York: Free Press, 1977), p. 13.

11   Ibid., p. 15.

12   Organization for Economic Cooperation and Development (OECD), *Energy Production and Environment* (Paris: OECD, 1977), p. 11. See this study for a comprehensive report on environmental problems relating to the *production* of energy.

13 These examples are drawn from Donald N. Dewees, "Energy Consumption and Environmental Quality," in *The Energy Question: An International Failure of Policy,* Edward W. Erickson and Leonard Waverman, eds. (Toronto: University of Toronto Press, 1974), pp. 226–28.

14 OECD, *Energy Production* , p. 75.

15 Dewees, "Energy Consumption," pp. 226–27.

16 OECD, *Energy Production,* p. 30.

17 See Sam H. Schurr et al., *Energy in America's Future* (Baltimore: Johns Hopkins University Press, 1979), for a full discussion of this set of concerns.

18 These examples are drawn from Dewees, "Energy Consumption," pp. 228–31.

19 According to Dewees, ibid. (p. 228), 40 to 60 percent of the particulates can be removed by mechanical collectors and up to 99.5 percent by electrostatic precipitators. But increasing the efficiency of the latter from 90 to 99.5 percent more than doubles the cost of installing and operating the precipitators.

20 Ibid., p. 230.

21 See Schurr et al., *Energy in America's Future,* pp. 384–97, for a full discussion of catastrophic problems associated with energy consumption.

22 *Opinion Outlook* (2 November 1981): 1.

23 See Mason Willrich, *Energy and World Politics* (New York: Free Press, 1975), for a comprehensive discussion of this point.

24 "Securing America's Energy Future: The National Energy Policy Plan," *A Report to the Congress Required by Title VII of the Department of Energy Organization Act,* (Washington, D.C.: Department of Energy, July 1981), p. 13.

25 U.S. Congress, House of Representatives, "Oil Fields as Military Objectives: A Feasibility Study," prepared for the Special Subcommittee on Investigations of the Committee on International Relations, by the Congressional Research Service (Washington, D.C.: Government Printing Office, August 1975).

4 Energy Policy

1 Leon N. Lindberg, ed., *The Energy Syndrome: Comparing National Response to the Energy Crisis* (Lexington, Mass: D.C. Heath, 1977).

2 Bruce A. Bishop, Mac McKee, and Roger D. Hansen, *Public Consultation in Public Policy Information: A State-of-the-Art Report* (Washington, D.C.: U.S. Energy Research and Development Administration, 1978).

3 Dorothy Nelkin, *Technological Decisions and Democracy: European Experiments in Public Participation* (Beverly Hills: Sage Publications, 1977).

4 Dorothy Nelkin and Arie Rip, "Distributing Expertise: A Dutch Experiment in Public Interest Science," *Bulletin of the Atomic Scientists* 35 (May 1979): 22.

5 Dorothy Nelkin and Michael Pollak, "The Politics of Participation and the Nuclear Debate in Sweden, the Netherlands, and Austria," *Public Policy* 25 (Summer 1977): 333–57.

6 Richard C. Dorf, *Energy, Resources & Policy* (Reading, Mass: Addison-Wesley, 1978).

7 William H. Witherell, "Recycling Oil Revenues," *Journal of Energy and Development* 1 (Autumn 1975): 28–37.

8 Nazli Choucri, "OPEC: Calming a Nervous World Oil Market," *Technology Review* 83 (October 1980): 36–45.

9 Guy de Carmoy, *Energy for Europe: Economic and Political Implications*

(Washington, D.C.: American Enterprise Institute for Public Policy Research, 1977).

10 Organization for Economic Cooperation and Development (OECD), *Energy Conservation in the International Energy Agency* (Paris, France: OECD, 1976).

11 John W. Sawhill, Keichi Oshima, and Hanns W. Maull, *Energy: Managing the Transition* (New York: The Trilateral Commission, 1978).

12 Raymond Goodman, "Managing the Demand for Energy in the Developing World," *Finance & Development* 17 (December 1980): 9–13.

13 Alvin M. Weinberg, "Can Technology Replace Social Engineering?" in *Technology and Man's Future*, Albert H. Teich, ed. (New York: St. Martin's Press, 1972), pp. 27–35.

14 Sawhill et al., *Energy*.

15 J. Herbert Holloman and Michel Grenon, *Energy Research and Development* (Cambridge, Mass.: Ballinger, 1975).

16 Milton F. Searl and Harry Perry, "Policies for Energy Research and Development," *American Journal of Agricultural Economics* 56 (May 1974): 408.

17 Peter L. Auer, "An Integrated National Energy Research and Development Program," *Science* 184 (19 April 1974), 295.

18 Nelson F. Sievering, Jr., "Statement by Nelson F. Sievering, Jr., Assistant Administrator for International Affairs, Energy Research and Development Administration, before the Environment, Energy and Natural Resources Subcommittee of the House Committee on Government Operations," 12 May 1977, pp. 22–25.

19 Herman Pollack and Michael B. Congdon, "International Cooperation in Energy Research in Development," *Law and Policy in International Business* 6 (Summer 1974): 677–724.

20 Ford Foundation, *Energy: The Next Twenty Years* (Cambridge, Mass.: Ballinger, 1979).

21 Sawhill et al., *Energy*.

22 Don E. Kash et al., *Our Energy Future: The Role of Research, Development, and Demonstration in Reaching a National Consensus on Energy Supply* (Norman: University of Oklahoma Press, 1976).

23 Resources for the Future, *Energy in America's Future: The Choices Before Us* (Baltimore: Johns Hopkins University Press, 1979), p. 2.

24 Lindberg, *The Energy Syndrome*.

25 Charles O. Jones, *An Introduction to the Study of Public Policy* (North Scituate, Mass.: Duxbury Press, 1977), p. 2.

26 Mason Willrich, *Energy and World Politics* (New York: Free Press, 1975).

27 Resources for the Future, *Energy in America's Future*.

28 Kash et al., *Our Energy Future*.

29 Ford Foundation, *Energy*, p. 51.

30 Robert C. Paehlke, "Canada: Energy and the Elections," *Environment* 22 (May 1980): 4–5.

31 Willrich, *Energy and World Politics*.

32 Ford Foundation, *Energy*, p. 264.

33 Frank N. Trager, ed., *Oil, Divestiture and National Security* (New York: Crane, Russak, 1977).

34 John Surrey and Charlotte Huggett, "Opposition to Nuclear Power: A Review of the International Experience," *Energy Policy* 4 (December 1976): 286–307.

35 Ford Foundation, *Energy*, p. 2.

36 U.S. Council on Environmental Quality and the State Department, *The Global 2000 Report to the President* (Washington, D.C.: Government Printing Office,

1980), p. 3.

37   Organization for Economic Cooperation and Development, *Energy Research and Development* (Paris, France: OECD, 1975).

38   Dennis Pirages, *Global Ecopolitics* (North Scituate, Mass.: Duxbury Press, 1978).

39   Resources for the Future, *Energy in America's Future*, p. 461.

40   Robert W. Rycroft, "Bureaucratic Performance in Energy Policy-Making: An Evaluation of Output Efficiency and Equity in the Federal Energy Administration," *Public Policy* 26 (Fall 1978): 599–627.

41   Richard B. Mancke, *Performance of the Federal Energy Office* (Washington, D.C.: American Enterprise Institute for Public Policy Research, 1975).

42   Ford Foundation, *Energy*, p. 167.

43   Margaret A. McKean, "Japan," in Donald R. Kelley, ed., *The Energy Crisis and the Environment: An International Perspective*, (New York: Praeger, 1977), pp. 159–88.

44   Robert W. Rycroft, "Energy Policy Feedback: Bureaucratic Responsiveness in the Federal Energy Administration," *Policy Analysis* 5 (Winter 1979): 1–19.

45   Melvin A. Conant and Fern R. Gold, *Geopolitics of Energy* (Washington, D.C.: Government Printing Office, 1977); Walter J. Levy, "Oil and the Decline of the West," *Foreign Affairs* 58 (Summer 1980): 999–1015.

46   Richard J. Barnet, *The Lean Years: Politics in the Age of Scarcity* (New York: Simon and Schuster, 1980), p. 45.

47   David Ronfeldt, Richard Nehring, and Arturo Gandara, *Mexico's Petroleum and U.S. Policy: Implications for the 1980s* (Santa Monica: Rand Corporation, 1980).

48   James O'Toole et al., *Energy and Social Change* (Cambridge, Mass.: MIT Press, 1976).

49   Kenneth P. Erickson, "Public Policy and Energy Consumption in Industrialized Societies," *Policy Studies Journal* 7 (Autumn 1978): 112–21.

50   Thomas F. Widmer and Elias P. Gyftopoulos, "Energy Conservation and a Healthy Economy," *Technology Review* 79 (June 1977): 30–40.

51   Bruce Hannon, "Energy, Labor, and the Conserver Society," *Technology Review* 79 (March–April 1977): 47–53.

52   Robert S. Pindyck, *The Structure of World Energy Demand* (Cambridge, Mass.: MIT Press, 1979).

53   OECD, *Energy Conservation*.

54   Resources for the Future, *Energy in America's Future*.

55   John H. Gibbons, "Long-term Research Opportunities," in *Energy Conservation and Public Policy*, John C. Sawhill, ed. (Englewood Cliffs, N.J.: Prentice-Hall, 1979), p. 220.

56   Norman L. Brown, ed., *Renewable Energy Resources and Rural Applications in the Developing World* (Boulder, Colo.: Westview Press, 1976).

5   Energy Futures

1   Workshop on Alternative Energy Strategies, *Energy: Global Prospects 1985–2000* (New York: McGraw-Hill, 1977), p. 38.

2   Ibid., p. 118.

3   R. Nehring, *Giant Oil Fields and World Oil Resources* (Santa Monica: Rand Corporation, June 1978), pp. 72–73: cited in U.S. Congress, Office of Technology Assessment, *World Petroleum Availability, 1980–2000* (Washington, D.C.:

Government Printing Office, October 1980) p. 24.

4   Ford Foundation, *A Time to Choose* (Cambridge, Mass.: Ballinger, 1974).

5   Ibid., p. 223

6   Ibid., p. 225.

7   Ibid., p. 229.

8   Ibid., pp. 95–96. In practice the taxes that bring about zero energy growth would most likely take the form of specific levies aimed at restricting growth in the specific activities mentioned earlier—i.e., state severance taxes to restrict development in certain areas, or taxes on CO_2 emissions. However, in the absence of clear indications of the most likely direct motivation for zero energy growth, and for purposes of studying the economic impacts of zero energy growth, a sales tax on energy generally will be the policy analyzed here.

9   World Coal Study, *Coal: Bridge to the Future* (Cambridge, Mass.: Ballinger, 1980), p. 160.

6   Global Energy

1   *Wall Street Journal*, 27 January 1983.

2   Daniel Yergin, "The Political Geology of the Energy Problem," in Dorothy S. Zinberg, ed., *Uncertain Power: The Struggle for a National Energy Policy* (Elmsford, N.Y.: Pergamon Press, 1983), p. 235.

3   *Christian Science Monitor*, 11 October 1983.

4   Central Intelligence Agency, *International Energy Statistical Review*, 20 December 1983, p. 4.

5   Yergin, "Political Geology," p. 241.

6   Daniel Yergin, "America in the Strait of Stringency," *Global Insecurity: A Strategy for Energy and Economic Renewal*, in Daniel Yergin and Martin Hillenbrand, eds. (Boston: Houghton Mifflin, 1982), p. 124.

7   *Christian Science Monitor*, 11 March 1983; *New York Times*, 18 October 1982.

8   CIA, *International Energy Statistical Review*, p. 1.

9   Ibid., p. 4.

10 M. King Hubbert, "The World's Evolving Energy System," *American Journal of Physics* 49 (November 1981): pp. 1025–26.

Bibliography

Energy as a Global Issue

For a good general introduction to energy issues, including resource availability, energy uses, environmental concerns, and energy politics, see Joel Darmstadter, Hans H. Landsberg, and Herbert C. Morton, *Energy: Today and Tomorrow* (Englewood Cliffs, N.J.: Prentice-Hall, 1983). To study in more detail the resource issues and historical relationships between energy and human society, see Earl Cook, *Man, Energy, Society* (San Francisco: W. H. Freeman, 1976). Also useful is the special issue of *Scientific American*, entitled *Energy and Power* (San Francisco: W. H. Freeman, 1971). For a discussion that gives a general orientation but also focuses on more contemporary issues, see Congressional Quarterly, *Energy Issues: New Directions and Goals* (Washington, D.C.: Congressional Quarterly, 1982).

There is much work that focuses on the relationship of energy to more specific societal issues. For instance, the linkages to economic issues are explored by Denis Healy in "Oil, Money and Recession" (*Foreign Affairs* 58, no. 2, Winter 1979–80, pp. 217–30). An already classic analysis of energy choices and societal development can be found in the article by Amory B. Lovins, "Energy Strategy: The Road Not Taken" (*Foreign Affairs* 55, October 1976, pp. 65–96).

An excellent history and analysis of U.S. energy policy is given by David Howard Davis, *Energy Politics* (New York: St. Martin's Press, 1982, third edition). For a discussion of policies in other countries, look to Wilfred L. Kohl, ed., *After the Second Oil Crisis*, (Lexington, Mass.: D. C. Heath and Co., 1982). An easy-to-read and comprehensive study of the global oil industry and politics surrounding it was written by Peter R. Odell, *Oil and World Power* (Baltimore: Penguin, 1983, seventh edition).

Finally, for future-oriented studies with an international perspective, turn to Robert Stobaugh and Daniel Yergin, eds., *Energy Future* (New York: Random House, 1983, third edition).

Actors

A number of sources serve as useful references for energy actors. Duane Chapman's *Energy Resources and Energy Corporations* (Ithaca, N.Y.: Cornell University Press, 1983) explores the basic economic dimensions of private-sector actors in the energy system. Concepts of competition, monopoly, market dynamics, and technological innovation are examined in the context of changing patterns of energy production and use, modifications in ownership and industry structure, and constraints on public policy.

Energy and Security, a volume edited by David A. Deese and Joseph S. Nye (Cambridge, Mass.: Ballinger, 1981), details the special problems faced by nation-states as they attempt to formulate and carry out energy decisions in a national security context. Chapters focus on military responses, global financial linkages, and international cooperative arrangements.

An article by Hans H. Landsberg, "Let's All Play Energy Policy!" *(Daedalus* 109, Summer 1980, pp. 71–84), outlines the very useful concept of "vicarious" participation in energy policy by actors whose involvement has little to do with any particular energy problem or issue. An example would be those participants whose concerns have to do with the potential for political centralization generated by high technology energy projects.

In David W. Orr's "U.S. Energy Policy and the Political Economy of Participation" *(Journal of Politics* 41, November 1979, pp. 1027–56), three perspectives of energy actors are delineated: supply, conservation, and energetics orientation. The latter is a substantial contribution to the literature, because it outlines the values and assumptions that enable some actors to make a causal linkage between the energy basis of a society and its social, political, and economic structures.

A clear picture of the ways private energy-producing companies have executed public policies is found in William G. Prast, *Securing U.S. Energy Supplies: The Private Sector as an Instrument of Public Policy* (Lexington, Mass.: D. C. Heath, 1981). In particular, the book assesses the performance of the large, integrated energy firms and develops recommendations for improving such performance in the future.

Finally, Daniel Yergin and Martin Hillenbrand's edited volume, *Global Insecurity: A Strategy for Energy and Economic Renewal* (Boston: Houghton Mifflin, 1982), develops the argument that energy insecurity extends beyond pricing and availability questions to fundamental issues of war and peace. Chapters look at energy policies of developed and underdeveloped societies, as well as the subject of political/military alliances as energy actors.

Values

Few works focus only on the general area of energy values although discussion of specific values is found in many volumes. One source that addresses the question of values in the American context is Ellis Cose's edited volume, *Energy and Equity: Some Social Concerns* (Washington, D.C.: Joint Center for Political Studies, 1979). A work focusing on the European experience is Hanns Maull's *Europe and World Energy* (London: Butterworths, 1980). This book addresses specific values such as security of supply, long-term availability, and the effects of pricing policies.

A volume examining the value system of today's society is the edited work of Melvin Kranzberg and Timothy A. Hall, *Energy and the Way We Live* (San Francisco: Boyd & Fraser Publishing Co., 1980). The Ford Foundation's *A Time to Choose* (Cambridge, Mass.: Ballinger, 1974) is becoming outdated, but it is one of the few books that mentions values specifically, again in the American context. The book offers three scenarios and addresses a number of issues where choices must be made. Among them are energy and the environment, private enterprise, electric utility regulation, and energy research and development.

Another work that merits some attention is *The Energy Controversy: Soft Path*

Questions and Answers, by Amory Lovins and his critics, edited by Hugh Nash (San Francisco: Friends of the Earth, 1979). This book presents a series of seventeen debates with Amory Lovins, who is a chief proponent of the values associated with "soft" energy paths. The topics range from solar collectors to conservation to nuclear wastes to the utility industry. While values are explicitly mentioned only a few times, it is difficult to miss them lurking beneath the arguments.

The link between values and government policy is explored in Robert B. Krueger's *The United States and International Oil* (New York: Praeger Publishers, 1975). Although cast in the American context, the discussion can be extended to the global context.

Policy

Six books serve as useful sources for understanding energy policy. Although its focus is more on general science and technology policy issues, Claude E. Barfield's *Science Policy from Ford to Reagan: Change and Continuity* (Washington, D.C.: American Enterprise Institute for Public Policy Research, 1982) contains an excellent discussion of the dramatic shift in energy research and development policies implemented by the Reagan administration.

A unique perspective on energy policy making can be found in Craufurd D. Goodwin, ed., *Energy Policy in Perspective: Today's Problems, Yesterday's Solutions* (Washington, D.C.: The Brookings Institution, 1981). Each chapter in this edited volume is organized around each of the last seven U.S. presidencies. The key arguments advanced have to do with the relative dominance of two competing philosophies: government intervention versus market regulation.

A good analysis of the role of various energy models, risk assessments, etc., in developing policy is Martin Greenberger's *Caught Unawares: The Energy Decade in Retrospect* (Cambridge, Mass.: Ballinger, 1983). There is also an interesting body of data reporting on survey research of energy elites.

In *U.S. Energy Policy: Crisis and Complacency* (Norman, Okla.: University of Oklahoma Press, 1984), Don E. Kash and Robert W. Rycroft present an overview of American energy policy in the period between 1973 and 1980, including a theoretical framework delineating the evolution of a stable energy policy system. They also provide a general critique of the ways in which the Reagan administration has destroyed this system.

Thomas J. Wilbanks' *Building a Consensus about Energy Technologies* (Oak Ridge, Tenn.: Oak Ridge National Laboratory, 1981) provides a thoughtful typology of alternative approaches to consensus building in energy policy. Categories include technological fixes (choices of technologies, improvements in technologies, and research and development) and social fixes (information improvements, incentives, legitimacy or institutional changes). The short monograph also undertakes a comparative assessment of these alternatives.

A good analysis of some often ignored aspects of energy policy making, including the role of media coverage of energy issues, state and local government perspectives, and the role of expertise in energy decisions, is found in *Uncertain Power: The Struggle for a National Energy Policy*, edited by Dorothy S. Zingerg (New York: Pergamon Press, 1983). A key contribution is the discussion of the tensions between democratic theory and energy policy.

Futures

There is substantial literature in the area of energy futures. Perhaps the most useful single resource book is *Energy: Global Prospects, 1985–2000*, by the Workshop on Alternative Energy Strategies (New York: McGraw-Hill, 1977). In this book w.a.e.s., an international group, examines trends in energy demand and conservation, as well as five other categories of energy: oil, natural gas, coal, nuclear energy, and "other fossil fuels and renewables." This group does a good job of presenting many facts, projections, and important issues for the future in a concise and relatively readable manner.

Two overviews of energy futures that concentrate more on the United States are Herman Kahn, William Brown, and Leon Martel's *The Next 200 Years* (New York: William Monoward Co., 1976), and Robert Stobaugh and Daniel Yergin's *Energy Future* (New York: Random House, 1983, third edition). The first is a result of a Hudson Institute study, and many of its forecasts are almost uniformly considered to be unduly optimistic. The latter is the product of a Harvard University study and focuses on five sources plus conservation, all in the United States context.

One recent effort that deals with energy modeling and forecasting is *Large-Scale Energy Models: Prospects and Potential*, edited by Robert M. Thrall, Russell G. Thompson, and Milton L. Holloway (Boulder, Colo.: Westview Press, 1983). This volume is written primarily from an economic perspective and reports the results of an American Association for the Advancement of Science symposium. Major topics include the viability of large-scale energy modeling, the need for linkage of micro- and macroeconomic models, and transfer and alternatives to transfer from large-scale models. A more textlike treatment of some of the same issues can be found in *Energy Economics: Quantitative Methods for Energy and Environment Decisions* by Seymour Kaplan (New York: McGraw-Hill, 1983). Rather than debating the issue, Kaplan tells students the "right" way to analyze energy questions. That "right" way is highly quantitative and emphasizes benefit-cost analysis.

In terms of the three scenarios outlined in chapter 5, the previously mentioned w.a.e.s. book and the Nash book give an overview of solar and nuclear paths. The best source for examining a high coal scenario is *Coal: Bridge to the Future* by the World Coal Study (Cambridge, Mass.: Ballinger, 1980). Like the w.a.e.s. book, this is a report of an international study group. Although it is quite comprehensive in treating almost any aspect of coal, it is somewhat biased in favor of expanded coal usage. A much shorter treatment of many of the issues involved in coal usage can be found in Stephen Chapman's "The Rebirth of King Coal" (*New Republic*, 182, no. 25, 21 June 1980, pp. 15-19).

Further explication of the solar path discussed in the energy futures chapter can be found in *Pathway to Energy Sufficiency: The 2050 Study*, by John S. Steinhart et al. (San Francisco: Friends of the Earth, 1979). In addition to laying out personal, business, and governmental aspects of a "low energy" scenario, the authors present systematic comparisons of sixteen previous energy forecasts from various sources.

Finally, a rather controversial article, at least when it appeared, was "The Energy Crisis Is Over" by William Tucker (*Harper's* 263, November 1981, pp. 25-36). It argues that the oil crisis of the early 1970s "was nothing more than a self-inflicted wound." Furthermore, the author believes that long-term problems are more easily solvable than most believe.

Global Energy: Issues and Prospects

The global energy environment is ever-changing. To follow the course of its development, one must evaluate interpretations that are often controversial and uncertain. The best sources for this purpose are therefore current analyses and current data found in periodical literature. National newspapers with reliable energy coverage provide one such course. These include; *The Christian Science Monitor, The New York Times,* and *The Wall Street Journal.* The *Oil and Gas Journal* publishes, in addition to articles on the petroleum industry, an annual and mid-year review of oil production and consumption. The American Petroleum Institute produces the *Basic Petroleum Data Book* on a periodic basis. A number of governmental agencies also publish periodic reports with wider coverage that provide current energy information. The Energy Information Administration of the U.S. Department of Energy issues three useful publications: a *Monthly Energy Review,* an *Annual Energy Review,* and the *International Energy Annual.* The Directorate of Intelligence of the Central Intelligence Agency publishes two biweekly reports that are useful: *International Energy Statistical Review* and *Economic and Energy Indicators.* The International Energy Agency publishes an *Annual Report* and a *World Energy Outlook.* This listing in no way exhausts current sources. There are many other publications to be found dealing with additional energy sources such as coal, solar, nuclear, and so forth.

Auer, Peter L. "An Integrated National Energy Research and Development Program." *Science* 184 (19 April 1974): 295–301.

Barnet, Richard J. *The Lean Years: Politics in the Age of Security.* New York: Simon and Schuster, 1980.

Bill, James A., and Robert W. Stookey. *Politics and Petroleum.* Brunswick, Ohio: King's Court Communications, 1975.

Bishop, Bruce A., Mac McKee, and Roger D. Hansen. *Public Consultation in Public Policy Information: A State-of-the-Art Report.* Washington, D.C.: U.S. Energy and Resource Administration, 1978.

Black, Robert A., Jr. "Western Europe: Energy and the Environment in the Nineties." In *The Energy Crisis and the Environment: An International Perspective,* edited by Donald R. Kelley. New York: Praeger Publishers, 1977, pp. 103–158.

Blair, John M. *The Control of Oil.* New York: Pantheon Books, 1976.

Brown, Lester R. *Building A Sustainable Society.* New York: W. W. Norton, 1981.

Brown, Norman L., ed. *Renewable Energy Resources and Rural Applications in the Developing World.* Boulder, Colo.: Westview Press, 1976.

Business Week. "The Petro-Crash of the 1980s." (8 October 1979): 76.

———. "The Petro-Crash of the 1980s." (19 November 1979): 176–90.

Carmoy, Guy de. *Energy for Europe: Economic and Political Implications.* Washington, D.C.: American Enterprise Institute for Public Policy Research, 1977.

Central Intelligence Agency. *International Energy Statistical Review,* 20 December 1983, pp. 1, 4.

Chancellor, W. J., and J. R. Goss. "Balancing Energy and Food Production, 1975–2000." *Science* 192 (16 April 1976): 213–18.

Choucri, Nazli. "OPEC: Calming a Nervous World Oil Market." *Technology Review*

83 (October 1980), pp. 36–45.

Christian Science Monitor, 11 March 1983 and 11 October 1981.

Conant, Melvin A., and Fern R. Gold. *Geopolitics of Energy*. Washington, D.C.: Government Printing Office, 1977.

Congressional Quarterly. *Continuing Energy Crisis in America*. Washington, D.C.: Congressional Quarterly, 1975.

————. *Energy Policy*. Washington, D.C.: Congressional Quarterly, 1979.

Cose, Ellis, ed. *Energy and Equity: Some Social Concerns*. Washington, D.C.: Joint Center for Political Studies, 1979.

Council on Environmental Quality and the Department of State. *The Global 2000 Report to the President*. Washington, D.C.: Government Printing Office, 1980.

Davis, David Howard. *Energy Politics*. 2nd ed. New York: St. Martin's Press, 1978.

Dewees, Donald N. "Energy Consumption and Environmental Quality." In *The Energy Questions: An International Failure of Policy*, edited by Edward Erickson and Leonard Waverman. Toronto: University of Toronto Press, 1974, pp. 225–38.

Doran, Charles F. *Myth, Oil and Politics*. New York: The Free Press, 1977.

Dorf, Richard C. *Energy Resources & Policy*. Reading, Mass.: Addison-Wesley, 1978.

Engler, Robert. *The Politics of Oil*. Chicago: University of Chicago Press, 1961.

Erickson, Kenneth P. "Public Policy and Energy Consumption in Industrialized Societies." *Policy Studies Journal* 7(Autumn 1978): 112–21.

Ford Foundation. *Energy, The Next Twenty Years*. Cambridge, Mass.: Ballinger, 1979.

————. *A Time to Choose*. Cambridge, Mass.: Ballinger, 1974.

Foreign Policy Association. *U.S. Foreign Policy, 1972–1973*. New York: Macmillan, 1972.

Freeman, David S. *Energy: The New Era*. New York: Random House, 1974.

Friedmann, Efrain. "Financing Energy in Developing Countries." *Energy Policy* 4 (March 1974): 37–49.

Garvey, Gerald. *Energy, Ecology and Economy*. New York: W. W. Norton, 1972.

Gibbons, John H. "Long-Term Research Opportunities." In *Energy Conservation and Public Policy*, edited by John C. Sawhill. Englewood Cliffs, N.J.: Prentice-Hall, 1979.

Goodman, Raymond. "Managing the Demand for Energy in the Developing World." *Finance Development* 17 (December 1980).: 9–13.

Hannon, Bruce. "Energy, Labor and the Conserver Society." *Technology Review* 79 (March–April 1979): 47–53.

Healey, Dennis. "Oil, Money and Recession." *Foreign Affairs* 58 (Winter 1979–80).

Holloman, J. Herbert, and Michel Grenon. *Energy Research and Development*. Cambridge, Mass.: Ballinger, 1975.

Hubbert, M. King. "The World's Evolving Energy System." *American Journal of Physics* 49 (November 1981).

Jones, Charles O. *An Introduction to the Study of Public Policy*. North Scituate, Mass.: Duxbury Press, 1977.

Kash, Don E., et al. *Our Energy Future: The Role of Research Development and Demonstration in Reaching a National Consensus on Energy Supply*. Norman, Okla.: University of Oklahoma Press, 1976.

Kranzberg, Melvin, and Timothy A. Hall, eds. *Energy and the Way We Live*. San Francisco: Boyd and Fraser, 1980.

Krueger, Robert B. *The U.S. and International Oil*. New York: Praeger Publishers, 1975.

Lantzke, Ulf. "The OECD and Its International Energy Agency." In *The Oil Crisis*, edited by Raymond Vernon. New York: W. W. Norton, 1976, pp. 217–27.

Lenczowski, George. "The Oil-Producing Countries." In *The Oil Crisis*, edited by Raymond Vernon. New York: W. W. Norton, 1976, pp. 59–72.

Levy, J. "Oil and the Decline of the West." *Foreign Affairs* 58 (Summer 1980): 999–1015.

Levy, Walter J. "The Years that the Locust Hath Eaten: Oil Policy and OPEC Development Projects." *Foreign Affairs* 57 (Winter 1978–79): 287–305.

Lindberg, Leon N. *The Energy Syndrome: Comparing National Responses to the Energy Crisis*. Lexington, Mass.: D.C. Heath, 1977.

Lovins, Amory B. "Energy Strategy: The Road Not Taken." *Foreign Affairs* 55 (October 1976): 65–96.

Mancke, Richard B. *Performance of the Federal Energy Office*. Washington, D.C.: American Enterprise Institute for Public Policy Research, 1975.

Maull, Hans. *Europe and World Energy*. London: Butterworths, 1980.

McFarland, Andrew S. *Public Interest Lobbies: Decision-Making on Energy*. Washington, D.C.: American Enterprise Institute for Public Policy Research, 1976.

McKean, Margaret A. "Japan." In *The Energy Crisis and the Environment: An International Perspective*, edited by Donald R. Kelly. New York: Praeger Publishers, 1977, pp. 159–88.

Mikdashi, Zuhayr. "Energy and Minerals: Some Developmental Issues." *Journal of Energy and Development* 1 (Spring 1976): 279–90.

Mosely, Leonard. *Power Play: Oil in the Middle East*. Baltimore: Penguin, 1974.

Nau, Henry R. "Continuity and Change in U.S. Foreign Energy Policy." *Policy Studies Journal* 7 (Autumn 1978): 121–31.

Nehring, R. *Giant Oil Fields and World Oil Resources*. Santa Monica: Rand Corporation, June 1978.

Nelkin, Dorothy. *Technological Decisions and Democracy: European Experiments in Public Participation*. Beverly Hills: Sage Publications, 1977.

Nelkin, Dorothy, and Michael Pollack. "The Politics of Participation and the Nuclear Debate in Sweden, the Netherlands, and Austria." *Public Policy* 25 (Summer 1977): 333–57.

———— and Arie Rip. "Distributing Expertise: A Dutch Experiment in Public Interest Science." *Bulletin of the Atomic Scientists* 35 (May 1979): 20–23, 54.

Odell, Peter R. *Oil and World Power*. 3rd ed. Baltimore: Penguin, 1974. *Opinion Outlook* (2 November 1981).

Organization for Economic Cooperation and Development. *Energy Conservation in the International Energy Agency*. Paris: OECD, 1976.

————. *Energy Production and Environment*. Paris: OECD, 1977.

————. *Energy Research and Development*. Paris: OECD, 1975.

O'Toole, James, et al. *Energy and Social Change*. Cambridge, Mass.: MIT Press, 1976.

Paehlke, Robert C. "Canada: Energy and the Elections." *Environment* 22 (May 1980): 4–5.

Pindyck, Robert S. *The Structure of World Energy Demand*. Cambridge, Mass.: MIT Press, 1979.

Pirages, Dennis. *Global Ecopolitics*. North Scituate, Mass.: Duxbury Press, 1978.

Pollack, Herman, and Michael B. Congdon. "International Cooperation in Energy Research and Development." *Law and Policy in International Business* 6 (Summer 1974): 677–724.

Roberts, Marc. "Is There an Energy Crisis?" *The Public Interest* 31 (Spring 1973): 17–37.

Ronfeldt, David, Richard Nehring, and Arturo Gandara. *Mexico's Petroleum and U.S. Policy: Implications for the 1980s.* Santa Monica: Rand Corporation, 1980.

Rycroft, Robert. "Bureaucratic Performance on Energy Policy-making: An Evaluation of Output Efficiency and Equity in the Federal Energy Administration." *Public Policy* 26 (Fall 1978): 599–627.

———. "Energy Policy Feedback: Bureaucratic Responsiveness in the Federal Energy Administration." *Policy Analysis* 5 (Winter 1979): 1–19.

———. "The United States Oil Industry." *Current History* 75 (May/June, 1978): 193–97.

Sawhill, John W., Keichi Oshima, and Hanns W. Maull. *Energy: Managing the Transition.* New York: The Trilaterial Commission, 1978.

Schipper, Lee, and A. J. Lichtenberg. "Efficient Energy Use and Well-Being: The Swedish Example." *Science* 194 (3 December 1976): 1001–12.

Schumacher, E. F. "Intermediate Technology and the Individual." In *Appropriate Visions,* edited by Richard C. Dorf and Yvonne L. Hunter. San Francisco: Boyd and Fraser, 1978, pp. 68–75.

Schurr, Sam H., ed. *Energy, Economic Growth and the Environment.* Baltimore: Johns Hopkins University Press, 1972.

——— et al. *Energy in America's Future: The Choices Before Us.* Baltimore: Johns Hopkins University Press, 1979.

Sear, Milton F., and Harry Perry. "Policies for Energy Research and Development." *American Journal of Agricultural Economics* 56 (May 1974): 408.

Sievering, Nelson F. "Statement by Nelson Sievering, Jr., Assistant Administrator for International Affairs, Energy Research and Development Administration, before the Environment, Energy and Natural Resources Subcommittee of the House Committee on Government Operations," 12 May 1977.

Stobaugh, Robert, and Daniel Yergin, eds. *Energy Future.* New York: Random House, 1979.

Stoker, Stephen H., Spencer L. Seager, and Robert L. Capener. *Energy: From Source to Use.* Glenville, Ill.: Scott, Foresman, 1975.

Swidler, Joseph C. "The Challenge to State Regulation Agencies: The Experience of New York State." *Annals of the American Academy of Political and Social Sciences* 410 (November 1973): 106–19.

Surrey, John, and Charlotte Huggett. "Opposition to Nuclear Power: A Review of the International Experience." *Energy Policy* 4 (December 1976): 286–307.

Trager, Frank N., ed. *Oil, Divestiture and National Security.* New York: Crane, Russak, 1977.

U.S. Congress, House of Representatives. "Oil Fields as Military Objectives: A Feasibility Study." Prepared for the Special Subcommittee on Investigations of the Committee on International Relations by the Congressional Research Service. Washington, D.C.: Government Printing Office, August 1975.

U. S. Congress, Office of Technology Assessment. *World Petroleum Availability, 1980–2000.* Washington, D.C.: Government Printing Office, October 1980.

U.S. Council on Environmental Quality and the State Department. *The Global 2000 Report to the President.* Washington, D.C.: Government Printing Office, 1980.

U.S. Department of Energy. "Securing America's Energy Future: The National Energy Policy Plan." *A Report to the Congress Required by Title VII of the*

Department of Energy Organization Act. Washington, D.C.: DOE, July 1981.

Weinberg, Alvin M. "Can Technology Replace Social Engineering?" In *Technology and Man's Future,* edited by Albert H. Teich. New York: St. Martin's Press, 1972, pp. 27–35.

Widmer, Thomas F., and Elias P. Gyftopoulus. "Energy Conservation and a Healthy Economy." *Technology Review* 79 (June 1977): 30–40.

Wilkins, Myra. "The Oil Companies in Perspective." In *The Oil Crisis,* edited by Raymond Vernon. New York: W.W. Norton, 1976, pp. 159–78.

Willrich, Mason. *Energy and World Politics.* New York: The Free Press, 1975.

Witherell, William H. "Recycling Oil Revenues." *Journal of Energy Development* 1 (Autumn 1975): 28–37.

Wall Street Journal, 27 January, 1983.

Workshop on Alternative Energy Strategies. *Energy: Global Prospects, 1985–2000.* New York: McGraw-Hill, 1977.

World Coal Study. *Coal Bridge to the Future.* Cambridge, Mass.: Ballinger, 1980.

Yergin, Daniel. "America in the Strait of Stringency." In *Global Insecurity: A Strategy for Energy and Economical Renewal,* edited by Daniel Yergen and Martin Hillerbrand. Boston: Houghton Mifflin, 1982.

———, and Martin Hillerbrand. *Global Insecurity: A Strategy for Energy and Economic Renewal.* Boston: Houghton Mifflin, 1982.

———. "The Political Geology of the Energy Problem." In *Uncertain Power: The Struggle for a National Energy Policy,* edited by Dorothy Zinberg. Elmsford, N.Y.: Pergamon, 1983.

Index

Contributors

James E. Harf is Professor of Political Science and Mershon Senior Faculty at The Ohio State University, a member of the faculty since 1969. He received his Ph.D. from Indiana University. He was Visiting Professor at Duke University in 1978–79 and an American Council on Education Fellow in Academic Administration in 1975–76 at The Pennsylvania State University. He served for six months as the principal staff for undergraduate education on President Carter's Foreign Language and International Studies Commission. Harf has been the recipient or co-recipient of nineteen grants that have focused primarily on materials and faculty development. He is the author or editor of many books and articles on international relations, including *National Security Affairs: Theoretical Perspectives and Contemporary Issues* and *International and Comparative Politics: A Handbook.* He is Executive Director of the Consortium for International Studies Education.

Barry B. Hughes earned a B.S. in Mathematics from Stanford in 1967 and a Ph.D. in Political Science from the University of Minnesota in 1970. He taught at Case Western Reserve University for ten years where he was actively involved in construction of computer simulation models for economic, energy, food and population forecasting. He is now Professor at the Graduate School of International Studies, University of Denver. Hughes has consulted for the governments of West Germany, Iran, Egypt, and the United States. He has written *The Domestic Context of American Foreign Policy, World Modeling,* and *World Futures: A Critical Analysis of Alternatives,* as well as numerous articles.

Robert W. Rycroft is Associate Professor of Public Affars and Political Science and Deputy Director of the Graduate Program in Science,

Technology, and Public Policy at The George Washington University. He received his Ph. D. from the University of Oklahoma and has held research and teaching positions at Oklahoma, Princeton, and the University of Denver. Rycroft specializes in science and technology policy, energy policy, and technology assessment and policy analysis. He is co-author of *U.S. Energy Policy: Crisis and Complacency, Energy from the West,* and *Our Energy Future,* as well as articles in *World Politics, The Journal of Politics, Public Administration Review* and numerous other professional journals and volumes of collective works.

Donald A. Sylvan is Associate Professor of Political Science at The Ohio State University. His research interests include foreign policy decision making, the design of public policy, and forecasting and computer simulation in both international relations and public policy. He has recently co-edited *Foreign Policy Decision Making: Perception, Cognition, and Artificial Intelligence.* He has authored or co-authored articles in such journals as *Journal of Conflict Resolution, Policy Sciences, International Studies Quarterly, Simulation and Games, International Interactions,* and *Journal of Peace Science.*

B. Thomas Trout is Associate Professor of Political Science at the University of New Hampshire. His graduate degrees are from Indiana University. He serves as Chairman of the Consortium for International Studies Education and is co-editor and author of the recently published text *National Security Affairs: Theoretical Perspectives and Contemporary Issues.* His research interests include United States-Soviet relations and both American and Soviet foreign and defense policy. He has published articles in the *American Political Science Review, International Studies Quarterly, Naval War College Review,* and other journals.